ETHICS
for CHRISTIAN
MINISTRY

ETHICS
for CHRISTIAN
MINISTRY

Moral Formation
for Twenty-First-Century Leaders

Joe E. Trull *and* R. Robert Creech

Baker Academic
a division of Baker Publishing Group
Grand Rapids, Michigan

Published by Baker Academic
a division of Baker Publishing Group
P.O. Box 6287, Grand Rapids, MI 49516-6287
www.bakeracademic.com

Printed in the United States of America

Library of Congress Cataloging-in-Publication Data
Names: Trull, Joe E., author.
Title: Ethics for Christian ministry : moral formation for twenty-first-century leaders / Joe E. Trull and R. Robert Creech.
Description: Grand Rapids : Baker Academic, 2017. | Includes bibliographical references and index.
Identifiers: LCCN 2017023372 | ISBN 9780801098314 (pbk. : alk. paper)
Subjects: LCSH: Clergy—Professional ethics.
Classification: LCC BV4011.5 .T778 2017 | DDC 241/.641—dc23
LC record available at https://lccn.loc.gov/2017023372

To
all good ministers
who faithfully serve
Jesus Christ and his church
with integrity

Wide was his parish, houses far asunder,
But never did he fail, for rain or thunder,
In sickness, or in sin, or any state,
To visit the farthest, regardless their financial state,
Going by foot, and in his hand, a stave.
This fine example to his flock he gave,
That first he wrought and afterwards he taught;
Out of the gospel then that text he caught,
And this metaphor he added thereunto—
That, if gold would rust, what shall iron do?
For if the priest be foul, in whom we trust,
No wonder that a layman thinks of lust?

Geoffrey Chaucer, *The Canterbury Tales*

Contents

Preface

Few voices were raised on the subject of ministerial ethics in the latter half of the twentieth century—seldom did theological seminaries offer training on the topic, and texts written on pastoral ethics were scarce. Although not many books on ethics in ministry appeared during the final years of the twentieth century,[1] a handful of excellent texts on the subject were written.[2] During the last two decades, little has changed—the lack of adequate resources for the study of ministerial ethics continues.

A corollary truth adds to this serious deficiency in pastoral education—very few seminaries offer even one course in this subject. Ironically, the most conservative Bible schools and theological seminaries are the ones most lacking in the study of ministerial ethics. Most divinity schools speak to this subject in pastoral ministry classes. However (as is so often true), the subject usually is left until last and thus often left out completely!

To be fair, many religious schools and seminaries have accepted greater responsibility to develop moral character in their students through studies in spiritual formation.[3] Emphases on spiritual growth and ethical character form a good foundation for ethics in ministry, but the complexity of moral issues in the minister's home, church, and society requires more than a "character development" course.

Rightly or wrongly, churches formerly assumed Christian ministers were persons of integrity who could be counted on to be ethical. No longer is this presumption possible, if it ever were! In 2002 clergy sexual misconduct by Roman Catholic priests, coupled with an apparent cover-up by church officials, shocked the nation and captured the news. Lawsuits threatened to bankrupt several dioceses. Leaders in all religious groups reassessed the need for ethics in ministry among their own clergy. Since then, hardly a week goes by without a revelation of a "fallen minister." On April 15, 2016, the new director of the Ethics and Religious Liberty Commission of the Southern Baptist Convention wrote: "This week another high-profile pastor was removed from ministry for immorality, this time a friend of mine."[4]

Add to this the number of knotty social issues faced by the modern minister, which increases annually—especially those ethical dilemmas exacerbated by our complex technological society. More than ever, the minister in today's world must be prepared to grapple with intricate moral problems and community conflicts, as well as ethical dilemmas in his or her own church and personal life.

The purpose of our text is twofold: First, this book intends to teach Christian ministry students the unique moral role of the minister and the ethical responsibilities of that vocation. The second purpose is more practical: to provide for new and established ministers a clear statement of the ethical obligations contemporary clergy should assume in their personal and professional life. The text begins with the minister's unique role as a professional (chap. 1), followed by an elaboration of those ethical responsibilities of the clergy to self, family, ministry colleagues, and society (chaps. 2–6). Chapter 7 addresses the particularly difficult issue of clergy sexual abuse, and chapter 8 uniquely outlines the way a minister may write their own personal code of ethics. Dr. Trull prepared chapters 1, 2, 7, and 8. Dr. Creech prepared chapters 3, 4, 5, and 6.

Four appendixes at the close of the book provide the reader with "A Procedure for Responding to Charges of Clergy Sexual Abuse" (app. A), "Early Denominational Codes of Ethics" (app. B), "Contemporary Denominational Codes of Ethics" (app. C), and "Sample Codes of Ethics" (app. D).

We wish to express our gratitude to our wives, Melinda Creech and Audra Trull, whose counsel, proofreading, and constant support were invaluable during the research and writing of this text. In addition, we wish to thank Baker Publishing Group for support and encouragement to publish this text, especially acquisitions editor Robert N. Hosack, whose patience and extra-mile efforts made this textbook possible.

1

Walking with Integrity

A Profession or a Calling?

Ours is an age of ethical uncertainty. In Walker Percy's novel *The Thanatos Syndrome*, a minister faces an ethical dilemma. Percy capsules his moral confusion and ours in one line: "This is not the Age of Enlightenment, but the Age of Not Knowing What to Do."[1] One writer calls this quote an apt aphorism for our age and adds: "Politicians, scientists, physicians, business leaders, everyday citizens, and our clergy increasingly find themselves in situations where they really do not know what to do. As a result, ethics has become a boom industry, and moral failure a regular front-page phenomenon. Conventional wisdom seems glaringly inadequate in the face of our environmental, technological, political, economic and social situations."[2] Ministerial ethics can no longer be assumed, if ever they were.

During the election year of 2016, many prominent evangelical ministers became involved in the political campaigns of candidates. One, the pastor of the renowned First Baptist Church of Dallas, Texas, even traveled to another state during a primary campaign to give his ringing endorsement of a candidate for president, although the candidate was himself not considered religious or even mildly moral.[3] Not only was this a violation of federal law for clergy but the act was also an obvious breach of all ministerial codes of conduct.[4]

To this seeming confusion about ministerial morality, add the present decline in organized religion. Martin Marty, eminent church historian at the University of Chicago, calls the present trend a "drift away" from traditional churches, quoting author Linda Mercadante: "'No matter how organized religions try to ignore, challenge, adapt, or protest it, our society is being changed by this pervasive ethos.' Her studied types, 'dissenters, casuals, explorers, seekers, and immigrants (to new beliefs)' are often 'millennials' who cannot return to the religion of their youth, 'in part because many of them never had one.'"[5] All studies indicate that today's youth are often more skeptical of the country's institutions than the youth in the generations that preceded them.

George Bullard, an expert on church ministry and cultural change, asks whether the millennial generation (those born from 1982 to 2000) brought radical change. His answer: "During their birth years, we saw the emergence of the postmodern age, in which paradigms shifted and many understandings of reality retuned to zero and reset. The heavy focus on vision . . . has shifted to a focus on relationships. . . . Absolute truth has morphed into the story of each person's truth. . . . Information previously imparted only by experts is now free on the Internet. . . . The fastest growing denomination beginning about 20 years ago is called nondenominational."[6]

Somewhat like the Earl of Grantham in *Downton Abbey*, I have difficulty accepting the fact that something I love and to which I have given my life is changing. Yet the last two decades have brought many alterations to the shape of American church life. Things are different. Among the many challenges faced by churches and denominations in this second decade of the twenty-first century, ministerial ethics ranks near the top.

An annual poll of the top ten religious stories in 2014 listed clergy wrong-doing as number eight. Catholic communities are still reeling from the sordid revelations and costly court cases involving priests who sexually abused young people—the Archdiocese of Chicago released more than twenty-one thousand pages of evidence related to such clergy abuse. Mark Driscoll, the leader of a Seattle-based megachurch network in five states, resigned following a series of charges that included financial misconduct, plagiarism, and a harsh, hyper-macho theology. In the nation's capital, Barry Freundel, a prominent Orthodox rabbi, was accused of voyeurism and secretly spying on naked women in the *mikvah*, the ritual bath.[7]

Moral failures in the ministry are all too common today. Chaucer asked, "If gold would rust, what shall iron do?" Obviously, it too rusts—perhaps more rapidly. "For if the priest be foul, in whom we trust," continued the author of *The Canterbury Tales*, "no wonder that a layman thinks of lust?"

The present crisis in ministerial ethics is both a reflection of our times and an influence on our society. Ethical failure in the pulpit affects the pew. At the same time, clergy morals seem to mirror the general decline in morality among the laity. In a day fraught with political cover-ups, insider trading on the stock exchange, corporate scandals, and media manipulation, people are seldom shocked when they hear of an immoral minister.

Today's minister walks an ethical tightrope. At one moment, she or he may serve as a prophet, priest, or educator; in the next, a cleric may be an administrator, a counselor, or a worship leader. Each of these roles raises ethical dilemmas and exposes moral vulnerability not faced by doctors, lawyers, or other professionals. For example, most church members trust their minister without hesitation. Yet this intimate relationship often involves parishioners sharing their souls, which makes a church minister vulnerable to many subtle temptations. The most obvious danger is sexual misconduct. Many clergy catastrophes involve adulterous relationships, sexual liaisons, pedophilic acts, and other sexual transgressions.[8]

Equally immoral, though often overlooked, are certain ministerial habits that may be considered part of the "job description." Pulpit exaggeration is accepted as a normal trait of preachers. More serious is the unethical conduct of an autocratic leader who misuses power, manipulates people, and practices deception and dishonesty. Blaise Pascal warned that people "never do evil so completely and cheerfully as when they do it from religious convictions" (*Pensees* 894). The American culture stimulates in many clerics the desire to succeed. To be called as a pastor of a large, prestigious church is a goal that has led many good ministers to sacrifice their integrity on the altar of success.

A foundational question must be asked at the beginning: Is Christian ministry a career or a profession? Is church ministry simply a vocational choice based on aptitude tests, personality profiles, or job opportunities? Should a person prepare to be a church minister without a sense of divine calling?

Oliver Sacks begins his book *The Man Who Mistook His Wife for a Hat* with the fascinating story of a person suffering from agnosia.[9] Dr. P. (the patient) was a distinguished musician and teacher in Berlin. His students first recognized his strange behavior when he was unable to identify people he knew well. In addition, he often mistook objects such as parking meters and fire hydrants for young children. At the close of one session with Dr. Sacks, Dr. P. started looking for his hat. Finally, he reached toward his wife's head and tried to put it on his own. *Agnosia* is the psychiatric term for the loss of the ability to recognize familiar objects. Although Dr. P. retained a highly abstract cognitive ability, his illness prevented him from recognizing people, for he saw faces only in bits and pieces. Incredible as it seems, Dr. P. got along quite well despite his disability and was able to work until the end of his life.

Amusing and yet tragic, the case of Dr. P. is a metaphor for the practice of ministry and for ministerial ethics.[10] Every seminarian knows that a call to become a minister of a church is a call to various tasks. Preaching, teaching, counseling, visiting, administrating, promoting, recruiting, leading worship, and doing community service are just a few of those tasks. Today's minister must wear many hats. The unseen danger for the busy religious worker is "clerical agnosia," becoming a minister who mistakes a parishioner for one of his or her hats! In short, people can get lost in the midst of an active ministry.

What caused this multiplication of roles, which increases the risk of contracting clerical agnosia and overlooking persons? James Gustafson observed three primary developments during the past century that precipitated this role change for ministers:

> The first is the voluntary character of religion in the United States, which in its various dimensions makes the clergy unusually responsive to the desires and needs of the laity and to changes in the culture. The second is the breakdown of a sense of independent authority in the clergy; in the absence of wide acceptance of the traditional bases of their authority, clergymen seek substitute ways to make themselves legitimate. The third is the effort of the clergy to find new ways to make religious faith relevant to changing social and cultural patterns.[11]

These changes have led to clergy confusion and a condition Gustafson calls *anomie*, a lack of clear delineation of authority. The typical minister is bewildered, not only about what to do but also about whom to serve. Who has the final word: the individual member, the congregation, the denomination, or God?

Dr. P.'s story is a parable of what can happen to any church overseer. Without realizing it, pastors and other ministers can slip into believing that as long as the "bits and pieces" of people are visible, all is well. Ministry can become impersonal. Church members begin to look like consumer-oriented clients, and the church itself takes on the appearance of a corporation, whose chief executive must work to keep "profits" high and "customers" happy. In the midst of this busyness, the real purpose of ministry can be lost.

As we propose in the next chapter, the moral ideal for a minister is integrity, a life of ethical wholeness and moral maturity. How does the person called by God to serve the church achieve integrity of character and conduct? The most naive believe that since a minister is set apart by God, ethics will take care of itself, for God calls only good people. Others assume that those who preach the gospel must surely live by the Bible's precepts and principles. Most laypersons admire the dedication of those who devote their lives to a Christian vocation and suppose that this commitment ensures a Christian lifestyle.

Ministerial integrity is neither simple nor automatic. Clergy ethics, however, does begin with a proper understanding of the minister's vocation. Therefore, the purpose of this chapter is to reexamine the vocational role of the clergy. This begins with the minister's understanding of "calling." Is it to a career or to a profession? To answer this basic question, we must also define *profession*. A brief review of the history of professions, which originated in religious orders (whose members "professed" something), will aid an understanding of the term. This chapter also explores a significant change in cultural values that precipitated a crisis for professionals. Many believe that because of a change in professionalization in American society, the professional ethics model is fundamentally inappropriate for today's clergy. Finally, we will attempt to determine whether the minister is indeed a true professional, and if so, how the professional ethics model can be a tool for "doing" clergy ethics.

The Call to Ministry

A basic prerequisite for an ethical ministry is a clear understanding of the minister's calling. How does a person enter vocational Christian service? Does a candidate receive a divine calling from God or simply choose a career? Is the ministry an occupation or a profession? What does the office itself require of the ordained: an inspiring moral life, effective church leadership, polished ministry skills, sound theological beliefs, unerring professional conduct, or some combination of these ministerial attributes?

H. Richard Niebuhr called the ministry of his generation a "perplexed profession." The situation today has not improved, for contemporary clerics are equally puzzled. Like butterflies newly hatched, seminary graduates flutter away from ivy-covered campuses planning to fly high, only to crash into the brick wall of "Old First Church." Young ministers quickly discover that pastoral ministry, rather than the spiritual enterprise they expected, is more like running a secular business. The weekly calendar is crammed with financial meetings, publicity decisions, personnel problems, and laity complaints. When will there be time for theological discussions, spiritual disciplines, or the real mission of the church?

A survey of recent graduates conducted by two seminary faculty members revealed that the major concern of these first-time ministers was coping with uncertainties regarding their roles in ministry. "We found beginning clergy-persons almost completely at the mercy of the expectations of their first parish without counterbalancing claims from denomination or profession. Formation of clerical identity depended on satisfying the first congregation."[12]

If this be true, it is important for first-time clergy to have a clear understanding of their role. Every church has an unwritten list of expectations for its ordained leaders, and similarly, each new church shepherd arrives with a notebook filled with plans and priorities. The two sets seldom match. Much disappointment and many tensions arise during the first years because of such misunderstandings. The result can be catastrophic: increasing conflict, ministerial fatigue, and even forced termination. Yale professor Gaylord Noyce asserts, "Clergy 'burnout,' so publicized, results more from a blurred pastoral identity than from overwork. Professional ethics well taught counteracts that kind of haziness."[13]

So the question arises again: To what is a minister called—a career or a profession? An occupation or a unique vocation? Each cleric must also ask, "Whom do I serve, Christ or the congregation?" Or to put it another way, "Am I serving Christ as I serve the congregation?" Building a ministry based on integrity requires that a minister's sense of calling and concept of service be biblical, ethical, and Christlike.

Most evangelical ministers would identify with Jeremiah's account of his calling: "The word of the LORD came to me, saying, 'Before I formed you in the womb I knew you, before you were born I set you apart; I appointed you as a prophet to the nations'" (Jer. 1:4–5 NIV). This messenger to Israel believed that the sovereign Lord had graciously planned for him to be a spokesman for God from the beginning of his existence. Christian ministers should likewise be confident of God's plan for their lives as revealed in their call to Christian ministry. This conviction about the will of God is more than a choice of career based on personality inventories; it is an acknowledgment of a divine appointment. As Yahweh chose Abraham to lead a new people (Gen. 12:1–3) and sent Moses on a redemptive mission (Exod. 3:10), so God calls and sends ministers today. Their response to God's calling must be like that of Isaiah: "Here am I; send me!" (Isa. 6:8).

Yahweh's prophets are not only called but also given a message and a mission. Such was the case with Deborah (Judg. 4–5), Isaiah (6:8–9), Amos (7:15), and John the Baptist (John 1:6–8). The apostle from Tarsus was so convinced that God had appointed him as a missionary to the gentile world that he wrote, "I am compelled to preach. Woe to me if I do not preach the gospel!" (1 Cor. 9:16 NIV). There can be no doubt that the minister of the gospel of Jesus Christ is set apart and sent forth by God to fulfill a divine mission. The ministry is a *vocatio*, a calling from God.

At the same time, the minister usually fulfills this calling through service to a congregation of God's people. This body of believers pays the salary of the church leader and expects some type of ministerial service in return. How should a person set apart by God to minister to the Christian community interpret his or her relationship to the church?

Simon Peter wrote a clear word about pastoral responsibility to the *ekklesia* of Christ: "Be shepherds of God's flock that is under your care, watching over them—not because you must, but because you are willing, as God wants you to be; not pursuing dishonest gain, but eager to serve; not lording it over those entrusted to you, but being examples to the flock" (1 Pet. 5:2–3 NIV).

It is impossible to discuss ministers and what they do apart from the church, for what the clergy most needs is a function of what the church most needs. "At a very early date, from among the ranks of the baptized, the church found it good to call some of its members to lead, to help the congregation nurture within itself those virtues needed for the life and work of the colony. Call these leaders preachers, priests, pastors, prophets, or just plain Jane—this is their particular vocation: building up a congregation."[14]

Although a minister's primary loyalty is to God, this devotion must never be an excuse for avoiding pastoral duties. Ministry involves both privilege and responsibility. A minister's calling always must be fleshed out in some kind of community, usually a local congregation. One cannot serve Christ without serving people, for to serve people is to serve Christ (Matt. 25:31–46).

As we seek a clear understanding of the minister's calling, we should note that the terms *vocation, profession,* and *career* have multiple meanings. William May of Southern Methodist University has suggested that this confusion of terminology has created tensions. He points out that every Christian has a vocation, which traditionally has meant a commitment to God and neighbor. A career, however, is a more selfish thing; it is a means to pursue one's own private aims and purposes. Instead of asking what the community needs, a career person asks, "What do I want to be, and where do I want to go?"[15] If these two questions are uppermost in your mind, does that not mean you are pursuing a career rather than answering a call?

In the biblical sense, as Martin Luther and John Calvin both emphasized, all Christians are "called" to serve God in and through their vocation. The minister stands somewhere between this generalized concept of vocation for all Christians and a specific career. She or he is fulfilling a calling and not just choosing a career. Yet something more is involved. The unique calling to be a Christian minister has features that result in unusual obligations.

Historically, the word *profess* meant "to testify on behalf of" or "to stand for something." Being a professional person carried implications about knowledge and moral responsibility. "The professional knows something that will benefit the wider community, and he or she has a responsibility to use that knowledge to serve the wider human community."[16] Let us now explore how this traditional concept of a professional relates to the vocation of the minister.

The History of Professions

John Piper wants his fellow pastors to know "we are *not* professionals."[17] His book with that title is a collection of essays that urges his preaching colleagues "to quit looking at their jobs through the eyes of secular society." He believes professionalism leads to spiritual decline and has nothing to do with the essence and heart of Christian ministry.[18]

This misunderstanding is common. The term *professional* is often considered a secular title reserved for reverends who are more concerned with status and prestige than spiritual ministry. In fact, the very opposite should be true. Indeed, only if a minister is truly a professional will that person's ministry be truly biblical and Christian.

To understand the true meaning of the word *professional*, it is necessary to review briefly the history of professions, how professionalization began, and what changes have occurred over the years. This is especially crucial for comprehending the present-day crisis facing all professionals, including ministers.

Darrell Reeck believes that the roots of contemporary professions can be traced back to those early priests, healers, and chiefs who promoted human values in primitive societies. Unlike the modern version, these "prototypical professionals" were unspecialized and usually perpetuated themselves through inheritance rather than through achievement. Nevertheless, these traditionalists did use their rudimentary skills to meet basic human needs in their cultural groups.[19]

In early Israel, a special class of religious professionals developed—namely, priests and prophets. They became the supreme authorities in law and religion and also performed some medical functions. The wealthy commercial and political "professionals" were castigated by prophets such as Amos for crushing the poor through dishonest and unethical business practices. The concept of the prophet in ancient Israel was a "religious-cultural creation of the highest order," because this religious profession "presuppose[d] the very source and meaning of the life of the individual and of the covenanted community."[20]

By the time of Jesus, a variety of professions had emerged: priests, teachers, lawyers, physicians, and soldiers. Although Christ often denounced the clerics and legal experts of his day as hypocritical and legalistic, Jesus himself became known as a rabbi from Galilee, a member of the teaching profession. In the Gospels and Acts, we meet another professional, the "beloved physician" Luke, who ministered to Paul and wrote two books of the New Testament.

During the Middle Ages, particularly in northern Europe, little change occurred. With the established church in control, the clergy became the dominant professional group. The religious leaders of the medieval period also controlled education, allowing them to write the rules governing the practice of all other professions. There were some benefits of this control. Medicine, law, business, and teaching all existed within a common framework of shared values and beliefs.

During this time and afterward, many occupations and commercial groups organized into guilds. The guilds served to maintain standards, train recruits, and discipline the wayward. After the Industrial Revolution, some guilds evolved into professions.

Important to an understanding of modern professions and the ministry is the revival of a key biblical doctrine during the Reformation. Before the Reformation, it was generally believed that the only people who received a divine calling were those chosen by God to enter the spiritually superior monastic way. This calling (*vocatio*) was reserved for religious professionals alone. Martin Luther and John Calvin challenged this tradition, basing their argument on the biblical teaching of calling prominent in the Pauline Epistles (Rom. 12:6–8; 1 Cor. 7:20–24; 12:28; Eph. 4:11). Both Reformers asserted that every worthwhile form of work was a divine calling. The farmer, the merchant, and the cobbler, not just the priest, had a call from God to serve the world in their work.

Luther, being a bit more conservative, felt that each person should labor in the occupation of his forebears. Calvin disagreed. He taught that the call to serve God and people was through whatever vocation best suited that person. According to his view, admittance to a profession should be based not on inheritance but on achievement. The importance of this teaching for professional life is difficult to overestimate. "The Judaeo-Christian culture from Biblical times through the Reformation imbued the concept of profession with the moral principle of service grounded in a religious vision of God working together with people for the improvement of all creation. The doctrine of the vocation or calling became the religious and moral theme that most illuminated the meaning of the professions and professional work."[21]

After 1500, most professions stagnated, remaining small in number and exclusive. Members of the professions led the "good life" of leisurely gentlemen, gaining high social status through attachment to the king and his court. Work that required labor was for the trades; professionals lived the life of refinement among the upper classes.

Even as late as the eighteenth century, the education and competence of professionals were deplorable. Physicians knew Latin and the Greek classics but very little about science or how to treat sick people. The law profession had actually deteriorated since medieval times, as barristers primarily served the gentry.

The clergy was not unaffected by these social trends. In eighteenth-century England, the minister's role was mainly "an occupational appendage of gentry status."[22] By the nineteenth century, many of the clergy were eager to be regarded as professionals with specific functions and duties. Regrettably, this desire was difficult to achieve, for a minister's role included many functions more related to his social position as patriarch of his rural parish than to his ordination. Often the local English pastor was also judge, doctor, lawyer, magistrate, and teacher.[23]

The professions in colonial America, however, took on a new character. Unhampered by the social class restrictions and institutional inheritance so rigid in England, the American professional "blithely ignored such hallowed distinctions as that between barrister and attorneys, or between apothecary and physician. Professionals were judged by the competency of their performance and not by the impressiveness of their credentials."[24]

This unique development of the professions in America also had a significant impact on religion. At first there were relatively few professions, the major ones being medicine, law, and ministry. As in rural England, in many towns in the new colonies the minister was the only professional, the one called on to help in matters of law and medicine as well as religion. At this time, all professionals felt a sense of service to the entire community, but they also believed their service was to God. For the minister, this sense of calling, of being chosen by God for this work, was even more intense. Yet Protestants, with their Reformation tradition, also insisted that every occupation was a holy calling. This generalization of the idea of calling led many in America to adopt an attitude of antiprofessionalism. "Lay preachers who were truly called by God could be seen as superior to an educated but spiritually tepid ordained ministry. The growth of the Baptist churches, which began to outnumber the older established Protestant denominations . . . offers an indication of this trend."[25] The social situation in America created a new history for professionals. Because there was no noble class, doctors, lawyers, and ministers attached to the middle class and offered to the young an avenue of expression and achievement.

The number of professions in the United States expanded rapidly in the twentieth century. One of the positive results has been a high degree of specialized knowledge and skills. Orthodontists straighten teeth, neurosurgeons correct spinal injuries, and ministers of music direct church choirs. However, because of the market orientation of American capitalism, the services of professionals have sometimes been seen as one more commodity for sale to the highest bidder. Lawyers often feel like hired guns; doctors appear more preoccupied with technology and economics than patients; ministers view themselves as slaves to laity expectations.

A large Southern Baptist seminary surveyed laity and clergy in eight south-eastern states concerning the role of pastors. About thirty-two hundred people responded. The results indicated unreasonably high expectations for pastors by laity, as well as wide differences of opinion between the two groups.

> Lay respondents showed a strong preference for a direct, aggressive, program-oriented leadership style, whereas professional ministers said they valued "shared, caring relational styles." . . . People in the pews expect pastors to be equally competent in virtually all aspects of ministry. . . . When laypeople were asked 108 questions about qualities for pastoral ministry, "they basically said all 108 are important. So there is nothing unimportant, which is in a way quite unrealistic."[26]

This is part of the crisis that ministers face today as they seek to clarify their role and define their ministry in the modern world.

What conclusions can be drawn from this brief history of the professions? The earliest use of the word *profession* was in relation to those who "professed" vows in a religious order. The essential services provided to society by these religious communities included both the sacred and the secular, as monasteries became centers of culture and education. Thus, these religious orders provided society with artists and educators, experts in law and medicine, political advisers and leaders, as well as theologians, priests, and ministers.[27] Gradually, the three vocations of medicine, law, and divinity came to be regarded as unique. The term *laity* originally referred to those untrained in these three professions. By the late Middle Ages, physicians and lawyers who took no religious vows were practicing their crafts. However, the original qualities the clergy "professed" continued to define the true professional.[28]

One ideal that emerges from this moral heritage of professional life is a theme that Darrell Reeck calls *enablement*, "the devotion of professional skills to meeting the needs of client groups and ultimately, to the common good."[29] The opposite of enablement is exploitation. Reeck believes that a critical question for all contemporary professionals, and especially for the modern minister, is: "Am I in my professional life an enabler or an exploiter?" Before that question can be fully addressed, however, we must first understand what it means today to be a professional and whether that term really fits the minister's role.

The Meaning of *Professional*

In popular language, the word *professional* is used in careless ways that confuse. Athletes call themselves "pros," and people with occupations such as exterminator and beautician advertise their work as "professional." This common usage of the term is intended to elicit from the public both respect and confidence, but it actually conceals the true meaning of the word.

Sociologists have written extensively about the true nature of professions, professionalization, and professionalism. Two major schools have developed: the "Harvard school," exemplified by Talcott Parsons, and the "Chicago school," represented by Eliot Friedson. The Harvard school is functionalist in approach, seeing a profession as a distinct occupation characterized by complex knowledge, social importance, and a high degree of responsibility. The Chicago school sees the category of professional as a "semi-mythic construct" created by members of an occupation to obtain social and economic advantage.[30]

The functional definition of a profession has been accepted by most researchers, and it is conceptually more substantial. Using Talcott Parsons's definition as a basis, James Adams characterizes a profession this way: "It performs a unique and essential social service; it requires a long period of general and specialized training, usually in connection with a university; it presupposes skills that are subjected to rational analysis; service to the community rather than economic gain is supposed to be the dominant motive; standards of competence are defined by a comprehensive self-governing organization of practitioners; a high degree of autonomy . . . ; some code of ethics."[31] Parsons also argues for certain moral obligations, such as competence and a lack of self-interest, as essential to performance of the social function of a profession.

Concerned about the moral drift in medicine, a health practitioner contends that there are four unchangeable characteristics of the helping professions: "The four features that are fundamental to a true profession are: (1) the nature of the human needs it addresses, (2) the vulnerable state of those it serves, (3) the expectations of trust it generates, and (4) the social contract it implies. Taken together, these features set the traditional ideal of a profession apart from other occupations that lay claim to the title."[32]

In a contemporary text on professional ethics, Michael Bayles outlines three central features necessary for an occupation to be a profession: (1) extensive training, (2) a significant intellectual component in the training, and (3) a trained ability that provides an important service in society. He also notes other features common to many professions—namely, credentialing, an organization of members, and autonomy in the professional's work.[33]

Other functional definitions of a professional devised by sociologists are similar, emphasizing four traits: (1) specialized training, (2) a sense of calling to serve the public, (3) self-regulation including a code of ethics, and

(4) autonomy. Reduced to the simplest terms, "a profession is intended to be a combination of *techne* and *ethos*—of technical knowledge and practice combined with responsible behavior . . . the joining of knowledge and character."[34]

A comparison of these professional characteristics with the vocation of minister reveals many points of identity. The role of minister matches all these characteristics except two, a code of ethics and autonomy, both of which are partially met in some denominations.[35]

Concerning the first, a code of ethics, some Christian groups have developed this document for their ministers, while others have not. The reasons for this inconsistency and the difficulty a code of ethics poses for ministers are explored in chapter 8. The second characteristic, autonomy, is the most critical dimension in an analysis of professions and one especially plaguing for the clergy. Professional autonomy is rooted in an authority based on superior competence. It is assumed, for example, that an orthopedic surgeon is competent in his or her area of specialized knowledge and therefore will assume responsibility for professional decisions. This issue of professional autonomy has become a major area of conflict between professionals and the organizations to which they belong.[36]

The autonomy of Protestant ministers is much more limited than other professionals because in most churches the clients (members) are also the directors and owners of the organization in which the ministers practice. There has been no small amount of church conflict over pastoral authority and congregational control.

One of the reasons many sociologists are reluctant to include clergypersons in the category of professional is that the pastoral role has become an occupational conglomerate. There are not only various specializations, such as education minister, church counselor, church administrator, and youth minister, but also a multiplicity of tasks in each category. "The job means different things to different people, depending upon who these people are and what they do. In fact, the overall image of the clergy appears confused, and to many, both in and outside the ministry, unattractive."[37]

Another research team, A. M. Carr-Saunders and P. A. Wilson, in a standard volume on the professions, excludes the church from consideration because "all those functions related to the ordinary business of life . . . which used to fall to the Church, have been taken over by other vocations. The functions remaining to the Church are spiritual."[38]

An adequate definition of *professions* is critical because "one of the most revealing ways of grasping the character of any civilization is precisely through discerning the ultimate orientation and the types of leadership which the civilization adopts."[39] Our culture could be judged by the nature of professional life today. A widening gap is developing between the traditional definition of a profession and the way professions function at the beginning of the twenty-first century.

Before we attempt to determine whether the minister is a true professional, then, one other task remains: to understand the cultural crisis that threatens professional life today. It may well be, as a result of the shift of values in modern American society, that the possibility for a minister to be a professional is no longer an option.

The Crisis in Professional Life Today

Michael Bayles begins both editions of his contemporary and often-quoted book *Professional Ethics* with this paragraph:

> The ethics of professional conduct is being questioned as never before in history. Lawyers, physicians, engineers, accountants, and other professionals are being criticized for disregarding the rights of clients and the public interest. Perhaps society is reconsidering the role of professions and professionals. In any event, many difficult ethical challenges are being faced by both professionals and the public. Given the important roles professionals are playing in society during the last decade of the twentieth century, everyone is concerned with professional ethics.[40]

The Alban Institute sponsored a study in 2001 on the status of leadership in American religion. The study concluded that professional ministry today evidences two basic pictures: crisis and ferment.[41] What has happened?

Between the Reformation and modern professionalization, the twin Christian doctrines of vocation and covenant changed decisively. The sense of calling was broadened to the "priesthood of all believers" and eventually included every individual. The doctrine of covenant encouraged the formation of religious communities whose members believed they served the purposes of God by serving others.

> The idea of vocation has been replaced by the idea of career as the governing notion of professional life. And the idea of covenant has been replaced by the idea of contract. "Career" comes from a word that referred to the race course in the ancient Roman world. It is a word that refers to achievement by competitive combat, getting ahead, and triumphing over others—even if such achievement involves merely going around in circles. . . . The word "contract" refers to the utilitarian agreements between parties whereby we establish a give-and-take relationship in which goods or services are exchanged on a tit-for-tat basis.[42]

This secularization of vocation and covenant into career and contract has seriously threatened the recovery of the traditional virtues of professionalism. A physician, Edmund Pellegrino, is alarmed that the central ideas of a profession—altruistic service and effacement of personal reward—are today downplayed. The shift is in the direction of self-interest and away from moral commitments. Pellegrino believes that the present moral character defects of many doctors, lawyers, scientists, and even ministers constitute a grave danger to professional life and to our present society.[43]

The crisis has both a personal and a social dimension. On the personal side, contemporary professional life poses certain risks. A researcher who has studied the professions in American history has warned that teachers, doctors, lawyers, and pastors face three present dangers: to become more self-reliant, more success oriented, and more convinced of how deserving they are. He concludes: "The church of Christ does not need smug professionals, preoccupied with managing their own careers. The church does not need success-oriented members who reach out only to other winners. The church does not need those who expect the good life because of how hard they work. Instead, Christians are to live out the original ideal of the professions: to serve rather than to be served."[44] On the other hand, Dennis Campbell has analyzed some realities in American society that threaten a Christian approach to professional practice. Three major movements in Western culture that are wearing away the underpinnings of professionalism are secularization, pluralism, and relativism.[45]

The United States, like most other nations in the Western world, is predominantly secular. Life is no longer informed by a vision of God or the church. Many views of reality compete in the marketplace of ideas, and thus no one view commands the ultimate loyalty of a majority of Americans.

During the Middle Ages, when the professions were emerging, a Christian worldview prevailed. All aspects of personal and social life were defined by the church and a religious interpretation of life. Society was unified by common religious beliefs and shared values. Concepts of professionalism developed during a time when Christian moral values were widely accepted.

Secularization, like weeds in an unmanaged garden, gradually outgrew the Christian monopoly of Western civilization. As new views challenged the traditions of the past, a plurality of ideas about the meaning and value of life emerged. This pluralism created many problems for the common life of Americans because it bred another cultural monster: relativism. Relativism contends that there is no one absolute view of reality; therefore, all perspectives are equal in value.

With nothing of ultimate meaning to believe in, the average American must turn to material reality for salvation. Religious affirmations make no sense for people who believe that only what is, is now, and there is no more. When it comes to values and virtues, modern Americans are diverse, divided, and often disinterested.

This absence of shared values is a serious problem for the professions. Since the devastating attacks by radical Islamic terrorists on September 11, 2001, the American public has become acutely aware of multiculturalism in our society. Tolerance of all views and values is the new order of the day. Yet if America encourages a pluralism of worldviews, and if all these views and their ethical teachings are of equal value, how can anyone make judgments about moral actions? "Unless judgments can be made about moral decisions, they are not *moral* decisions, but simply decisions of individual idiosyncrasy. Ethical reflection requires clearly stated assumptions to which one can appeal when reasons for action are examined."[46] Developing guidelines for ethical conduct among professionals requires some consensus about values. The social crisis facing all professionals today is the increasing lack of shared values in American society.

Professional ethics also faces a crisis that has other personal and social dimensions. In many ways, it is an outgrowth and reflection of the social changes discussed above. The authority and identity of the professional person is in jeopardy as never before. Traditionally, the authority of doctors, lawyers, and ministers was never questioned because of their vocational competence and their dedication to serve. In the contemporary world, however, the lay public is challenging the professionals at both points. As laypeople have become more knowledgeable, they have become more critical of professional practice. Public disclosures of negligent physicians, incompetent lawyers, and misguided ministers have increased society's skepticism. Lawsuits have escalated dramatically.

A lack of public confidence in professional competence has paralleled the charge of diminishing professional dedication. Historically, those practicing medicine, law, and religion were trusted because people assumed their only interest was the welfare of those they served. Today, people are not so sure a professional practitioner can be trusted. "Reports abound of unnecessary surgery, unreliable dental practice, questionable legal advice, and poor-quality teaching."[47]

Since 1977 Gallup has asked the public to rate the honesty and standards of various professions and occupations. In 1985 the clergy had its highest positive rating of 67 percent. In the 1989 poll 12 percent of the public said the clergy rated "very high" on ethical standards, and 43 percent gave a rating of "high"—a 55 percent favorable rating, second to pharmacists and druggists (62 percent), followed by physicians and dentists (52 percent). In

2002, 52 percent of Americans gave "very high" or "high" ratings to clergy, compared to 64 percent in 2001. Researchers attributed the decline in large part to the highly publicized sex scandals that plagued the Roman Catholic Church in 2002, but religious leaders believed there was more to it.[48] (This number dropped to 45 percent in 2015.)

The point is obvious. Doctors, lawyers, teachers, and even ministers do not command the aura of respect and admiration they once did. Professionals themselves do not share common values, which has no doubt contributed to this question of competence and dedication. Ministers in particular are confused about their identity. James Glasse reported over three decades ago what seems to be true even today: "The image of the ministry is cloudy, confused, and unattractive."[49] In particular, he noted that three images of ministry create an identity crisis for the clergy: the ministry as (1) a calling for a particular kind of person, (2) a calling from a particular kind of institution, and (3) a calling to a particular kind of work.[50] In an analysis of the role of the minister, James Gustafson further points out: "The problem the minister faces in any social context is that of determining *who he is* and *what he is doing* within the complexity of his functions. He frequently lacks, more than anything else, an awareness of what he is about, and therefore he has no central focus for the integration of his various activities."[51]

The crisis faced by ministers is like that of other professionals because both groups have been significantly affected by the shifts in cultural values in America. Perhaps the situation is best summed up by Martin Marty in a text on clergy ethics in America. The highly respected historian contends that the context for clergy ethics has changed to "a more privately contracted entrepreneurial understanding."[52] Five elements have intensified this centuries-long trend: (1) a secular view of the clergy, (2) the legal subordination of religion to the state, (3) modernity and modernization, (4) the moral specialization of the clergy, and (5) theological accommodation. Using show-business lingo, Marty explains that in days past a minister's identity was determined by being part of a church establishment or denomination, but now "you are only as good as your last act."[53] After extensive research, an Alban Institute leader concludes: "If professional ministry is to take its new place in our postmodern world, it need not compete with other professional jurisdictions. . . . The new jurisdiction that awaits professional ministry depends upon a return to the theological vocation of interpretation—a prophetic role filled by the professional minister."[54]

An exploration of the factors that have contributed to a crisis in the professions has revealed that Americans lack a shared moral tradition. This cultural change has created a social and personal crisis for professionals. An absence of shared values has contributed to skepticism from without and an identity crisis from within. In a secularized, materialistic culture in which moral values are relative, what is a minister to be and to do?

This brings us then to the crux of the matter: Is the minister a true professional? If the minister does "profess" something, what is it they profess, and in what way does this "profession" affect ministerial ethics?

The Minister as a Professional

To summarize, then, we can now define a professional as a broadly educated person with highly developed skills and knowledge who works autonomously under the discipline of an ethic developed and enforced by peers, who renders a social service that is essential and unique, and who makes complex judgments involving potentially dangerous consequences.[55] A professional is more concerned with communal interest than with self, and with services rendered than with financial rewards.[56] The question we must now answer is this: Does the minister's vocation fit this general characterization of a profession?

First, the concept of a professional does not neatly describe the minister. Many ordained ministers do not have a higher education, and even more lack professional (theological) training. Although the clergy was the historical setting to which the modern professions owe their origin, intellectual training among modern ministers varies greatly.[57]

Another sphere of difference is the social role of the minister, which today includes not only pastoral responsibilities but also many other parish skills. The contemporary minister, for example, must be adept in business administration and public relations, tasks for which most ministers do not have technical competence.[58] At the same time, theological education has moved away from the study of divinity to provide "a cafeteria-like offering of studies in specialized disciplines and an accumulation of professional skills."[59] Too often this effort to prepare ministers for the multiplicity of vocational demands they will face is incomplete and superficial.

Peter Jarvis has raised another question: Is the ministry an occupation, a profession, or a status? He notes two major difficulties: the concept of profession has undergone a transformation from status to occupation, and there are no universally accepted criteria for a profession. Jarvis concludes that the minister is something less than a professional because (1) the ministry is so heterogeneous that it is impossible to argue that it is either an occupation or a profession, and (2) the ministry has become a status profession with no high social position and thus is anachronistic in a world emphasizing achievement and specialization.[60]

Although a lack of autonomy and specialization may prevent ministers from being considered professionals, Jarvis believes this "neither denies the possibility of individual ministers being professionals nor that they may develop expertise which makes them highly skilled practitioners."[61]

In an opposite sense, the minister of a Christian church is something more than or other than a professional. Similar to Søren Kierkegaard's distinction between the apostle and the genius, there is a "nonprofessional" ingredient in the vocation of the religious calling. The minister's *vocatio* is not of this world.[62] This distinction underscores the minister's unique authority, which is grounded not ultimately in technical competence but in religious and moral tradition. This means the clerical office is legitimized by its charismatic witness, which does not maintain cultural tradition as much as reject a self-sufficient culture, bringing it under the judgment of the One who transforms both church and culture.[63] Perhaps for this reason Jacques Ellul contrasted vocation and profession, seeing them as a "total divorce between what society unceasingly asks of us and God's will. Service to God cannot be written into a profession."[64]

Two Duke University professors, Stanley Hauerwas and William Willimon, also believe the ministry is something more than one of the "helping professions." They resist placing the minister in this category because of the implied presumption that ministry is simply a matter of meeting the needs of people. This "sentimentality" makes a ministry of integrity impossible, for people "not trained to want the right things rightly" will shape ministry more than the gospel narrative. "Being a minister (like a pastor) is not a vocation merely to help people. We are called to help people 'in the name of Jesus.'"[65]

Having admitted these ways in which the modern minister of the gospel is unlike the traditional professional, let us also note some ways in which the ministerial vocation fits that designation. Unlike typical specialists today, ministers are usually concerned with the total person; they are generalists with broad educational backgrounds, traditionally a trait of the professional. As the status of professionals depends on technical competence in their field, so the status of the clergyperson depends on competence in certain theological disciplines, both theoretical and practical.[66] Church clerics, for example, must be able to explain the meaning of Christian marriage as well as perform a wedding service.

As leaders in the colony that exists as God's redemptive community in the world, pastors and other ministers render service that is both unique and essential. The message they preach and teach is "dangerous knowledge," for it reveals the real meaning and purpose of life, as well as knowledge of the One who is "the way, and the truth, and the life" (John 14:6).

As a professional, the minister of the gospel is dedicated to serving others. Financial reward and social status are not primary motivations; the minister puts the needs of others before his or her own, for this is what it means to be a called minister and a follower of Jesus.

Many ministerial bodies have developed codes of ethics for their clergy. As will be explained in chapter 8, these codes are usually developed by peers for guiding ministerial conduct, particularly in areas of unusual vulnerability. At the same time, there is a conspicuous absence of codes of ethics for large groups of ministers, particularly those of the "free church" tradition.

The classic defense of the minister as a professional is set forth by James Glasse in *Profession: Minister*. Urging church leaders to reaffirm their vocational identity as professionals, Glasse suggests that a religious professional should embody five important characteristics. The Christian minister is:

1. an *educated* person, the master of some body of knowledge. This knowledge is neither esoteric nor mundane but essential to ministry and available through accredited educational institutions.

2. an *expert* person, the master of a specific group of vocational skills. These abilities, while requiring some talent, can be learned and refined through practice and with supervision.

3. an *institutional* person, relating to society and serving persons through a social institution, of which the minister is partly servant and partly master. Ministers are also part of an association of clergy, usually a denomination, to which they are uniquely responsible.

4. a *responsible* person who "professes" to act competently in any situation that requires the minister's service. This includes the highest standards of ethical conduct.

5. a *dedicated* person who also "professes" to provide something of great value for society. The minister's dedication to the values of Christian ministry is the ultimate basis for evaluating ministerial service.[67]

Glasse builds his concept of "the professional perspective" on these five points, which all professions have in common. To identify the minister as a professional, Glasse traces the relationship of doctor, lawyer, teacher, and clergy to these factors.[68]

Adapting this model, Gaylord Noyce develops a grid that compares five professions (he adds business manager) in like manner. Although his list of elements is similar, he includes several additional characteristics. For him a professional (1) is educated in a body of knowledge, (2) makes a commitment of service, (3) is part of a peer group that sets standards of practice, (4) is in an institutional matrix that claims allegiance, and (5) serves immediate goals in the name of certain ultimate values that are (6) specific to that profession.[69] Noyce graphically illustrates how these aspects of obligations apply to the religious professional. Reflecting on the grid, Noyce concludes that the minister belongs in the category of a professional. "The ordained minister learns theology, and steps into service in relation not only to a denomination and through it to the whole church, but also to peers in the ordained ministry. Entry into the colleagueship is celebrated as the ordinand pledges churchly participation and loyalty. All of this is clearly designated for the mission of Christ and the extension of Christian faith, by means of the proximate goals of pastoral care and the building up of the church."[70]

In an article in the *Christian Century* titled "The Pastor Is (Also) a Professional," Noyce adds, "Thus, rightly understood, the professional tag is not destructive. Quite the contrary. It can firm up our sense of purpose and our understanding of how to go about the work of ministry."[71]

What then can we honestly conclude? Should the minister today accept the title "professional," or should it be rejected? It is our conviction that there is more to be gained than lost by a minister assuming the designation of a professional. This is not to say that this title fits neatly or that there are not some drawbacks to the proposal. Nevertheless, as Glasse and many others observe, there are two main reasons for seeing ministers as professionals: traditional identification and rational definition.[72]

On the one hand, many clergy today fit the traditional description in the historical sense: university educated, full time, resident, tenured, and salaried. On the other hand, even among denominations that allow less than these standards, expectations for ministers continue to rise toward professional standards in all categories. Most Protestant churches view their ministers as professional, whether they use the title or not.[73]

If we who are ministers call ourselves professionals, what significance does this have for ministerial ethics? Acknowledging the danger of being redundant, let us once more affirm that if Christian ministers are professionals, they are committed to certain ideals. The standards of professional practice that apply to Christian ministry include these six ethical obligations:

1. *Education.* The minister will prepare for Christian service by experiencing a broad liberal arts education, followed by specialized training in theology and ministry. Ministers will also be committed to a lifelong process of study and growth that prepares them for continued service (2 Tim. 2:15).

2. *Competency.* The church shepherd will develop and refine pastoral gifts and vocational skills in order to act competently in any situation that requires his or her services (1 Cor. 12:7–11; Eph. 4:11–12).

3. *Autonomy.* The minister is called to a life of responsible decision making involving potentially dangerous consequences. As a spiritual leader, the minister will make decisions and exert pastoral authority in light of the servant-leader model exemplified by Christ (John 13:1–16).

4. *Service.* The minister's motivation for ministry will be neither social status nor financial reward but rather *agape* love, to serve others in Christ's name (1 Cor. 13).

5. *Dedication.* The minister will "profess" to provide something of great value, the good news of God's salvation and the demonstration of God's love through Christian ministry. To these values the called of God are dedicated (Rom. 1:11–17).

6. *Ethics.* In relation to congregation, colleagues, and community, as well as in personal life, the ordained will live under the discipline of an ethic that upholds the highest standards of Christian morality (1 Tim. 3:1–7).

One intangible factor is the honor all professionals seek: the esteem of others in their profession.[74] Anyone familiar with Harper Lee's novel *To Kill a Mockingbird*, later an Academy Award–winning movie, will remember the climax of the story. Atticus Finch fails to gain an acquittal for Tom Robinson, the black man who had been falsely accused of raping a white woman in a small Alabama town. As the white lawyer leaves the courtroom, the black observers who had been segregated in the balcony all rise. One of them says to the young narrator of the book, "Miss Jean Louise, stand up. Your father's passin'." Justice has failed, but the pursuit of it brought professional honor.

In conclusion, vocation, in the sense of a calling by God, is the essential element that prevents the concept of a professional minister from degenerating into an enterprise for personal success. While not demanding that a minister exemplify the notion of the professional in every way, we are convinced that there are good historical and theological reasons for asserting that the Christian minister is a professional. If this is the case, then the recovery of the religious and social meaning of the clergy vocation and profession can revitalize the church as well as build a foundation for an ethical ministry. Perhaps Paul Camenisch sums it up best: "I would argue that the professional ethics model is useful and appropriate for the clergy as far as it goes. Seen positively as the standards that guide professionals in their relations to clients and the larger society in light of the special skills and knowledge they claim to have, the distinctive goal they pursue in their professional activity, and the atypical moral commitment they aspire to, professional ethics sets a floor below which the clergy ought not fall."[75]

The heart of this book is an attempt to explain what this commitment to an ethical ministry means in these various arenas of the minister's life. Without being legalistic, we will attempt to apply and illustrate the ethical demands the gospel makes on the professional life of the Christian minister. It is our hope that by the time we reach the last chapter, you will be prepared to write a personal code of ethics as a guide for your ministry.

The task of the next chapter is to review the art of ethics. To evaluate the ethical life of the minister, a clergyperson must first have a clear understanding of the role of character, conduct, and moral vision in the process of making good moral choices.

Suggested Reading

Bayles, Michael D. *Professional Ethics*. 2nd ed. Belmont, CA: Wadsworth, 1989.

Campbell, Dennis M. *Doctors, Lawyers, Ministers: Christian Ethics in Professional Practice*. Nashville: Abingdon, 1982.

Glasse, James D. *Profession: Minister*. Nashville: Abingdon, 1968.

May, William F. *Beleaguered Rulers: The Public Obligation of the Professional*. Louisville: Westminster John Knox, 2003.

Noyce, Gaylord. *Pastoral Ethics: Professional Responsibilities of the Clergy*. Nashville: Abingdon, 1988.

Reeck, Darrell. *Ethics for the Professions: A Christian Perspective*. Minneapolis: Augsburg, 1982.

Theology Today 59 (October 2002): 349–420.

Wind, James P., Russell Burck, Paul F. Camenisch, and Dennis P. McCann, eds. *Clergy Ethics in a Changing Society: Mapping the Terrain*. Louisville: Westminster John Knox, 1991.

2

Being Good and Doing Good

Moral Formation for Ministry

On January 31, 1872, renowned minister Henry Ward Beecher traveled to Yale to deliver the first of the Beecher Lectures on preaching. His biographer notes:

> He had a bad night, not feeling well. Went to his hotel, got his dinner, lay down to take a nap. About two o'clock he got up and began to shave without having been able to get at any plan of the lecture to be delivered within the hour. Just as he had his face lathered and was beginning to strop his razor, the whole thing came out of the clouds and dawned on him. He dropped his razor, seized his pencil, and dashed off the memoranda for it and afterwards cut himself badly, he said, thinking it out.[1]

A century later another renowned minister, Frederick Buechner, commented, "And well the old pulpiteer might have cut himself with his razor because part of the inner world his lecture came from . . . was the deep trouble that he was in or the deep trouble that was in him."[2] Rumors about Beecher's relationship with the wife of a parishioner had gone beyond the gossip stage. Embarrassing letters and tearful confessions had surfaced. A public trial for adultery was not far away. So as Beecher stood gazing into the hotel mirror,

---

Although the method of moral decision making outlined and discussed in this chapter is mainly applied to ministerial ethics, this procedure could also serve as an outline for the study of the broader discipline of Christian ethics.

with soap on his face and a razor in his hand, what he saw was not himself, for everything he believed in and stood for and had come to Yale to talk about was not reflected in that mirror. "Henry Ward Beecher cut himself with his razor and wrote out notes for that first Beecher Lecture in blood because, whatever else he was or aspired to be or was famous for being, he was a man of flesh and blood, and so were all the men over the years who traveled to New Haven after him to deliver the same lectures."[3] All ministers who stand behind pulpits less prominent than the one at Yale can also "cut themselves badly."

In 2016 the director of the master of divinity program for the Disciples of Christ Church at Oklahoma Christian University wrote a passionate plea for ministerial ethics, stating: "An ethical crisis exists in ministry . . . with sexual scandals and abuses, homosexuality, financial irregularities frequently in the news . . . [and] less visible ethical issues that tempt ministers daily in their choices, goals, and obligations. . . . Twenty years ago ministerial ethics was seldom discussed. Today, a quick survey of the Internet reveals hundreds of sites with policy statements, disclaimers, and resources for ministerial ethics."[4]

Again, how do ministers keep their lives unscarred by ethical misconduct? Is there a single formula for learning to do the right thing? Are "good ministers" born with moral character, or do they acquire the ability to make right moral decisions?

Some moral choices are fairly ordinary, such as choosing between recreation with the family or sermon preparation. Others are quite complex. A teenager reveals in counseling that she is pregnant but asks you not to tell her parents. What do you do? Every day ministers must make decisions that touch other people's lives, as well as their own. In the process they often ask, "Did I do the right thing? How does one know? Can I improve my ability to make the right choices?"

A hotly debated topic is whether ethics can be taught. In a *New York Times* article, Michael Levin asserts that "ethics courses are an utterly pointless exercise. . . . Abstract knowledge of right and wrong no more contributes to character than knowledge of physics contributes to bicycling."[5] Teachers of ethics responded vigorously. Acknowledging Levin's contention that right living is mainly a matter of instilling good habits of the heart, they nevertheless asked, "Is there no place for reason?" A decent ethics class, they claimed, accomplishes three things: it stimulates moral imagination, hones moral analysis, and elicits a sense of moral obligation.[6] Indeed, these three goals spotlight the aims of this chapter.

In religious circles, the argument against learning ethics takes a different form. There is a popular myth that ministers automatically know the right thing to do. As noted in chapter 1, most ministers believe their vocation is a calling from God. In addition, the laity often assumes that God calls only persons of good moral character to begin with. Some believe that a minister develops moral sensitivity through education and experience so that by the time of ordination, an articulate ethical expert walks forth with credentials in one hand and a résumé in the other. However, no one knows better than pastors that Solomonic wisdom is rare, even among the clergy. For ministers to develop skills in moral decision making, they must understand the role of virtues in character, the place of values in conduct, and the way to develop integrity through moral vision.[7]

In light of the continuing moral failures of prominent preachers, it is surprising that anyone believes ministers are innately endowed with moral character or discernment. Nevertheless, it is not uncommon (especially in seminary classrooms) to hear a young theologue say, "Why do I have to take ethics? I know what's right. I believe the Bible, and I am committed to do the will of God." Many experienced ministers also believe they need no special training in moral decision making. Somehow they feel that their enlightened conscience, Scripture, or common sense will carry them through.

This last statement raises a basic ethical question, that of authority. Who, or what, determines right or wrong for the minister? Is the answer found within the person? Has God given a trustworthy "inner light" to ministers—a moral gyroscope that always points northward toward God's perfect will? Thomas Aquinas saw reason as an infallible teacher. Joseph Butler, on the other hand, elevated the conscience to the role of unerring guide. Quakers such as George Fox listened for the voice from the "inner light" in order to decide what was right or wrong.

Most Christian ministers look beyond themselves for a dependable ethical compass to help them navigate through moral storms. Evangelical clerics normally turn first to the Bible. Worshipers often hear their ministers proclaim, "Look to the Bible. It has the answer for every question." Certainly, most Protestant clergy accept Scripture as the "main tangible, objective source for a knowledge of the will of God."[8] Yet sometimes our understanding of Scripture is so limited that we view the Old Testament simply as a book of moral rules and the New Testament simply as an advanced ethic of principles. Closer examination, however, reveals that the entire Bible includes a diversity of ways to do moral reasoning.[9]

Two contemporary ethicists have appealed to their colleagues to reconsider the role of the Bible in Christian ethics. In *Bible and Ethics in the Christian Life*, Bruce Birch and Larry Rasmussen build a strong case for seeing the Bible as the major "formative and normative" authority for Christian character development and moral decision making.[10] Yet simply saying "follow the Bible" does not solve all our moral questions. Some ethical issues, such as divorce and war, seem to be both condoned and condemned in Scripture. Also, a number of modern moral concerns, such as artificial insemination and media morality, did not exist in biblical times. Properly applying the ethical teachings of Scripture to these and other issues requires skillful exegesis and sound hermeneutics.[11] The Bible has a rich vein of ethical gold to be mined by the minister "who correctly handles the word of truth" (2 Tim. 2:15 NIV).

Taken as a whole, then, the Bible is the primary resource for doing ethics. "The Biblical writers do offer a helpful lead. They suggest what sort of ethical approach is appropriate for the Christian—even if a lot of the details remain to be filled in."[12] One way the "details are filled in" is through the work of the Holy Spirit, the subjective means of revelation. As Christ is the pattern for morality, the Spirit is the power that makes Christian living possible (Rom. 8:13–14). The apostle John wrote, "But when he, the Spirit of truth, comes, he will guide you into all the truth" (John 16:13 NIV). The word *truth* presumably includes moral truth, the Spirit's help and guidance in moral choices. The apostle Paul reminds us that the *paraclete* of God is our abiding moral guide (Rom. 8:9–14; 1 Cor. 6:19–20). Sometimes we limit the Spirit's work to sudden inspiration or direct prompting regarding a certain action. While the Spirit can certainly guide in this way, he also gives insight to Christians in the midst of serious reflection on moral decisions.

What about the Christian tradition—the documents of early Christianity as well as the thoughts of present-day writers? Some of the best insights about Christian living are found in the writings of Augustine and Aquinas, Teresa of Àvila and Catherine of Siena, Luther and Calvin, along with those of modern ethicists such as Lisa Sowle Cahill, Stanley Hauerwas, Karen Lebacqz, Richard J. Mouw, and Allen Verhey.[13] Ethically serious ministers should read widely from the great books that inform and inspire.

Reflection and the ability to analyze situations are also extremely important aids in moral decision making. Prayer is a vital link to the mind of God and often the final way of confirming God's will; this was true in Jesus's life (Matt. 26:42; Luke 6:12; John 17). Many modern ethics scholars contend, "The primary question of Christian ethics is not 'What should I do?' but 'What has been given to us?'"[14] Sam Wells, Anglican cleric and former dean of Duke University Chapel, counsels Christian ministers to "discern what is fitting in the moment."[15] However, these latter situational approaches can be quite subjective and individualistic.

In light of all of the various ways to determine the Christian ethic, how does a church leader discover and do the right thing? In sum, the Christian minister must utilize every means at his or her command in order to discern the will of God. The chapters that follow will seek to illustrate and amplify the application of Christian ethical principles to ministry.

This list of resources brings to mind an important distinction. Is ethics a matter of character or conduct? Which is more important, virtues or values? Does what I *am* determine what I *do*, or does what I *do* shape who I *am*? The answer to these last two questions is yes. Being affects doing, and doing shapes being.

Although some ethicists believe the key to morality is character development, an equal number argue that the secret to correct conduct is how one does ethics. In fact, both "being good" (character) and "doing good" (conduct) are necessary. The two elements are interdependent. Like the bow and the violin, they work together to produce the harmonious music that we call moral vision—a lifestyle of "living good." The best word to describe the minister's moral life is *integrity*, a term that is the theme of this book and the "integrating" element that unifies character, conduct, and moral vision into a "life worthy of the calling you have received" (Eph. 4:1 NIV).

Discovering the will of God and discerning the right thing to do are not always easy; doing the right thing is equally difficult. In Dante's *Inferno*, the first group in hell whom the poet meets are those who could not make a moral decision. The process of learning what is moral for the Christian minister, as well as developing the fortitude to do the right thing, is a lifelong challenge. Growing in the ability to analyze each situation correctly, applying Christian principles and perspectives wisely, and walking in the pathway that leads toward the ultimate will of God are the goals of an ethical ministry.

As we begin the larger discussion of ministerial ethics, let us be sure that we understand the basics of moral decision making. There are three major components in this task: character, conduct, and moral vision or integrity. Sometimes ethicists use the terms *virtues*, *values*, and *vision* to define these three dynamics in the moral life.[16] Being a good minister is obviously a matter of *being*; however, it is also a matter of *doing* and a matter of *living*. As with each leg of a three-legged stool, each of these ethical supports is needed to keep us from falling and failing in our moral choices.

Being Good—the Ethics of Character

Henry Ward Beecher saw two images in his hotel mirror the night before the Yale lectures. He gazed at both the man he wanted to be and the person he had become. Although Rev. Beecher had an ideal image of himself in his mind, the face he viewed as he shaved troubled him. He was ashamed to look himself in the eye, for that meant facing his own failure and folly. Perhaps that is why he "cut himself badly."

Beecher is certainly not the only preacher who bleeds, "for all have sinned" (Rom. 3:23 NIV). In one way or another, every person of the cloth has felt the weight of his or her own humanity. We have all cut ourselves—if not in the flesh, then in the spirit. But the question is not "Have I ever failed?" Rather, it is "How do I live as a human being in the world and not be controlled by my human appetites?"

A large part of the answer is found in the merging of those two images in the mirror, synthesizing the ideal person we ought to be with the real person we are capable of becoming. It all begins with the development of the inner life—something called *character*.

The Meaning of Character

Character is basic to all ethical decisions. Who we are determines what we do. Jesus stressed that truth in his teachings, especially in the Sermon on the Mount (Matt. 5–7). Scholars agree that this monumental message contains the essence of Christ's ethic. Jesus emphasized again and again that character precedes conduct and that morality is a matter of the heart (5:3–48). It is futile to pray or give gifts to the poor in order "to be seen by others," Jesus said, for wrong motives nullify good deeds (6:1–8). Christ condemned the superficial righteousness of many scribes and Pharisees, not because the act was wrong but because the actor played the role of hypocrite (5:20; 6:5). Albert Knudson notes that Jesus upheld two principles that all Christians accept: the principle of love and the principle of moral inwardness.[17] The first is the supreme Christian virtue (1 Cor. 13:13); the second is the key to Christian morality: character.

Though we all have an idea of what the term *character* means, it is not that easy to define. Character refers to the kind of person who acts in a certain way. It is the inner realities of the self. Theologian-ethicist Stanley Hauerwas describes character as "the qualification or determination of our self-agency, formed by our having certain intentions rather than others."[18] William Willimon calls it the "basic moral orientation that gives unity, definition, and direction to our lives by forming our habits and intentions into meaningful and predictable patterns that have been determined by our dominant convictions."[19] According to Willimon, character is formed consciously and unconsciously in a community or a social setting.

Sondra Ely Wheeler praises character and virtue ethics as those "skills, dispositions, and habits that enable us to behave rightly under pressure," stating the paradoxical classical insight that "you cannot act virtuously without possessing virtue, and you cannot develop virtue without acting virtuously."[20]

No one-sentence definition or paragraph description can begin to do justice to the complexity of the concept of character. More important to the task at hand, however, is the need to understand how moral character is formed and how it functions in a Christian's ethical life.

The focus of decision making has shifted to the role of character and the place of its source: community. Perhaps no modern writer has emphasized the place of character in Christian ethics more than Stanley Hauerwas. In his view, what we *are* is the ultimate determinative of what we *do*. As Glen Saul writes, individuals do not approach a moral choice objectively; "rather, each person brings the dispositions, experience, traditions, heritage, and virtues that he or she has cultivated."[21] We develop these "habits of the heart" within the communities to which we belong: family, church, schools, and society.

If character is that inner "moral orientation" that shapes our lives into "meaningful and predictable patterns," then the Christian minister must internalize "both the demands and limits of professional life to the point of behaving ethically most of the time as though by instinct."[22] This reality, that being shapes doing, influences an approach to personal and social ethics. "The first task of Christian social ethics, therefore, is not to make the 'world' better or more just, but to help Christian people form their community consistent with their conviction."[23]

Like Beecher, we look into the mirror each morning, gazing at two images. One is clear and distinct; it is the real person we are. The other is a hazy projection from our inner being; it is the person we hope to be. Rather than always asking "What should I do?" we should also ask "What should I be?"

The Role of Virtues in Character

Darrell Reeck describes character ethics as "expressive ethics." The question he poses is, "What moral values do you wish to manifest through your life and practice?"[24] As traditional Catholic moral theology states it, *agere sequitur esse*, we act out of who we are." "Character refers to the kind of person who acts in a certain way. It focuses on inner realities of the self: motives, intention, attitudes, dispositions. We do not see character directly. We see it in its fruits."[25] Character consists of those personality traits that are moral and traditionally have been called *virtues*. Historically, character ethics has encouraged the cultivation of moral excellences considered essential to the "good life."

Ancient Greek philosophers saw four traits as cardinal virtues: prudence, justice, temperance, and courage. Prudence is practical wisdom, not to be confused with intelligence. Such wisdom always leads to good choices. Justice centers on fairness, honesty, and the rule of law. Temperance is self-discipline, the capacity to control one's impulses to gratify immediate desires that are harmful in the long run. Courage, also called fortitude, is the capacity to do what is right or necessary, even in the face of adversity. "It is not good enough to get two out of three or three out of four. That might be great for baseball, but it is bad for society. The core virtues make each other possible. A sense of justice is ineffectual if one lacks the courage to stand against injustice. Courage without wisdom is simply foolhardiness. And all the other virtues are undercut when one lacks self-control."[26]

Christian theologians such as Augustine and Aquinas accepted these ideal traits as the very best natural humans could discover through reason. To these cardinal virtues they added the theological virtues of faith, hope, and love, virtues received through revelation. "For the Greeks, as well as the Christians, virtue was the central concept for moral reflection. Although there was no complete consensus about what constitutes virtue or which virtues should be considered primary, it was accepted that consideration of morality began with descriptions of the virtuous life."[27]

For many centuries, the Christian moral life was mainly a matter of pursuing the right virtues. In a general sense, once the virtuous life was achieved, one was believed to be a "good person." Although virtue has had an important place in Christian ethics from the beginning, there has also been some suspicion of it. Reformers such as Luther saw the inherent danger in such a quest. Much evil is the corruption of good, and much vice the perversion of virtue. The very pursuit of morality, Luther felt, inevitably led to self-righteousness. Rejecting the Aristotelian idea that ethics was a movement from vice to virtue, the German Reformer said that if there is a "movement," it is from vice *and* virtue to grace.[28]

Modern theologian Reinhold Niebuhr has also reminded us that human nature has a tremendous capacity for self-deception and evil in the guise of good.[29] In our zeal to defend orthodoxy and uphold righteousness, we may sometimes manipulate the truth to suit our purposes, read data with a bias, or use people to achieve our grand goals. Despite these built-in dangers, character remains the single most important factor in ethical decision making. A person must *be* something before they can *do* anything. A person of integrity not only tells the truth but is also truthful.

Writing to ministers, Karen Lebacqz pleads for two basic character traits: trustworthiness and prudence. Ministerial character absolutely requires trustworthiness. A clergyperson must be "a person of integrity who not only does the 'right' thing, but is an *honorable person*."[30] Trustworthiness, writes

Lebacqz, means that a minister is a "trustworthy trustee," one who can be trusted to be honest, fair, helpful, and not hurtful. The minister must be not like Judas but like Jesus.[31]

No real Christian ministry can exist without the ability to discern the truth. *Prudence* is Lebacqz's word for it. This virtue helps a minister perceive what is required in any situation. Prudence, or discernment, is the ability to make right decisions and thus is central to ethical decision making.[32] Lewis Smedes agrees. A key element in Christian decision making, declared the late Fuller Seminary professor, is "the ability to see what is really going on, the small things . . . the difference between things . . . what is new and what is bizarre . . . what is excellent and what is only good."[33]

Yale professor Gaylord Noyce has addressed the professional responsibilities of the clergy in his book *Pastoral Ethics*. The basic character trait necessary in ministers, Noyce contends, is "faithful integrity." A responsible shepherd of God strives to be "a person of religious integrity, a person of faith and spiritual wisdom."[34]

Seminary professors Walter Wiest and Elwyn Smith have written a basic ministerial ethics text in which they center ethical ministry on the nucleus of truth, "which includes both truthfulness and being true."[35] These Presbyterian ministers believe that a primary requirement of clerical ministry is being honest about one's self, the gospel preached and taught, and the conduct of ministry.[36]

In a contemporary text produced by the Chicago Area Clergy Ethics Study Group, Dennis McCann proposes a unique character trait as the distinctive of clergy ethics: "I will argue that a capacity for self-sacrifice is and ought to be the indispensable first principle for clergy ethics, regardless of specific denominational traditions, precisely because the role of the clergy in any society is to be the institutional bearers of whatever learning and teaching about sacrifice inevitably goes on in that society."[37]

Although these various writers have differing opinions regarding the most important clergy virtue, they unanimously agree that ministerial morality always begins with character.

Lewis Smedes's book *A Pretty Good Person* explains the necessity of a cluster of significant virtues for a moral life. Living the "good life" and becoming a "pretty good person" require living with qualities such as "gratitude, guts, simple integrity, self-control, discernment, and fair love."[38] Individual virtues not only help us to be better persons but, when taken together, also produce a whole person. To achieve good character, wholeness is needed. Smedes concludes that character is a living network that links all virtues, each depending on the other. "Without gratitude there can be no integrity; ingratitude falsifies life at the start. But integrity needs courage when honesty runs the risk of trouble. And courage needs discernment so that we can see what is going on and know when bravery calls us to act and when it calls us to stay where we are. But discernment needs self-control because when we fly off the handle we cannot see what is going on; and when we cannot see what is going on we usually end up making a mess of things."[39]

The Centrality of Character

Character ethics, then, are basic to ministerial ethics. The clerical collar does not guarantee ethical conduct; rather, what exists under that collar significantly affects every moral choice. In fact, character is the link between a person's past and future. A minister who has proven to be trustworthy in previous church relationships usually can be counted on to continue that pattern in the future.

There is an overwhelming consensus that character is central to the clergy role. Bishop Nolan Harmon put it succinctly years ago: "The Christian minister must *be* something before he can *do* anything. . . . His work depends on his personal character."[40] Numerous writers throughout the years have sounded that same note of conviction: "What the minister *is* will be his greatest sermon";[41] "What he does is sometimes not nearly so important as what he is";[42] "I do not just *perform* a ministry, I *am* a minister."[43] Although ministry has changed over the years, this theme of *being*, not merely *doing*, has remained at the forefront of ministerial ethics.

A three-year study by the Association of Theological Schools identified qualities church people look for in young ministers. Of the five leading characteristics, four focused on the minister as a person. Similarly, the three images ranked least desirable also dealt with issues of character. All forty-eight denominations agreed that "service in humility" was most important. Lebacqz believes the phrase stresses humility rather than service and thereby affirms that character, not just function, is central to the clergy role.[44]

Character ethics enables ministers and other professionals to fulfill their roles by providing "a certain sense of calmness in doing the right thing and courage in resisting the wrong" and "a measure of discretion" that leaves "final judgment up to the individual."[45] However, in this individuality lies one of the weaknesses of character ethics. Social and institutional moral values are not often based on personal ethics; they are usually based on social survival goals such as economic profit. Wise ministers, while retaining their inner convictions, must learn to deal with social structures inside and outside the church. The correct way to express ministerial virtues in real-life dilemmas is not always clear.

Thus, acting ethically always involves more than just having a sterling moral character. That is certainly basic, but the moral life is more than simply being a good person or playing out one's character in society.[46] Along with a healthy wholeness of *being*, a consistent method of *doing* is needed. To character and its virtues must be added conduct and its values: the perspectives, obligations, and aspirations that guide the Christian minister in making right choices.

Doing Good—the Ethics of Conduct

Traditionally, books addressed to pastors have focused on certain areas that seem to tempt ministers more than others. Because of the nature of the profession and the unique vulnerability of the minister, clergy ethical misconduct seems to concern sex, money, and power. These topics are discussed fully in chapter 3.

Quaker theologian Richard Foster has called attention to these triple temptations. To help Christians reconsider the monastic quest for spirituality, he reviews the early struggle of the religious hermit with worldliness. To renounce the material values of society, the monk took a vow of poverty. To flee the follies of the flesh, the celibate pledged chastity. To conquer the inner will, the recluse pledged obedience to ecclesiastical authority. Warning our generation not to misjudge the monastics, Foster calls us to reexamine the monastic dilemma. He does not accept the monastic ideal uncritically, however. Instead, he bases his concept of the disciplined Christian life on the monastic pursuit and makes it relevant for today. "We are faced with the necessity for framing a contemporary response to the issues of money, sex and power."[47] Modern ministers are especially vulnerable to this trilogy of temptation, and the three are uniquely related. "Money manifests itself as power. Sex is used to acquire both money and power. And power is often called 'the best aphrodisiac.'"[48] The minister's world often seems like the ancient Roman Colosseum, where lurk three voracious lions: greed, lust, and power.

Earlier we noted that Wiest and Smith identified truthfulness as the central issue of ethics in ministry. For these seminary professors, the principle of truthfulness applies to the ordained in five areas of ministry: letters of recommendation, plagiarism, theological differences with the laity, theological growth, and confidentiality.[49] The point made by these authors is this: ministerial behavior is a crucial ingredient in the performance of ministry. Acting in ways both unethical and indiscreet can seriously jeopardize a person's ability to serve the church of Jesus Christ.

A prominent pastor of one of the largest churches in the South led a campus revival at a seminary in New Orleans where I taught. He encouraged the students to bring their wives on Friday to hear his famous sermon on the family. The auditorium was filled with over fifteen hundred people who marveled at his message. The very next day the deacons of his church confronted him with evidence of his many sexual affairs with women in the congregation. Whatever gifts he possessed were overshadowed by his moral failure.

The Meaning of Values

Just as *being* centers on virtues, *doing* revolves around values. What are values? Values are "moral goods to be realized in society."[50] They are the ideals and concepts considered by a group of people to be of great worth. In the United States, for example, freedom and justice are important values. One function of a value is to highlight the consequences of behavior in society. When someone acts in a way that violates an accepted value, the unifying beliefs of that community are weakened and threatened.

The people of faith, the Christian church, have been called forth to be an alternate community, "a society shaped and informed by the truthful character of the God we find revealed in the stories of Israel and Jesus."[51] The biblical writers often use the word *good* to identify moral and spiritual values.

> He has told you, O mortal, what is good;
>   and what does the LORD require of you
>   but to do justice, and to love kindness,
>   and to walk humbly with your God?
>   —Micah 6:8

Over the centuries, certain values kept appearing as reminders to God's people that they were "resident aliens . . . a colony, an island of one culture in the middle of another."[52] These essential "goods" revealed the nature and character of God, especially in the story of Jesus in the Gospels. From these values come the theological perspectives that ground us, the obligations that bind us, the norms that guide us, and the goals that motivate us.

The Theological Question

Just as virtue emphasizes moral character within, values stress moral ideals realized without. As the minister considers the role of values in her or his ethical life, the first question raised is a theological one: What moral values stabilize the clergy?

Basic to an understanding of ministerial ethics is comprehension of the moral nature of God. Leviticus 19:2 is the *shema* of ethical belief: "Be holy because I, the LORD your God, am holy" (NIV). Biblical faith is an ethical faith because the one and only true God is inherently holy, righteous, and just. Throughout the canon, the moral character of God is revealed, in both God's actions and God's expectations.

The climax of God's revelation was the incarnation—the life, death, and resurrection of Jesus Christ of Nazareth. "The Word became flesh and made his dwelling among us. We have seen his glory, the glory of the one and only Son, who came from the Father, full of grace and truth" (John 1:14 NIV). Jesus's entire life was in perfect harmony with the ethical ideals he taught. In no other religion has there been a founder who was himself the norm and the illustration of the values he professed.

One statement captures the essence of Jesus's ethics. When asked, "Teacher, which is the greatest commandment in the Law?" (Matt. 22:36 NIV), Jesus replied using two key Old Testament passages, Deuteronomy 6:5 and Leviticus 19:18: "'Love the Lord your God with all your heart and with all your soul and with all your mind.' This is the first and greatest commandment. And the second is like it: 'Love your neighbor as yourself'" (Matt. 22:37–39 NIV). These two commandments of love, one vertical and one horizontal, are the fulfillment of the entire Old Testament revelation (v. 40). In other words, the Christian faith is an ethical one because Yahweh, the God whose nature is steadfast love (Hosea 11:1–4), expects his covenant people to love as God loves.

Theologian Reinhold Niebuhr has reminded contemporary believers, however, that self-sacrificial love generally does not work in society because of different sets of values in social groups. As Niebuhr put it, individuals and groups have different moral possibilities (as the title of his book *Moral Man and Immoral Society* suggests).[53] Although love is the ideal for personal relationships, in social organizations justice is often the best humans can achieve.[54] For ministers of the church, this is a reminder that social groups (committees, churches, denominations) usually operate by a different set of values. Christian love may seem to be absent from decisions concerning, for example, who pays for medical benefits for the minister; fairness is probably a more realistic goal.

Moral values, such as love and justice, are guides for ministerial ethics. One of the ways we discern the "good" we are to follow is through our understanding of God and his will. This is the theological basis for an ethical ministry.

The Question of Obligations

After determining the theological perspectives that ground us, we face additional inquiries: What obligations bind the minister? Are there moral imperatives the clergy must always follow? The deontological question is, What duties are necessary for the minister?

The ethics of obligation seeks to define the moral principles or laws that must be obeyed. Darrell Reeck points out that "if one of the weaknesses of character ethics is to specify with clarity what a person ought to do," then "that deficiency is satisfied to some extent by . . . the ethics of obligation."[55] Biblical examples of deontological duties are numerous. The two tablets of the law Moses brought down from the mountain were neither ten suggestions nor ten multiple-choice options. The Ten Commandments were moral absolutes for Israel to follow (Exod. 20:1–17). New Testament moral imperatives, such as the Golden Rule (Matt. 7:12) and the call for nonretaliation (Matt. 5:38–39), are "ethical ideals and principles which are implicit in that new relationship to God into which a man enters when the Kingdom is established within him."[56]

Philosopher Immanuel Kant is sometimes called the "dean of the deontologists." Kant concluded that universal moral absolutes, which he called "categorical imperatives," must be followed without exception. One is the maxim always to treat persons as an end, never as a means.[57]

Ethicist W. D. Ross developed his own list of absolutes, which he called prima facie ("on first appearance") duties. Examples of prima facie duties are fidelity, gratitude, justice, duties of beneficence (helping those who cannot help themselves), and duties of nonmaleficence (no injury to others).[58] Applying this to ministers, Lebacqz writes that "certain acts tend to be right because of the nature of the act that they are."[59] This ethics professor sees the following responsibilities as compulsory for the clergy, all other things being equal: promise keeping, truth telling, beneficence, nonmaleficence, and justice.[60]

Obligations also include rules. Just how should biblical norms, church codes, and governmental edicts be understood by the minister? Laws are written to be obeyed. The Bible gives specific guidance on many subjects and admonishes, "Fear God, and keep his commandments; for that is the whole duty of everyone" (Eccles. 12:13). Both Testaments define in detail behavior that is considered moral and immoral. Can a prophet of God take these commandments seriously without becoming a legalistic Pharisee?

First, let us affirm that rules have value. Biblical norms give guidance for ordinary, everyday decisions. This is especially true for new Christians, who are moral and spiritual infants as they begin their new life in Christ (1 Cor. 3:1–2). Several lists of vices and virtues appear in the Pauline Letters; new gentile converts in a pagan, immoral Roman world needed immediate guidance for their daily lives. Rules also describe the kind of people Christians ought to be. They spell out in specific ways how those who have been captured by

Jesus Christ act in certain situations. Biblical norms also show the unbelieving world what they can expect from disciples of Jesus.

What about a code of ethics for the church professional? Many professional roles carry obligations specific to them, often expressed in an ethical code. Doctors, lawyers, and scientists practice within self-imposed limits that are usually expressed in a code of ethics sanctioned by an oversight committee. The professional nature of the minister's work suggests that a similar set of mutually accepted rules of conduct is needed. Chapter 8 addresses that need and poses the possibility of developing a code or covenant of ethics for ministers.

At this point, however, the question of ministerial codes relates to the value of rules and the dangers of prescriptive ethics. Legalism has always been a virus of religion. In Jesus's day, Sabbath laws had become burdensome restrictions. In their zeal to keep the letter of the Torah perfectly, orthodox rabbis missed the spirit of the law, even accusing Jesus of breaking the law of Moses (Mark 2:23–24). Jewish casuistry, with its meticulous regulations, continues to transform the faith of Abraham into a book of rules.

Christian ministers are also tempted to fall into legalism. Most evangelical pastors resist papal pronouncements, church dogmas, and authoritative creeds of conduct, which eliminate the priesthood of every believer. Yet how easy it is for ministers to turn the Bible into a rule book, to rely on the judgments of a religious hero, or to allow a church tradition to become a rule of faith. Ministers ought to know better, yet many are guilty on occasion of regressing to an ancient list of dos and don'ts rather than seeking the will of God.

Legalism is an inadequate approach to decision making for several reasons. First, any list of laws is never long enough. A code can never cover every possible circumstance. Also, keeping some laws requires breaking others. To save a life, it may be necessary to tell a lie (Exod. 1:19). Finally, perhaps the greatest weakness of legalism is that it almost always hinders moral maturity and stimulates egoistic pride.

To guard against even subconscious legalism, the minister must understand the relationship between rules and values. Every biblical rule expresses a value, which is the reason behind the rule. For example, the seventh commandment, "You shall not commit adultery" (Exod. 20:14), does not condemn sexual desire. The value expressed in this rule is the sanctity of marriage and family life. Stated as a principle, this commandment declares, "Marriage is an intimate sexual union that excludes all sexual partners except husband and wife." The ethical emphasis of the Bible, as T. B. Maston often stressed to his students, is on principles rather than rules.[61]

The Question of Consequences

Values also deal with teleology, the ethics of aspiration. *Telos* is the Greek word for "end" or "goal," and such ethics ask, "What is the purpose or end result of an action?" This focus on consequences raises another ethical issue: how to act in such a way as to bring about a better state of affairs.

Nineteenth-century social philosopher and reformer John Stuart Mill articulated a policy called utilitarianism. In short, his goal was to bring the greatest good to the greatest number of people. The value of utilitarianism is that it forces a person to consider all the relevant factors in a decision and their consequences. Its weakness, of course, is that one can never know for sure what a consequence may be. A minister may believe that if she reveals a teenager's drug problem to a parent, the family will respond positively. Just the opposite may occur. Consequentialism is present in both the Old and New Testaments.[62] Wisdom literature seldom takes the imperative form but usually gives practical advice about how to achieve the good life (Prov. 9:10). Hebrew midwives who "feared God" made their decision to deceive Pharaoh on the basis of consequences: to save the male babies. God apparently approved of their decision (Exod. 1:15–20).

Jesus had numerous conflicts with religious leaders over the observance of Sabbath laws. The Lord of the Sabbath was concerned that the purpose of the day of rest not be lost in Jewish casuistry: "The sabbath was made for humankind, and not humankind for the sabbath" (Mark 2:27). In the Sermon on the Mount, Christ stressed motives, noting that good deeds may be corrupted by wrong reasons. The apostle Paul often evaluated consequences before making a final decision. Once he took a vow and shaved his head, not because of religious obligation but probably to conciliate Jewish Christian leaders (Acts 18:18), a practice of accommodation he followed on other occasions (Acts 15:29; 16:3). The end result of any moral choice must be taken into account as part of the final decision.

The teleological question is usually raised when two values seem to be in conflict. When Nazis came knocking on Corrie ten Boom's door during World War II, the heroine of the historical story *The Hiding Place* faced a dilemma. Should she tell the truth and reveal the Jews hiding in her house, or should she lie to the Gestapo to protect them? Her decision involved consequences; to tell the truth meant Auschwitz and the "final solution." With much courage and some anguish she chose a lesser evil in order to achieve a higher good; she sent the soldiers away. Her decision was like Rahab's misleading of the king of Jericho (Josh. 2) and Elisha's deception of the foreign soldiers (2 Kings 6).

Sometimes a minister must decide whether revealing the whole truth will do more harm than good. A wife asks her pastor, who is counseling her husband, whether her spouse is having an affair. Is the minister guilty of breaking the eighth commandment if they conceal the truth? Does this jeopardize their integrity?

Though it may appear to be the best you can do in a certain situation, never forget that a lesser evil is an evil and not a good. A repentant spirit is in order. The Christian minister should always regret the necessity of such a choice and should work toward the day when such conflicts are eliminated or at least minimized. Lewis Smedes reminds us that in the "crooked ways of the world" we can deceive ourselves into believing that our loving lies are gallant when they may be only a way to save us from trouble. "Telling one loving lie does not turn a person of integrity into a liar any more than one wrong note turns a concert violinist into a barn dance fiddler. But if you get used to getting away with a wrong note, you may get careless with yourself, and become just another fiddler when you could have been an artist."[63]

Being a good minister is a matter of learning how to *do good*. Doing good is a matter of values, deciding which moral goods are worth preserving and which rules, principles, and ideals apply to each moral question. Theological perspectives are basic; what we believe about God as creator, redeemer, and governor influences our ability to make good moral choices. For the minister, there are moral duties that must be followed, relevant norms that must be heeded, and social consequences that must be considered.

Yet making good moral choices is more than being a good person (character) and doing the right thing (conduct). There is also a third component, called moral vision or integrity, which is unique among the three. This approach to decision making creates a new way to perceive ourselves and others.[64] This moral vision not only completes the trilogy of major components in ethical decision making but also unifies both character and conduct into a wholeness of life that is best described by the moral ideal of integrity.

Living Well—the Ethics of Integrity

In his hotel room the night before he delivered the Yale lectures, the Reverend Beecher wiped blood from his cleanly shaven face. He had cut himself, for in the mirror he had faced a contradiction between the person he saw and the message he preached. His life lacked integrity as he prepared to deliver the first lectures on preaching in New Haven.

In vivid contrast is the testimony of another person who later delivered a Yale lecture on preaching. George Wharton Pepper, one of the few laypersons to deliver such a lecture, spoke for the laity when he said, "It is impossible to exaggerate the weight that the man in the pew attaches to the integrity of the preacher."[65] No professional is expected to model integrity as much as a church minister. "Misconduct is inexcusable among professionals, but glaringly so among preachers."[66] After challenging the notion that ministers are superhuman and not subject to normal human faults and foibles, Lebacqz nevertheless states: "The minister is expected to embody trustworthiness in such an integral way (i.e., to have such integrity) that even the slightest failure becomes a sign of lack of integrity. This does not mean the minister is permitted no faults. It means that the minister is permitted no faults *that have to do with trustworthiness.*"[67]

The term *integrity* best describes the ethical wholeness of life demanded of the Christian minister. The morally mature minister experiences concomitant growth in three vital areas: character, conduct, and moral vision. These three elements interface to produce a morally complete person. Each is necessary, and none is complete without the other two.

Virtuous people who lack the ability to discern values usually fail to touch the world around them. Restricting the ethical life to the task of discerning right and wrong values often causes people to lose touch with the world around them. The absence of responsible "being" and "doing" in a minister prevents the development of moral vision, the world within. As Birch and Rasmussen concur, "Moral vision establishes the reference point for the other elements in the moral life. It sets the terms for that which will be included and excluded. It confers status upon that which is of greater importance, lesser, and, indeed, of no importance at all. Formation of moral character, together with decision making and action, are pervaded by the reigning moral vision."[68]

As three interlocking circles form a new shape at the center where the trio overlaps, so in the minister's moral life a dynamic center is formed that integrates character, conduct, and moral vision into one complete life of integrity.

The Meaning of Integrity

The term *integrity* appears sixteen times in Scripture. The Hebrew word for it is *tom* or *tummah* and means "whole," "sound," "unimpaired," "perfection." It is used to describe biblical characters such as David (Ps. 7:8), Solomon (1 Kings 9:4), and Job (2:9). None of these men was morally perfect, but they each modeled a life of wholeness and maturity.

In the New Testament, Paul reminds Timothy that a pastoral overseer must be blameless (1 Tim. 3:2). In personal character, family relationships, and spiritual commitments, the one called to shepherd God's flock must be above reproach (1 Tim. 3:1–7). The apostle counsels the young preacher Titus, "In your teaching show integrity" (Titus 2:7). Jesus is the supreme example of integrity. Even his enemies admitted, "Teacher, we know that you are a man of integrity. You aren't swayed by others, . . . but you teach the way of God in accordance with the truth" (Mark 12:14 NIV).

Modern dictionaries define *integrity* as "soundness, adherence to a code of values, the quality or state of being complete or undivided." Charles Swindoll adds, "When one has integrity there is an absence of hypocrisy. He or she is personally reliable, financially accountable, and privately clean, . . . innocent of impure motives."[69] Integrity includes both who one is and what one does. It involves the way one thinks as well as acts. It is "ethical soundness, intellectual veracity, and moral excellence. It keeps us from fearing the white light of close examination and from resisting the scrutiny of accountability. It is honesty at all cost . . . rocklike character that won't crack when standing alone or crumble when pressure mounts."[70]

The Creation of Integrity

How does a minister develop character, conduct, and moral vision into one organic whole called integrity? Theology and ethics emphasize the role of narrative, or story, in the Bible and in the Christian life. Narrative ethics asserts that we create ourselves and write our own stories according to moral convictions we receive from the communities to which we belong. As noted earlier, our character is shaped by our communities and their stories. Stanley Hauerwas contends that this claim about the significance of narrative and community for theological understanding is not "just to make a point about the form of biblical sources, but involves claims about the nature of God, the self, and the nature of the world. We are 'storied people' because the God that sustains us is a 'storied God,' whom we come to know only by having our character formed appropriate to God's character."[71]

As believers identify with God's story and make it their own story, they become a part of the Christian community, which nurtures and reinforces in them the virtues and values of the kingdom of God. When they make this story their own, they receive moral guidance and hear the moral demands of the gospel. Sometimes called the ethic of discipleship, narrative ethics focuses on the life and teachings of Jesus as a call to radical obedience. "Rather than reducing Jesus' teachings to principles or values, costly witness is called for. It is to live in the liberty that the new age has dawned in Christ."[72]

In short, the approaches called narrative, community, and discipleship ethics all point to the importance of integrating character and conduct in decision making. The virtues and values revealed in Scripture are not isolated from the biblical story, which is the story of the people of God, who share a new vision.

The ultimate test of any story is the sort of person it shapes. Ministers of Jesus Christ and proclaimers of "the story" are compelled to ask, "Does my story fit God's story?" At the beginning of the twentieth century, Charles Sheldon wrote the devotional classic *In His Steps*, which poses the ethical question "What would Jesus do?"[73] Though idealistic in its application, the novel was accurate in its basic theme. The example of Jesus is our guiding story.

How do we follow the example of Jesus? Is it possible in this modern world for a minister to live the way Jesus lived and to love the way Jesus loved? Acceptance as a disciple involves learning to imitate a master. It is not a matter of merely doing our duty. It means living Jesus's story. "The problem lies not in knowing *what* we must do, but *how* we are to do it. And the how is learned only by watching and following."[74]

Whether you call it discipleship or moral vision or integrity, the challenge is the same: We are to walk as Jesus did (1 John 2:6). T. B. Maston's last book, *To Walk as He Walked*, was based on this his favorite Scripture passage. The renowned ethicist called for Christians to reexamine the historic Jesus and the life he lived. "The major recurring question for us is, How much do we walk as He walked?"[75] What gives a minister integrity is the way the events of her or his life embody the gospel story, the life and teachings of Jesus the Messiah.

For example, the stories told by Christ, such as the parable of the good Samaritan, teach us how to perceive people. Lebacqz reminds us that we often miss the point Jesus makes here. The question introducing the story—"Who is my neighbor?"—was addressed to Jews. The parable tells the injured Jew lying on the roadside, your neighbor is your enemy! The Samaritan you hate and the race your friends despise is the compassionate one who stopped and gave you aid. "The meaning of the story goes far beyond simple rules about helping others. . . . It has to do with vision."[76]

The Practical Question

At this point you may be thinking, "All of this sounds well and good, but specifically, how does a minister put this into practice?" First, let us agree that every person called to the ministry wants to be a person of integrity—wants to achieve that wholeness of life and soundness of character that result in good moral choices.

Second, let us reaffirm the inadequacy of singular approaches. Any list of moral rules fails at several points, even if the rules are from the Bible or from orthodox church teachings. Likewise, great ethical principles such as love and justice, though important values, do not by themselves give complete guidance. Listening for an inner voice alone is also inadequate, for it is too subjective. Even looking for the lesser evil or the greater good does not resolve all moral conflicts.

What, then, can a church's moral leader do? Different styles of moral reasoning fit various moral questions. In a book written to help professionals, Darrell Reeck concludes:

> Astute people in actual practice use a mix of types of ethics. In day-to-day situations they may operate with reference to a set of principles that are perhaps even only somewhat dimly perceived. When they face unique, nonrepetitive decisions, they may bring calculations of consequences into operation. If really pushed to the wall in a situation in which they cannot compromise, they may act according to principle without any regard to consequences. As people mature in decision making they achieve an artful ability to make appropriate ethical responses by drawing selectively from their repertoire of ethical knowledge.[77]

"Artful ability" seems to allude to the quality called moral vision.

Perhaps the most important characteristic not mentioned until now is consistency. For the minister to be inconsistent in moral thinking and actions is not only irrational but also raises serious questions about personal integrity. The vice Jesus condemned with his harshest words and most scathing denunciation was hypocrisy (Matt. 23). "Hypocrisy can mean a failure to practice what one preaches; it can also entail an attitude of rigorous moral scrupulosity in one area co-existing with an attitude of libertarian indifference in a comparable area. Hypocrisy may consist in a failure to carry through the implications of one's moral stances consistently."[78]

For example, if a minister denounces explicit sexual scenes on television, does that minister also condemn excessive violence? Are a minister's views about war and peace compatible with those regarding euthanasia and abortion? Would a minister be honest if it were possible to get away with not being so?

Our contention has been that of all the methods used to make good moral decisions, three are basic: character, conduct, and moral vision. The character of a Christian minister is foundational; being precedes doing. Developing the right virtues is absolutely essential to effective ministry. The ability to discern and apply social values is also crucial. A well-grounded minister recognizes which duties are obligatory and which goals serve as guidelines for achieving the will of God. Finally, through personal identification with Jesus Christ and full participation in the gospel story, *an ethical leader gains a moral vision that synthesizes and harmonizes being, doing, and living into a life of moral integrity—living the truth.*

Fyodor Dostoyevsky eloquently described the effects of living a lie in his novel *The Brothers Karamazov*: "Above all don't lie to yourself. The man who lies to himself and listens to his own lie comes to such a pass that he cannot distinguish the truth within him, or around him, and so loses all respect for himself and for others. And having no respect he ceases to love, and in order to occupy and distract himself without love he gives way to passions and coarse pleasures, and sinks to bestiality in its vices, all from continual lying to other men and to himself."[79]

We return to the initial question of this chapter: Are a minister's moral choices endowed or acquired? By now, the answer should be clear. Ethical integrity is not genetically inbred at conception or miraculously infused at baptism or ordination. The prophet of God must grow in faith and morals, as do all believers. Learning how to make good moral choices is a lifelong process called Christian discipleship.

Thus far we have attempted two tasks. First, we have explored the meaning of the minister's vocation, suggesting that the traditional professional role of the clergy has significant ethical implications. Second, we have sought to establish a method for making good moral choices by properly combining character, conduct, and moral vision to form a life of ethical integrity.

Now it is time to move into the more practical aspects of ministerial ethics by addressing what it means to be an ethical minister in relation to one's personal life (chap. 3), congregational life (chap. 4), life with colleagues (chap. 5), and life in the community (chap. 6).

Suggested Reading

Gula, Richard M. *Just Ministry: Professional Ethics for Pastoral Ministers*. New York: Paulist Press, 2010.

Hauerwas, Stanley. *A Community of Character*. Notre Dame, IN: University of Notre Dame Press, 1981.

Stassen, Glenn H., and David P. Gushee. *Kingdom Ethics*. 2nd ed. Grand Rapids: Eerdmans, 2016.

Trull, Joe E. *Walking in the Way: An Introduction to Christian Ethics*. Nashville: Broadman & Holman, 1997.

Wiest, Walter E., and Elwyn A. Smith. *Ethics in Ministry: A Guide for the Professional*. Minneapolis: Fortress, 1990.

3

Looking in the Mirror

Integrity in Your Personal Life

The Challenges of Integrity in Ministry

Writing to gentile believers, Paul affirms the good news that by God's grace in Christ they have received a calling to be the people of God, standing in equal status with Israel. The wall of partition that once separated Israel and the nations has been eliminated (Eph. 2:11–22). Just as God's covenant with Israel placed moral and ethical demands on them (Exod. 20:1–17), so the church, both Jew and gentile, is exhorted to live a life befitting the people of God (Eph. 4:1). Paul uses the word *axios* (worthily) to describe how they ought to live. The root of the word means to weigh an object on a scale, to evaluate it.[1] Paul urges the believers to place the weighty calling to be God's people on one side of the scale and then to place on the other a life lived morally and ethically corresponding fully to that calling, balancing the scale. In Ephesians 4–6 the apostle describes such a life in detail.

Although this calling is shared by all believers, another kind of calling belongs to those who serve the church as its pastors, one that William Willimon describes as "a particular adaptation of the vocations of all Christians to ministry, to be sure, but nevertheless a vocation—a call, a summons from God, an assignment to a work that we could not, would not, take up on our own."[2] The calling to vocational ministry also demands a worthy life, one that balances the scales. Paul writes in the verses that follow: "The gifts he gave were that some would be apostles, some prophets, some evangelists, some pastors and teachers, to equip the saints for the work of ministry, for building up the body of Christ" (Eph. 4:11–12). To claim to be called by God to serve the church is to accept the call to a holy, worthy life. Such a life is lived with integrity, finding a congruence between the claim to be called and the moral and ethical choices one makes.

Of all the roles of leadership in the church mentioned in the New Testament, only two come with a list of moral qualifiers: deacons and overseers, or elders (1 Tim. 3:1–13; Titus 1:5–9). The reason is clear: the work of making disciples of Jesus requires a practice of discipleship. A life that fails to back up the gospel message makes ministry impossible. The call to ministry necessitates a commitment to the service of Christ and the church with a life of integrity matching the gospel that is preached. Although holy living is intended for all of Christ's followers, it cannot be optional or compromised for those who serve as their pastors and teachers. This is a kind of double standard, to be sure, but it is a necessary one. James warns, "Not many of you should become teachers, my brothers and sisters, for you know that we who teach will be judged with greater strictness" (James 3:1). The failure to live in this direction can disqualify one for the work (1 Cor. 9:26–27).

The integrity demanded by the call places ministry in a unique category among the professions. One may be an excellent math professor and yet live a life of moral decadence. One may be a skilled surgeon in the hospital but an ethical failure in marriage. An outstanding courtroom attorney may nevertheless be addicted to illegal drugs. The ministry cannot survive with such a distinction between one's personal and professional lives. What one is on the inside is what one brings to the work. Integrity is not negotiable in a work in which trust is among the most important resources. Character matters.

The Question of Ethics in Ministry

Ethics and morality are essentially issues of relationships. Cain, the first murderer, asked the first truly ethical question in the biblical story, however ironically: "Am I my brother's keeper?" (Gen. 4:9 NIV). In defense of his own lack of love for those different from him, a lawyer asked essentially the same question of Jesus: "Who is my neighbor?" (Luke 10:29 NIV). Ethical questions are essentially considerations of our relationship to the world around us—how do we rightly relate to the world of people and things about us? Everything is included—family, friends, strangers, and enemies. The physical world is involved as well—money, possessions, power, and institutions. Our relationship to everything from our own bodies to the entirety of the

creation itself is part of the question. As Wendell Berry notes, "Our bodies
. . . are not distinct from the bodies of plants and animals, with which we
are involved in the cycles of feeding and in the intricate companionships of
ecological systems and of the spirit. They are not distinct from the earth,
the sun and moon, and other heavenly bodies."[3] He observes, "It is hardly
surprising, then, that there should be some profound resemblances between
our treatment of our bodies and our treatment of the earth."[4] The ethical life
is a unified whole, like Jesus's tunic, seamless, woven in a single piece (John
19:23). Virtue is not divided so that one might exhibit love, for example, but
not gentleness or patience or perseverance. The Spirit who bears fruit in the
life of the disciple does so wholly (Gal. 5:22–23).

When the question of ethics is brought to bear on the work of ministry, it becomes focused on four sets of relationships: the minister's personal
life (relationship to God, self, and family), the minister's relationship to the
congregation, the minister's relationship to partners in ministry (one's peers
and colleagues), and the minister's relationship to the wider community in
which the ministry occurs (the immediate community, the state, the people
of the world and the very earth itself). The word for a right relationship to
this network is *integrity*. To live an integrated life ethically is to consider our
relationship to all that is about us in light of the gospel of the kingdom of God.

A focus on the integrity of the moral life of the disciple considers a variety
of approaches to ethical decision making, as noted earlier. Virtue and character underlie such a life as they are formed with faithful spiritual practices
and in connection with faithful Christian communities. Principles and rules
of life are woven into the fabric of ministry, not arbitrarily but with reflection
and understanding. Moral values are clarified as one lives within a faithful
community, listening to the biblical texts that have given birth to and shaped
that community while worshiping and obeying the God who is holy, just, and
compassionate (1 Pet. 1:15–16; Lev. 19:1–2). Along the way one incorporates
such principles and rules as the Ten Commandments, Jesus's instructions in
the Sermon on the Mount, or the instructions of the prophets and apostles,
considering the implications these words hold for life lived in this world. We
understand that we have obligations to others, that they can rightfully expect
certain things of us. So we begin to expect them of ourselves. In this community of faith, disciples learn that life is not simply about themselves and
their desires, but that decisions and actions have consequences in the lives of
others and are to be made thoughtfully, carefully, and lovingly.

Living in such a community as the church, attending to the Christian
Scriptures, we develop what was earlier termed a moral vision, a way of
imagining our lives in light of what it means to follow Jesus. We learn to

live out of his vision of the kingdom of God, to be part of this community called the church. We experience what Richard Hays describes as living in "imaginative obedience" to "the moral vision of the New Testament."[5] For those who pursue the path of vocational ministry, who serve as teachers and leaders in this community, the pursuit of such integrity is nonnegotiable (1 Tim. 3:1–7; Titus 1:5–9; James 3:1). The entire life of the minister is part of the ministry.

James McClendon Jr. produced a three-volume systematic theology dealing with ethics, doctrine, and witness. These three aspects of theology, he believed, were essentially grounded in the same subject—"the convictions of the community in relation to the triune God and to all else."[6] Doctrine asks, "What must the church teach in order truly to be the church?" Witness asks, "What stance must the church take vis-à-vis the world in order truly to be the church?" Ethics asks, "How should the church live in order truly to be the church?" McClendon gives ethics the first word and begins his project with that question.

To bring McClendon's question of ethics to bear on the life and work of the minister would be to ask, "How should a Christian minister live in order to truly to be a minister of Christ?" The question, so framed, recognizes that the ethics of ministry are firmly rooted in the context of the gospel and discipleship—what God has done redemptively in Jesus Christ, what it means to follow Jesus, and what God has done in calling out the church to be God's people. How does one live a life of integrity in all one's relationships as a minister of this gospel and as a prophet/priest/shepherd among these people?

As we explore those relationships through the next four chapters, consider imaginatively how God longs for your own relationships to look in the light of your calling to serve in God's kingdom.

A Failure of Trust

Unfortunately, not all those who engage the work of ministry have always balanced the scales well. The annual Gallup Honesty and Ethics ranking has charted the decline of public trust in the clergy. In December 2015, the survey indicated that less than half (45 percent) of Americans regarded clergy as highly ethical, the lowest percentage since 1977.[7] Ministers can no longer simply assume their congregations trust them. Many people have been disappointed by pastors who misused power, lacked character, or failed morally. According to a 2009 study by Diana R. Garland of Baylor University's Diana R. Garland School of Social Work, 3 percent of women who attended a congregation in the past month reported that they had been the object of clergy sexual misconduct at some time in their adult lives.[8] In a congregation of five hundred adults, perhaps as many as seven to ten women might be victims of such behavior.

Additionally, as the church in North America is increasingly marginalized in the culture, pastors are no longer held in the popular esteem they once enjoyed. The best apologetic in such a setting is a ministry offered with integrity. Trust will have to be earned. Glenn E. Ludwig affirms, "Without soundness of character, a pastor's credibility is seriously threatened. I would contend that a pastor who lacks integrity will not have the emotional and psychological maturity to survive over the long haul. When lack of integrity is exposed, any trust that had been developed between a pastor and a congregation is seriously threatened. And when trust does not exist, the opportunities for future ministry will be limited."[9]

Sustaining ministry over decades requires moral and ethical integrity and an authentic spirituality. The trust required to minister effectively is something ministers must earn through lives of moral and ethical integrity. Like a paycheck, it is not earned once and for all but must be worked for week after week.

Pastors Are Human Beings

Those who pursue a life of vocational ministry must eventually come to terms with their own humanity—their limitations and their vulnerabilities. In 1952 Welsh priest and poet R. S. Thomas wrote a long, dramatic poem that BBC Radio broadcast on Good Friday.[10] Thomas tells the story of a young priest, Elias Morgan, freshly minted from the university, who was assigned to a backward parish in the hill country of Wales. He resisted the people and the place and eventually died of tuberculosis. Job Davies, one of Morgan's adversaries in the congregation, was the wealthiest farmer in the area (he had a large Dutch barn and four cows instead of two). Job ran the congregation's affairs (and one of his own) and had the principal say in selecting a new pastor. Thomas describes the process:

> They chose their pastors as they chose their horses
> For hard work. But the last one died
> Sooner than expected; nothing sinister,
> You understand, but just the natural
> Breaking of the heart beneath a load
> Unfit for horses. "Ay, he's a good 'un,"
> Job Davies had said: and Job was a master
> Hand at choosing a nag or a pastor.[11]

One issue in this troubled relationship between priest and people, in which both parties played a part, was the heavy set of expectations placed on the pastor.

> And Job was right, but he forgot,
> They all forgot that even a pastor
> Is a man first and a minister after,
> Although he wears the sober armor
> Of God, and wields the fiery tongue
> Of God, and listens to the voice
> Of God, the voice no others listen to.[12]

Pastors are human beings first, mortal and sinful, frail children of dust, like those they serve. For either party to forget this fact is to lay the groundwork for one or the other to be abused—the people by a pastor's taking advantage of the power bestowed, or the pastor by expectations beyond her or his ability to deliver. As Paul confessed to the people of Lystra when they were about to worship him and Barnabas as gods come among them, "Friends, why are you doing this? We are mortals just like you" (Acts 14:15). Next to Peter's confession at Caesarea Philippi, "You are the Messiah, the Son of the living God" (Matt. 16:16), the humble recognition of one's humanity is the most significant confession a pastor makes.

The power, influence, affection, and devotion that often accompany an effective pastoral ministry can be a temptation to forget that we too are mere mortals. Speaking for God from God's Word does not make our voice the voice of God. Representing Christ in pastoral ministry, fulfilling our priestly role, does not make us anything other than fallen and redeemed human beings, just like those we serve. This confession is not an excuse but a recognition of our need to depend on Christ for our very lives. The failure to do so will inevitably result in our attempting to be a god or our moral collapse in some other area of vulnerability.

Perhaps among the many who do the work of vocational ministry, a percentage of charlatans can be found who see this profession as a means to abuse people or acquire money or power for themselves. The presence of such hypocrites, however, does not negate the sincerity and authenticity with which most pursue this calling. The existence of counterfeit bills does not mean that we stop accepting all currency. We just become more cautious, less naive. Most clergy by far desire to live lives of moral and ethical integrity that are worthy of the calling to which they have responded. Men and women do not ordinarily enter this profession expecting to fail morally, damaging their reputation, their ministry, their congregations, and their families. Yet failures occur far too frequently.

The apostle Paul warned of the possibility of such moral collapse. He offered this caveat to the "spiritual" ones in the Galatian congregations who might be attempting to restore a brother or sister "caught up" in a sinful behavior: "Take care that you yourselves are not tempted" (Gal. 6:1). Literally, he says, "watch yourselves." The work of ministry and the life of holiness require a kind of humility that knows we always remain vulnerable to moral failure ourselves. The apostle warns believers in Corinth who thought themselves above the fray of temptation, "So if you think you are standing, watch out that you do not fall" (1 Cor. 10:12). For those in ministry these warnings underscore the necessity of keeping our "moral immune system" healthy and sensitive.

A Moral Immune System

The human body's ability to fight off infection and disease is remarkable. The immune system is a complex interaction of various biological structures and chemical processes that allow us to detect and respond to a wide variety of threats to our physical health. If this system becomes compromised by stress, lack of sleep, or poor nutrition, for example, we find ourselves more vulnerable to environmental threats we might otherwise easily have resisted. Pastoral moral failure often occurs in a context of what we might understand as a compromised moral immune system.[13]

Vulnerability to moral failure increases when we neglect important areas of our lives. Folks in the recovery movement sometimes refer to an acronym, HALT. The word reminds them that they are most vulnerable to their addictive behaviors when they allow themselves to become Hungry, Angry, Lonely, or Tired. In the same way, pastors who fail to maintain a healthy moral immune system increase their vulnerability to moral failure.

Consider the inherent vulnerabilities pastors face. The pastoral role can often be an isolated one. The pastor and the pastor's family are often the only ones in the congregation without a pastor. Relationships with congregational members, however warm and affectionate, still retain something of an equivocal nature—we are not exactly "equals" in the equation. We may be friends, but we remain their pastor. Additionally, many in the congregation with whom we have only a superficial connection may have the sense that they know us. After all, each Sunday they hear us talk about our thinking, our lives, and our beliefs from the pulpit. But we do not know them at that level, and they know only the pulpit version of us. Not to be known is a kind of loneliness that pastors frequently experience. Relationships with fellow staff members also have that ambiguity of supervisor/pastor/friend that can leave a residue of loneliness. When this kind of pastoral isolation combines with other elements, such as marital or family struggles, depression, or other forms of intense stress, the minister's moral immune system becomes compromised.

Henri J. M. Nouwen speaks of loneliness as one of the deepest wounds of the minister. The wound exists at two levels.[14] On the one hand, the minister shares the wound of personal loneliness with all of humanity. Lonely people keep hoping, falsely, that the wound is going to be cured by some man or woman, some friendship or experience, some accomplishment or community. Nouwen observes, "Many marriages are ruined because neither partner was able to fulfill the hidden hope that the other would take his or her loneliness away. And many celibates live with the naive dream that in the intimacy of marriage their loneliness will be taken away."[15] He warns ministers especially to be aware of the dangers of this fantasy: "When the minister lives with these false expectations and illusions he prevents himself from claiming his own loneliness as a source of human understanding, and is unable to offer any real service to the many who do not understand their own suffering."[16]

On the other hand, Nouwen identifies an additional aspect of loneliness in the life of the minister—professional loneliness. He sees the isolation and marginalization of the work of ministry intensifying, for the pastor, the common human pain of loneliness: "So we see how loneliness is the minister's wound not only because he shares the human condition, but also because of the unique predicament of his profession."[17] Nouwen calls on the minister to "bind" those wounds so that ministry to others might be possible. He writes, "It is this wound which he is called to bind with more care and attention than others usually do."[18] Wounds left untended remain susceptible to infection. The wound of loneliness, unbound in the life of the minister, can leave one weakened in moral strength and susceptible to choosing destructive means of easing the pain.

In a sufficiently depleted condition, all that is required for severe ethical failure may be the right set of circumstances. Lonely and struggling with financial matters at home, a pastor may begin to resent the salary the congregation pays and blame them for the difficulties. In time, the minister may rationalize cheating on expense accounts, misreporting taxes, cutting back on the effort that goes into preaching by plagiarizing sermons from the internet, or even resorting to embezzlement of funds from the church. Or that loneliness, coupled with a loss of intimacy in the pastor's marriage, may increase susceptibility to an experience of transference in a series of pastoral conversations with a parishioner struggling in their own marriage. Few pastors set out to commit clergy sexual abuse with a church member, but such failure becomes possible when the moral immune system is suppressed.

David Pooler uses identity theory to demonstrate how a pastor can become vulnerable to various forms of clergy misconduct.[19] He argues that the more completely a pastor becomes absorbed into the "role" of pastor, the more at risk that minister becomes to various kinds of ethical failure. Pastors become vulnerable to ethical failure when they see themselves as "set apart from or even above their congregants, and congregations may be complicit in this process."[20] This perspective contributes to the loneliness pastors often experience. Because of the idealized nature of the pastoral role, ministers find it difficult to acknowledge to others, or even to themselves, that they face problems in their lives akin to the issues of those they serve, adding further to their loneliness. Eventually the pastoral role can become not simply what one *does* but who one *is*. As pastors attempt to live into this idealized role, unsuccessfully, they can become depleted spiritually and emotionally, "at risk for loneliness, burnout, distress, and even sexual misconduct."[21] These conditions leave pastors at risk of making choices that run contrary to their own moral and ethical commitments.

A healthy immune system in the human body is sustained by such things as rest, exercise, nutrition, and the management of one's level of stress.[22] The moral immune system requires attention as well. Paul's metaphor of the church as the body of Christ encourages us to consider the role of the congregation in developing a moral or ethical immune system. Health is not a condition that pertains simply to an individual—it is the condition of the entire system.[23] Paul Stevens and Phil Collins ponder the various subsystems of the congregation that parallel the various systems the human body comprises.[24] The moral immune system could easily be added to their list. Congregations that maintain appropriate forms of accountability and support for their pastors out of covenantal faithfulness should find themselves and their pastors less vulnerable to such failures. In the same way, pastors who work at developing such a system for themselves and for their congregations may find both themselves and their congregants less susceptible to such behaviors.

Pastor and Congregation: A Covenant Relationship in Ministry

Wise pastors and congregations can work to create a moral environment that may help them to avoid situations in which a depleted and vulnerable pastor fails to sustain ethical commitments. Such an environment for ministry cannot be left to chance, thinking ourselves or our congregations invulnerable to such diseases of the soul. Instead, we must act intentionally to protect God's people and God's pastors where we can.

The kind of action that is most effective will be taken by both the pastor and the congregation, working with a common moral vision for ministry. The relationship between pastor and congregation is a covenantal one in which both parties share responsibilities to the other out of love. In the twentieth century, however, the relationship took on more and more of a contractual tone. The pastor is "hired" by the congregation and can be fired by them as well.[25] The failure to see the relationship as mutual, reciprocal, and covenantal can play its part in a pastor's struggle to live with moral and ethical integrity.

Although the congregation is not necessarily "to blame" when pastors fail to act with moral and ethical integrity, they should be inquiring as to what part they play in making it possible. Some congregations can point to a series of such failures in their experience but write it off as doing a poor job in selecting pastors. They have difficulty understanding that their congregational emotional system might have something to contribute to the problem. Sometimes that may be a failure on the part of the congregational system to allow, or even expect, the pastor to engage in forms of personal and spiritual renewal. Sometimes it may be, like Elias Morgan, the eventual "Breaking of the heart beneath a load / Unfit for horses"—unrealistic expectations of the role.[26] At other times, the congregation's failure may be a naïveté that does not provide appropriate systems of accountability for the pastor, a comfortable assumption that all is well with their minister spiritually, emotionally, physically, and relationally. When pastors fail morally, an honest congregation should take an inward look at the system that allowed such failure to occur, to be repeated, or to go undetected for so long.

A wise congregation will ask those questions before a problem occurs. A proper question might be, "What kind of system do we need to build that supports and encourages our ministers and builds appropriate accountability into their lives?" Unfortunately, the expectations surrounding the pastoral role, both by congregations and pastors themselves, often leave pastors who struggle with problems feeling fearful of being punished or losing their jobs. Consequently, they are unlikely to admit their need and to seek help.

Pooler observes, "At a local church level, the people in the immediate accountability configuration around the pastor need to understand the potential vulnerability of the pastor and validate that aspect of their role. Healthy systems are created when organizational structures and congregations take more responsibility for supporting pastors, rather than blaming pastors or individuals when there are pastoral problems."[27] Few pastors set out to damage their lives, their families, their ministries, or their congregations through ethical failure. When they face struggles in their family life or ministry and do not have structures of support and accountability, they become vulnerable to such destructive moral choices.

A covenantal approach to the relationship between pastor and congregation requires us to ask what roles the congregation and the minister each play in creating and sustaining a healthy moral environment for leaders. What ethical responsibilities belong to the church? What duties belong to the pastor? We will explore areas in which pastors and congregations can and should work together to ensure the best possible environment for faithful ministry. Both the congregation and the minister have a better chance for success when they share a common commitment to creating a healthy moral environment that includes the pastor's spiritual, physical, emotional, and financial well-being; healthy social support systems; appropriate accountability structures; and sufficient opportunity for the pastor's renewal. We will then suggest two tools, or practices, that help a pastor engage moral formation and accountability: a code/covenant of ethics and time management.

The Means to Integrity in Ministry

Congregations that faithfully hold up their side of the covenant provide a context that supports physical and emotional health, as well as moral and spiritual strength, and makes possible sustainable ministry in partnership with their pastor.[28] Pastors committed to moral and ethical faithfulness in their personal lives will work with congregational leaders to build such an environment. They will take responsibility to provide as much of this on their own as possible, especially if they find themselves working in a context that does not share a commitment to such a vision. Whether the congregation works at this vision or not, the pastor must.

Unlike some professions, pastors bring every dimension of their lives to the work they do. When an important aspect of the pastor's life is unhealthy, ministry is deeply affected. That the pastor's relationship with God must remain vital might be assumed (although such assumptions are dangerous). However, physical well-being also greatly affects the energy brought to the work. Emotional and relational health impact the degree to which one can manage conflict, persevere through crises, and survive challenges in congregational and personal life. A lack of financial well-being may saddle the pastor with frustration, anxiety, and resentment that can contribute to destructive conflict within the clergy marriage. A healthy moral immune system requires that both pastors and congregations attend to these many facets of life so that faithful ministry can maintain its integrity over time.

The Pastor's Life with God

Relationship with God is the center out of which pastoral ministry radiates.[29] Preaching, caring, and leading are vitally connected to the pastor's sense of God's presence and power. Yet, ironically, the spiritual dimension can erode quickly in the day-in-and-day-out work of ministry. One who handles holy things routinely may soon find them routine. Glenn Ludwig notes that laypeople engage three primary spiritual practices: reading Scripture, praying, and worshiping. But, he observes, "When a pastor becomes ordained, there is the danger of losing all three of those. Scripture can become preparation, prayer can become a task, and worship can become a performance."[30] Charles Bugg advises pastors to be clear about the role of Scripture in their own lives: "One of the vocational hazards of ministry is that we begin to treat the Bible simply as the means to the end of getting our message for Sunday. What about approaching the Bible in a formational way instead of just as information to be explored? By this I mean, what about allowing the power of the Bible to speak to my own life and to continue to form and reform me?"[31] Faithful ministry requires the disciplined practice of engaging in those "holy habits" that keep one attentive to God.

Roy M. Oswald devotes a chapter to spiritual practices in his description of clergy self-care. He says, "As pastors, we may not always find spiritual nurture in our churches, so rediscovering some spiritual practices that help us deal with stress and burnout may take us beyond the organized church."[32] The Gospel accounts are clear that Jesus made such practices part of his life. Solitude, fasting, prayer, corporate worship, Scripture reading, and meditation are evident alongside his active, daily ministry. Robert Sizemore's study of key factors in long-term ministry identified spiritual disciplines as among the most frequently mentioned aspects of personal growth.[33] A life lived worthy of the calling to ministry requires the pastor to practice those disciplines that help them attend to God in the course of ministry week in and week out.

Maintaining such practices is the pastor's personal responsibility. Congregations, however, can be clear in their commitment to their pastor's life with God. Providing occasional days away from the office to be spent in solitude at a retreat center or other location is one way such a commitment can be expressed. They can also be explicit in their expectations expressed in job descriptions or covenants with their pastor that they both support and expect the maintenance of the pastor's life with God.

The Pastor's Physical Health

Faithful ministry requires attending to the physical well-being of pastors, not just their spiritual health. A pastor whose body is obese, whose mind is stressed, whose diet is poor, and whose life is sedentary puts at risk the future of their ministry. This amounts to poor stewardship of one's body and sets an inadequate example for one's congregation.

In the 1950s, "Protestant clergy had the lowest rates of disease for every major diagnosis and lived longer and healthier lives than people in any other profession." However, by the early 1980s they had the highest overall work-related stress among religious professionals and the next-to-the-lowest amount of personal resources to cope with the strain. A 1999 study indicated that clergy had one of the highest death rates from heart disease of any occupation. A 2003 Pulpit and Pew survey found that "76 percent of the clergy surveyed were either overweight (46 percent) or obese (30 percent), a significantly higher percentage than the population as a whole (61 percent)." Men struggled with this more than women, with eight out of ten of them being overweight, as compared to just over half of the women.[34]

Clearly pastors must take responsibility for their own physical health. Those who study the problem, however, increasingly recognize that the congregation has a role to play in this issue as well. Besides offering adequate medical insurance with wellness benefits, churches might also include a program of physical exercise in the pastor's job description or in their covenant with their pastors. Stephanie Paulsell, author of *Honoring the Body*,[35] acknowledges: "Clergy can't do it by themselves. They need to have the whole church and whole congregations behind them to say that honoring the body is important. Both clergy and laity need to understand that the body is a precious gift from God that has to be cherished. People need to understand that ministry isn't done by the disembodied mind, but by the whole embodied self."[36]

William Hendricks, who taught theology to seminary students for many years, often told his classes, "Bodily exercise profiteth little" (citing 1 Tim. 4:8 in the KJV), "but what little it profiteth, you needeth."

The Pastor's Emotional Health

Attention to clergy health includes the emotions as well as the body. Depression and other mental health issues affect pastors just as they do others. Kathryn Greene-McCreight, an Episcopal pastor, describes in detail her own struggle with bipolar disorder and the help she sought and received that allowed her to continue in ministry.[37] Suicide has ended the ministries of competent and caring pastors who perhaps could have been helped had they and their congregations been more sensitive to the indications and dangers of depression and burnout.[38]

Congregations can encourage pastors to lead healthier lives and to seek help and support, and can provide insurance and other resources to make it possible. Pastors can prioritize this aspect of self-care as a key moral and ethical issue in their ministry and can discipline themselves to attend to it. This is a vital element to maintaining a healthy, functioning moral immune system.

The Pastor's Family

Family pressures resulting from demands on the clergy's time, financial struggles, and role expectations for the clergy's spouse and children make ministry unviable for some. When marriage and family problems mount, a pastor's vulnerability to moral failure increases along with them. Congregations intent on experiencing a long and faithful ministry with their pastors will intentionally develop an environment that supports the pastor's marriage and family. Although the pastor bears responsibility for managing time and schedule, the congregation can learn to engage more family-friendly practices in order to sustain ministry. Fewer evening meetings, adequate vacation time, and sufficient financial support are among the practices congregations could choose to put into place. Pastors and their families certainly need to make their own heroic efforts to set boundaries of time and roles to guard against burnout and to ensure sustainable ministry. Thoughtful congregational leaders with a vision for moral integrity among their ministers, however, can play a role in creating such an environment as well.

The Pastor's Finances

Clergy want to be financially responsible—to support a family, manage health-care costs, plan for a college education for their children, anticipate retirement, and eliminate their own educational debts. They may, however, face issues related to financial well-being on two fronts: (1) the amount of salary provided by the congregation and (2) their own skill and discipline in effective money management. Seminary graduates now enter ministry with an average student debt burden of more than $35,000 from their undergraduate and graduate studies. And, unlike their colleagues in other professions, they enter a calling that will make the amortization of those loans a challenge. In a study reported by Auburn Theological Seminary, theological school graduates in 2011 still carried an average debt of $18,542 from undergraduate student loans. By the time they financed their graduate education, one-quarter of theological graduates had a personal debt in excess of $40,000.[39] The burden of debt creates a litany of issues that can affect the sustainability of ministry and challenge pastors ethically. The necessity of taking on additional work may leave pastors tired and with less energy for the congregation, or may send them looking for a higher-paying position. Pastors who cannot manage personal finances may find it a challenge to oversee the congregation's affairs well. Additionally, guilt over debt and ambivalent attitudes concerning money may hinder their leadership in congregational fund-raising efforts.[40] The Auburn study calls for a collaboration of students, theological schools, denominations, congregations, and laypeople to address these issues so that ministry can be more sustainable for clergy.

The issue of clergy compensation can be shown to affect the life of the congregation as well. The Pulpit and Pew study on pastors' salaries argued that, besides transforming ministry from a calling into a professional career by pushing pastors to "move up the ladder" in order to meet family financial needs, local churches can also be affected negatively by market approaches to clergy compensation.[41] Faithful ministry demands the financial well-being of pastors, which necessitates a just and generous approach from congregational leaders. Paul admonishes that those who labor in preaching and teaching are worthy of generous financial support (1 Tim. 5:17–18).

Managing money, adjusting lifestyle to live within one's means, learning contentment, and modeling generosity are ethical financial practices for clergy. The more faithful one is in these areas, the fewer financial pressures come to bear on the pastor's family. At the same time, providing adequate compensation, supporting the pastor's retirement fund, offering sufficient health insurance, and, when possible, helping the pastor find the kind of wise financial advice needed are actions congregations are ethically obligated to consider.

The Pastor's Support System

One can make a living as a pastor while having life drained from the soul by loneliness if the environment does not provide the needed sustenance. A pastor who lacks an adequate support system serves in a tenuous setting. Although the development and maintenance of a healthy support system may not be immediately identified as an ethical issue, the failure to attend to this component of a healthy moral immune system jeopardizes the ministry one has committed to, trained for, and invested in for years. It puts at risk one's family and one's congregation. Both the pastor and the congregation have an ethical obligation to protect these valuable assets by assuring the pastor's adequate relational support.

Interviews with ten Texas Baptist clergy engaged in congregational ministry for more than twenty years revealed a variety of factors that contributed to the support of those ministers. One of the frequently mentioned variables making possible their faithful ministry over decades was the presence of mentors in their lives.[42] Such relationships, along with relationships with ministry peers, offer significant resources to help overcome the loneliness that leaves pastors vulnerable to moral failure. Elizabeth Ann Jackson-Jordan's review of literature on clergy burnout identifies at least three studies pointing to the importance of such support.[43] Dean R. Hoge and Jacqueline E. Wenger found that a perceived *lack* of support from denominational workers, from other clergy, and from the congregation played a key role in the loneliness experienced by Protestant pastors who left ministry.[44]

Adequate, healthy social-support systems can help a minister continue through difficulties and challenges in their work. Pastors will need to seek out such systems and build them if necessary. Congregations would be wise to find ways of assuring that their ministers have such support available to them. Church personnel committees, deacons, or elders could engage their pastors in conversation about the ways this need is being met in their lives or help them find creative ways of meeting it. Mentors, spiritual directors, ministry peer groups, and authentic friendships all can serve to contribute to the support of a healthy ministry.

The Pastor's Accountability

Pastors frequently lead largely unaccountable lives. The congregation often affords them a level of trust that can be taken for granted and abused. A pastor in a large city may routinely leave the office to visit the local medical center and be gone half a day with no questions asked. Ministerial meetings associated with the local or state denominational offices might necessitate being away from home and the church for a day or more. People trust their pastors to act with integrity in the use of their time for such activities. With the lack of accountability in most settings, pastors might easily be tempted to take advantage of such situations, with disastrous results. Ministry with integrity requires personal accountability.

Additionally, congregations tend to assume that the pastor's life with God is richly maintained. Congregational leaders may not be comfortable routinely inquiring about the pastor's worship, life of prayer, engagement with Scripture, or the practice of other spiritual disciplines. These are simply assumed. Consequently, pastors, accountable to no one, are sometimes in a perilous situation regarding their spiritual lives.

Prudent pastors, and caring congregations, will not leave such matters to chance. If the congregation does not already have in place some means for professional, moral, and spiritual accountability for its staff, pastors should wisely build such structures into their own lives. In chapter 8 we will consider the use of a personally developed code/covenant of ethics as one way to establish a form of accountability. This code/covenant could be shared with the congregation, with other staff members, and with the congregation's governing board so that they will understand the pastor's commitment to moral integrity. Other accountability practices might include participation in a pastoral peer group, meeting with a spiritual director, or having some form of accountability with certain members of the congregation. Such arrangements can be helpful if they are approached with transparency, support, confidentiality, and mutuality. The possibility of a ministry marked by moral and ethical authenticity is greatly enhanced by accountability structures to assist the pastor in maintaining integrity with God, self, family, colleagues, peers, congregants, and the community.

Richard Foster identifies money, sex, and power as three dominant ethical issues Christians have wrestled with over the centuries. These three areas especially require personal accountability on the part of the minister. Ancient monastic movements called for vows of poverty, chastity, and obedience to counter the abuse of these aspects of human life and relationships.[45] Pastors who intend to live with moral integrity will want to have appropriate accountability practices providing necessary moral boundaries.

The dangers of failure in the arena of sexual sin are as prominent today as ever. Chapter 7 will deal extensively with the nature and cost of clergy sexual abuse. Consider at this point, however, the practices at one's disposal for living accountably. Two specific aspects of the minister's life come into play.

The first aspect is the relationship between clergy and congregant that spins out of control morally when the pastor's depleted moral immune system encounters transference in pastoral conversations and relationships. Although occasionally clergy sexual offenders are female, the overwhelming majority are male. Isolation in the role as pastor and loneliness in one's own marriage often precede the offense. A female congregant, perhaps struggling in her own marriage, may find in the minister a man she trusts as spiritual and who genuinely listens to her. In such a case, the sexual boundaries of both the pastor and the congregant may become permeable. Consciously or not, the pastor begins to "groom" the victim. Choices are made about meeting places or times that provide more privacy. In time, the woman finds herself the victim of clergy sexual abuse, although neither intended for the relationship to go in that direction at the outset.[46]

Consequently, pastors need to have clear boundaries and accountability practices around their relationships with congregants of the opposite sex. Windows in the office doors provide one level of accountability while preserving necessary privacy. Meetings can be scheduled so that another person is in the vicinity at all times. Some pastors choose not to have private meetings with a parishioner of the opposite sex at all, including breakfast or lunch meetings. Should something inappropriate be said or sensed in a relationship with a parishioner, pastors who are choosing moral accountability will report the incident to their spouse, their spiritual director, or a designated person in their congregation, such as the deacon chair or personnel committee chair. Wise pastors will listen to their own spouse, who may sense a person's attraction and call attention to it. In such a situation, measures may be needed to practice even greater accountability about that relationship. Boundaries such as these are not offered here as prescriptive. However, both the pastor and the congregational representatives, such as the personnel committee, should be clear about what steps ministers are expected to take to be appropriately accountable in relationship with members of the opposite sex. These steps could be thought through in discussion about the pastor's code of ethics or congregational covenant of ethics.

A second aspect of the minister's life that affects sexual accountability is the technology that is now readily available and that is a part of everyday life. Such technology has rapidly proliferated, affecting human relationships in a variety of ways, both positively and negatively. Smartphones, tablets, and personal computers make it possible for a pastor to communicate with the congregation as a whole or with individual members easily, removing limitations of both time and space. Effective pastors have learned to employ these tools to their advantage, enhancing their ability to care for their congregation. Email has made possible ongoing conversations about spiritual formation, dialogue about last week's sermon, and problem solving around leadership and management issues without calling another meeting. Texting has made the rapid exchange of pertinent information among staff members instantaneous. Websites have allowed potential church members to visit before they set foot on the property. Online video capacities make it possible for members to listen to sermons more than once, for those who miss a worship service to hear the message later, and for the pastor's preaching and teaching ministry to be extended around the world. The pastor's resources for preaching have increased unimaginably on the internet and available Bible software programs. Home visitation is made easier by GPS-enhanced map applications. In just a few years much of pastoral ministry has been revolutionized.

At the same time, these technological advancements, neutral in themselves, can feed into the dark side of ministers' lives when their moral immune system is depleted. Technology has introduced an unhealthy, unaccountable privacy into our lives. Cell phones mean that one does not have to sit in the kitchen talking on the phone in front of other family members. Texting, email, and smartphones make it possible for one to communicate inappropriately with others and maintain secrecy in the communication.

The online world has also introduced an element of anonymity. One can use social media to create a virtual self that is free to act and speak in ways one would not do in public. Pornography is no longer limited to magazines or even pay-per-view cable services. Forms of adult-only movies flow into our living rooms on some basic cable packages. Online pornography is available without charge from anywhere in the world and can be viewed on one's phone, tablet, or laptop in total seclusion. According to H. B. London and Neil B. Wiseman, "51 percent of pastors say that Internet pornography is a possible temptation for them; 37 percent admit that it's a current struggle. . . . 33 percent of the clergy and 36 percent of the laity have visited a sexually explicit website; of that number, 53 percent of the clergy and 44 percent of the laity say they have visited the sites a few times in the past year. A total of 18 percent of clergy respondents say they visit such websites between a couple of times a month and more than once a week."[47]

Other online services promote more than mere viewing. In August 2015 someone hacked the Ashley Madison website, which advertises "Life is short. Have an affair" and facilitates such relationships. The hacker released the names of the website's "clients." Based on conversations with denominational leaders in the United States and Canada, Ed Stetzer, former executive director of LifeWay Research, estimated that as many as four hundred church leaders (pastors, staff members, elders, deacons) would be resigning the following Sunday.[48] No research is available to validate Stetzer's speculation, but at least one pastor/professor committed suicide in the wake of the incident and a prominent theologian resigned his post.[49] This element of privacy and anonymity combined provides a dangerous temptation for anyone whose inner life or intimate relationships are in a deteriorating state.[50]

Clearly our members face these temptations, but we face them as well. How will you manage yourself in this morally and ethically challenging environment of technology? Accountability in this realm needs to be thought through carefully. When and where will you use your phone? Who besides you will have access to your accounts, your devices, your passwords? Do you want to have accountability software installed on your devices? What cable packages will you subscribe to? How will you manage the online relationships of social media? These questions and more expose the challenges that technology has brought to the personal ethical life of pastors. In the interest of transparency with those we serve, such matters as these might also be addressed in one's code of ethics or congregational covenant. Our congregation deserves to know how we are attempting to negotiate these paths with integrity.

Single ministers face the same set of challenges as do married ministers, but they do so without the benefit of a spouse to aid in the effort at accountability. Having someone to step into that accountability role, providing a sounding board or detached perspective, is useful. Additionally, single ministers may find themselves attracted to a church member and wanting to take the relationship deeper. Such relationships between ministers and congregants are fraught with potential dangers. The confusion of roles may create a conflict of interest for the pastor. If the two of them find themselves on opposite sides of an issue in the congregation, the pastor's leadership might be compromised, for example. Or, should the relationship end, the pastor may find the other person's friends or family members in the congregation angry or distant. No chapter and verse of the Bible dictates what one should do as a single minister, but clearly one should act thoughtfully and with a level of accountability to congregational leaders. Such relationships ought not be kept secret. Prayerfully seek the wisdom of others in the congregation and pay attention to it.

The Pastor's Personal Renewal

Pastors and congregations that desire to develop a healthy ethical environment must consider the minister's need for personal renewal. Few public speakers are expected to address the same audience forty-five to fifty times a year and still have something fresh to say. In the case of churches that hold Sunday evening or Wednesday evening services, pastors may be speaking to the same people as many as a 150 times a year. Pastors need intellectual and spiritual renewal to sustain this pace over time. Additionally, like others in "helping professions," pastors may find that the constant demand to be giving to others leaves them depleted spiritually and emotionally. Over time, without opportunities for renewal, pastors may be prone to develop symptoms of burnout, losing energy for the work and weakening their ethical immune response to temptations to cut corners in their work or compromise themselves in other ways.

William Willimon claims that pastors are susceptible to something worse than burnout. He calls it "blackout"—they forget why they are doing what they do, and they lose a sense of call and purpose in the work:

I was never happy with the metaphor of "burnout" as a description of why some pastors call it quits. "Burnout" implies that our problem, as pastors, is a lack of energy. One day we wake up and simply have no more fuel to give to the demands of ministry. From what I observe, our pastoral problem of constancy is more a matter of "blackout" or "brownout," the gradual dissipation of meaning in ministry, a blurring of vision, the inability to keep the theological rationale for ministry that is necessary to enliven our imagination. We wake up one day and no longer have a reason or purpose for doing the things that the church expects us, as pastors, to do.[51]

Willimon argues that the antidote to such a condition is "to cultivate the disciplines of Sabbath observance, refurbishment, re-creation, and remembrance of vocation."[52]

Congregations that desire effective preachers and teachers who live with consistent moral integrity will see to it that their pastors have weekly days off (Sunday is not a day off) and annual vacations, as well as opportunities to attend conferences, to take annual study leave, to purchase helpful resources, and to have a regular sabbatical experience. Sabbaticals are not extended vacations but an opportunity for needed renewal. They are good for both the pastor and the congregation.[53] Pastors, for their part, need to be faithful in adhering to their day off, to the practice of Sabbath, and to using their vacation days and other opportunities for renewal physically, spiritually, intellectually, and vocationally. Such practices will help counter the tendency of pastors, thinking themselves indispensable to the congregation's life, to become a busy, workaholic minister. A strong moral immune system requires experiences of renewal and refreshment.

Tools for Integrity in Ministry: An Intentional Approach to Life and Service

Building such a system to give pastors a better chance at a ministry marked by moral and ethical integrity over the long haul requires some tools for the minister and for the congregation. Two such tools are indispensable: a code/covenant of ethics and the practice of effective time/life management.

A Code/Covenant of Ethics

The development of an effective code/covenant of ethics will be described in detail in chapter 8, and samples of such documents can be found in appendixes B, C, and D. At this point, however, consider the way the code/

covenant can become a tool for moral integrity. A rule of life has long been an instrument for spiritual formation of individuals or communities. For fifteen hundred years, the rule of St. Benedict has served the Benedictine order and has provided a model for other monastic communities.[54] A code/covenant of ethics offers the same kind of formational instrument, both for individual ministers and for the communities they serve. The potential effectiveness of a code/covenant of ethics is increased to the degree that it is developed thoughtfully, out of the personal convictions of the pastor, and in covenant with others (congregational leaders or ministry peers). Although it will be helpful to read and study existing codes, simply adopting one that others have written without personal reflection, or to force a code on the minister, can turn the project into an exercise in legalism. On the other hand, the pastor's life can be shaped morally and ethically by making the effort to think through ethical principles and commitments, discussing them with congregational leaders or peers, and expressing them in the form of a code or a rule of life for ministry.

A ministerial code of ethics in a free church or congregational setting often lacks a means of accountability. This is where a code of ethics in the form of a covenant between ministers and the congregation can be a more effective practice.[55] Pastors and congregational leaders can develop such a code/covenant out of a common moral vision for ministry, affirming the responsibilities and commitments that both parties bring to the relationship. Appropriate forms of accountability can be written into the covenant. In those ministry contexts where no such community effort is possible, one might covenant with one's colleagues in ministry—those who serve on a church staff together or participants in a local ministerial peer group, for example. The commitment one makes to others who agree to some form of accountability for living by the code can preserve some of the communal or covenantal element. However you manage to implement such a practice, your life and ministry will be shaped by thinking through your values and principles, writing down those commitments, and sharing with others your intent to live by them.

Time/Life Management

Next to a personally and congregationally developed code/covenant of ethics, one of the most powerful tools you can master is your calendar. This is the place where you have opportunity to manage your life. "Time management" is something of a misnomer. We do not manage our time. We manage our lives. How we spend our time is how we live our lives. The more that we spend our time in line with what we most value, what we are most deeply committed to, the more our lives are formed ethically and morally. Too often time management practices are presented as a mere set of job competencies, a way to be more productive and to accomplish personal or corporate goals. Clearly those skills could be employed in such a way. But they also lend themselves as instruments for spiritual, moral, and ethical formation.

Consider this model for thinking about moral formation. Suppose you drew a circle and within that circle you wrote down all the things in life you value most—God, family, church, creation, your calling, your character—everything. Now draw another circle within which lies every detail of the way your life is actually lived, good and bad. Now allow those circles to overlap to the degree that they actually do. The space where they overlap would represent your true self, the place where you are fully living out all that you say you value. Outside that area on one side would be a version of what might be called a pseudo-self—the places where what you claim to value and believe do not find their way into the life you actually live. On the other side of the true self lies an area in which you are living in contradiction to what you claim to value and believe, which could be called your false self. The goal of moral formation might be seen as the gradual bringing of those two circles into complete congruence, where what we claim to believe and how we actually live are one and the same.[56]

One tool for such a task is our calendar, the place where we allow things into our lives. To claim to value family relationships and yet to have a calendar that squeezes them out reveals a lack of congruence in one's life. To profess to believe that physical health is important but to schedule no time for working out is to be living out of a pseudo-self that talks a good game but does not live it. Intentional practices can be built into our lives by means of learning to manage time/life.

Eugene Peterson, somewhat tongue-in-cheek, declares that the appointment calendar is "a gift of the Holy Ghost" that pastors can use to bring their lives more in line with their calling.[57] He says, "The trick, of course, is to get to the calendar before anyone else does. I mark out the times for prayer, for reading, for leisure, for the silence and solitude out of which creative work—prayer, preaching, and listening—can issue. I find that when these central needs are met, there is plenty of time for everything else."[58] Time-management expert Stephen Covey calls this practice "putting the big rocks in first."[59]

Systems for practicing effective time/life management abound. Pastors intent on moral and ethical formation and on ministering with integrity will find such a system and master it, finding the lives they live becoming increasingly congruent with their beliefs, values, and principles. This is a most necessary and effective tool.

Conclusion

Moral and ethical integrity are nonnegotiable in effective ministry. The minister's relationships—with God, family, self, congregation, colleagues, and the community—all come with legitimate ethical obligations. Even though clergy sometimes fail to live up to these expectations, by far most pastors genuinely desire to do so. On the personal end of the spectrum the minister looks at their own spiritual, physical, relational, and emotional well-being. These areas of life call for intentionality—their integrity cannot be assumed. Both the minister and the congregation have a part to play in keeping the pastor's "moral immune system" in a healthy condition. A thoughtfully developed code/covenant of ethics and an effective system for managing one's time are two necessary tools to aid in the minister's continuing personal ethical formation and moral integrity. We can now turn our attention to the ethical responsibilities the minister owes the congregation as its pastor.

Suggested Reading

Foster, Richard J. *The Challenge of the Disciplined Life: Christian Reflections on Money, Sex, and Power*. San Francisco: HarperOne, 1989.

Hays, Richard B. *The Moral Vision of the New Testament: Community, Cross, New Creation; A Contemporary Introduction to New Testament Ethics*. San Francisco: HarperSanFrancisco, 1996.

Hobbs, Charles. *Time Power: The Revolutionary Time Management System That Can Change Your Professional and Personal Life*. New York: HarperCollins, 1987.

London, H. B., Neil B. Wiseman, and James C. Dobson. *Pastors at Greater Risk: Real Help for Pastors from Pastors Who Have Been There*. Ventura, CA: Gospel Light Publications, 2003.

4

Looking at the Church

Integrity in Your Ministry

Wendell Berry's novel *A Place on Earth* is set in 1945 in the fictitious Kentucky town of Port William. Mat and Margaret Felton, whose son Virgil was serving in the Army, are notified that he was reported missing and presumed dead. These stalwart people of the land receive an awkward pastoral call from Brother Preston, who is inept at dealing with the embodied life of these farmers. They know it and he knows it. Berry describes the pastor's thoughts after the visit:

> He [Brother Preston] came away from the Feltner house grieved by the imperfection of his visit. It was not, as he had hoped it would be, a conversation. It was a sermon. This is the history of his life in Port William. The Word, in his speaking it, fails to be made flesh. It is a failure particularized for him in the palm of every work-stiffened hand held out to him at the church door every Sunday morning—the hard dark hand taking his pale unworn one in a gesture of politeness without understanding. He belongs to the governance of those he ministers to without belonging to their knowledge, the bringer of the Word preserved from flesh.[1]

The minister failed to connect with his congregation, to enter authentically into their lives and know them. As R. Paul Stevens and Phil Collins would put it, Brother Preston had failed to "join the church."[2]

Two days after the pastor's impotent call on the Feltners, Burley Coulter, a dear friend of Mat and Margaret, writes to his nephew, Nathan, who is also serving in the war. Burley has his own opinion of the pastor's ministry in Port William, since two years earlier he had been the recipient of such a visit when Nathan's brother, Tom, had died in the fighting. Burley refers to the minister as "Brother Piston." He recognizes the same pastoral failure Brother Preston himself acknowledged—the disconnect between himself and those he serves. Burley complains that the minister has no right to speak words of consolation to people whose lives he will not share:

> While he was having his say I sat there and thought my thoughts. Here in a way he'd come to have the last words over Tom. And what claim did he have to do it? He'd never done a day's work with us in his life, nor could have. He never did stand up in his ache and sweat and go down the row with us. He never tasted any of our sweat in the water jug. And I was thinking: Preacher, who are you to speak of Tom to me, who knew him, and knew the very smell of him?[3]

Pastors earn the right to enter intimately into the pain of those they serve by engaging them with authenticity and affection at other times. In other words, the pastor's relationship with the congregation comes with a set of ethical obligations. The congregation has a right to expect certain qualities and behaviors of their pastors. In a real sense, pastors "owe" their congregations a debt of love (Rom. 13:8). This pastoral love and affection is offered in tangible ways over the years in the form of a competent ministry delivered with moral and ethical integrity.

The Challenges of Integrity in Ministry: A Calling to Competence

Ministry Is Local

Ministry is a calling that is expressed locally or not at all. It takes place in *this* place among *these* people, never abstractly. The Word has to be made flesh in each place. The pastor is called to know that place, to engage that place, to know those people, and to love those people.[4] A congregation has every right to expect that of its pastors. Every pastoral task—proclamation, pastoral care, and leadership—is to conform to the particular congregation in which it is offered. Churches are not franchise operations. Pastors, like farmers, need to learn to attend to what Wes Jackson, borrowing from Alexander Pope, calls "the genius of the place."[5] The congregation has something specific to teach its pastors and to expect from its pastors, and it is the pastor's responsibility to discern what those things are. "Brother Piston" apparently missed that class in seminary.

Becoming a congregation's pastor is a bit like getting married. Couples often enter into their life together without explicitly voicing their mutual expectations. The minister declares them to be "husband and wife." Each now has a title, but neither has a job description—at least not a formal one. But both are mistaken if they fail to recognize the reality that each has *two* job descriptions and that they likely contradict each other in many places. He has in his head a set of expectations about what *husband* means and a set of expectations about what *wife* means. She, likewise, has her own ideas about those roles filed away in her head and heart. The problem is that they have derived those expectations from different sources. He, primarily from his own family, modified by things he has read, heard, observed, and come to believe. She, from her family and those influences that have shaped her thinking. If the two of them fail to hammer out something in common, coming to terms with these roles, they will inevitably clash. The recovery movement has an aphorism: "Unexpressed expectations are premeditated resentments."

After the courtship and saying "I do," pastor and congregation settle down to live life together as well. Perhaps the pastor is given a formal job description, but not always. And the congregation is certainly never given one. Even if a personnel committee has made the effort to thoughtfully develop a reasonable job description to hand the new pastor, expectations do not end there. Members of the congregation carry some expectations about what a pastor is and what a pastor is supposed to do based on relationships with previous pastors in their lives as well as, hopefully, on thoughtful reading of Christian Scriptures and discussions with other believers. In the same way, the pastor has a set of expectations about what the role will require. Pastors also have in mind some expectations about what the congregation will and will not do. These unexpressed expectations on the part of pastor and congregation easily become the breeding ground for resentment over time.

The new relationship between a pastor and a congregation provides an opportunity to think together about what each should expect of the other and what each owes the other morally and ethically. Because this relationship is mutual, thinking about integrity in the relationship is best done with pastors and congregational leaders in conversation with each other. A covenant that expresses this relationship can be developed to call both parties to the highest level of integrity in their work together.[6]

Ministry Comprises Multiple Tasks, Roles, and Expectations

The list of expectations for a pastor on the part of a congregation is potentially long. But the categories to be considered are few enough to be manageable. Because we are focusing on the life of the minister, we can think about these things in terms of what the minister reasonably owes the congregation. We will consider each of these categories in more detail later.

The minister owes the congregation a moral and spiritual example of following Christ—humility, integrity, and confidentiality in all aspects of the minister's relationships. The minister owes the congregation authentic affection and pastoral competence. The minister owes the congregation a commitment to servant leadership that helps them understand and engage God's call on the congregation's life. The minister also owes them an opportunity to participate in the ministry of the church, exercising their God-given gifts and callings. And when it is time to move on, either in retirement or in transition to another place of ministry, the minister owes the congregation integrity in that process.

The minister also owes the congregation a commitment to faithfulness to the gospel and discipleship. Eugene Peterson attempts to voice what a congregation is saying when they ordain or call a pastor to serve among them. In their best and deepest longings, they are saying,

> We need help in keeping our beliefs sharp and accurate and intact. We don't trust ourselves; our emotions seduce us into infidelities. We know we are launched on a difficult and dangerous act of faith, and there are strong influences intent on diluting or destroying it. We want you to give us help. Be our pastor, a minister of Word and sacrament in the middle of this world's life. Minister with Word and sacrament in all the different parts and stages of our lives—in our work and play, with our children and our parents, at birth and death, in our celebrations and sorrows, on those days when morning breaks over us in a wash of sunshine, and those other days that are all drizzle. This isn't the only task in the life of faith, but it is your task. We will find someone else to do the other important and essential tasks. This is yours: Word and sacrament.[7]

Part of the pastor's responsibility is to be clear on what the calling to ministry includes and does not include, which expectations—whether the congregation's or one's own—are legitimate and which are not. This sorting task goes on over the years and is itself a kind of ethical endeavor.

Pastoral ministry comprises a wide variety of roles and tasks. That variety is part of what keeps ministry interesting and part of what makes it maddening at times. On a given day a pastor might drive across town to a large hospital and sit at the bedside of a young mother in the last stages of cancer. Return-ing to the office, they may sit down with a Greek New Testament and seek to understand what message God would have them share with a congregation they have spoken to hundreds of times already. That evening might include gathering with the finance committee to explore ways the church can best develop a budget for the coming year. Scattered through the day they could be responding to various questions, complaints, or ideas from congregational leaders. In a given week a pastor might wear the hats of administrator, leader, supervisor, scholar, preacher, teacher, counselor, writer, editor, and grounds-keeper! Each of these roles implies expectations and ethical demands.

Ministry Requires Competence

Congregations thrive in the care of pastors who are able to deliver compe-tent proclamation, pastoral care, and leadership. Church consultant Kennon Callahan notes this as a characteristic of churches that minister effectively in their communities.[8] Lyle Schaller describes the necessity of a pastor's "paying the rent" during the first year of ministry in a new congregation. One does so by performing pastoral tasks competently.[9] That "rent" continues to be due in all the years to follow as well.

The competent pastor sustains an ethically faithful ministry by learning from the congregation. Sustainability results in part from the pastor's becom-ing a "reflective practitioner" of ministry.[10] The cycle of acting and reflecting becomes automatic, so that the one doing ministry is constantly being taught by the work of ministry. Over the years this practice develops in the minister a kind of acquired wisdom through experience, a "pastoral imagination."[11] Congregations need pastors who maintain a lifelong-learning posture, and wise congregations support that effort on the part of their pastors with funding and allowance for them to pursue their learning. This developing competence in ministry permits pastors to remain in place and serve over decades without growing stale or losing their edge.

An incompetent pastor is in some sense an unethical one. That is not to say that every pastor needs to be able to preach like Charles Spurgeon, provide pastoral care like Wayne Oates, lead like Bill Hybels, evangelize like Billy Graham, and serve like Mother Teresa! It does mean that a faithful response to the call of God is to develop the gifts and abilities one has in order to serve as effectively as possible. Competence in pastoral ministry is an achievable goal.[12] The apostle Paul admonished his protégé Timothy to pay attention to his life and his teaching (1 Tim. 4:11–16), to discipline himself in his ministry (2 Tim. 2:1–6), and to make every effort to present himself unashamed as a minister (2 Tim. 2:15). A call to ministry, far from making preparation unnecessary, makes it obligatory. Both God and our congregations can expect this of pastors, and we ought to expect it of ourselves.

In a world as rich in resources as ours is, pastors who do not grow professionally year after year are failing to live up to their calling. Increasing our competence in preaching, teaching, theology, pastoral care, and administrative skills over the years is part of a ministry offered with integrity. We expect our physicians to stay up with the latest developments in their field for the sake of our health. We expect our attorneys to be aware of every court ruling that might affect our rights. We actually expect our auto mechanics to stay certified in the rapidly changing technology of our cars! How much more ought congregations be able to expect their pastors to be learning their craft with increasing competence?

Ministry Demands Integrity

Congregations have a right to expect our ministry to have an integrity. That is, what we say in the pulpit on Sunday, for example, about prayer, the importance of Scripture, or the imperative to love one another, needs to show up in the building and grounds committee meeting on Tuesday evening. Preaching, teaching, pastoral care, and leadership are not discrete pastoral tasks that we perform, but are the cohesive acts of ministry we offer to God and our congregations. We will explore the ethical issues surrounding each of these aspects of ministry, but at this point simply note that these tasks belong to one another—they are interwoven, interlocking, and integrated.

The Means to Integrity in Ministry: The Domains of Pastoral Ministry

Pastoral ministry occurs in these three interlocking and overlapping domains: pastoral care, proclamation, and leadership and administration. I have often sat with boys and girls in Vacation Bible School to talk with them about the work of a pastor. I tell them that the word *pastor* in English once meant "shepherd," and that in the Greek language of the New Testament "pastor" and "shepherd" are two meanings of a single word, *poime*. With that metaphor in place we look at biblical passages such as John 21, Acts 20, or 1 Peter 5, in which church leaders are referred to as shepherds. Eventually I ask, "What kinds of things do shepherds do for sheep?" Even these young suburbanites soon come up with answers. Shepherds care for the sheep. Shepherds lead the sheep. Shepherds feed the sheep. Before long we are talking about the work of a pastor as care, leadership, and preaching/teaching. I draw three interlocking, overlapping circles on the board, and we think about the ways the tasks relate to one another. I have used the same exercise with adult church members as well as with seminary students. The mental model provides a kind of broad description of the domains of pastoral work.

These three primary pastoral tasks interlock and support one another. Competent preaching week after week allows worshipers to come to know and trust their pastor. When they are working with the pastor in church committees or ministries, they have a basis from which to work together. In the same way, pastoral care competently and compassionately delivered increases trust and affection, reduces conflict in the congregation, and makes the tasks of leadership more effective. At times, pastoral care and leadership are aspects of the pastor's proclamation. Pastors who devote themselves to competence in their work can maintain faithful and sustainable congregational ministry.

Because each of these three domains of pastoral ministry represents an interaction between the pastor and the people of the congregation, each has its own set of ethical demands and obligations. Thinking through our relationship to the congregation can easily be done by pondering the various roles and relationships our work creates.

Pastoral Care

Pastoral care is that interaction between a pastor and another person that occurs during some life event, often a crisis, in which the pastor's personal presence provides a reminder of God's own presence and care. The pastor's role in such times is not, like "Brother Piston," to deliver a sermon but to listen and to help the person have a sense of God's presence in the moment. The pastor is to help them think about what they are facing and to find a way to move forward in hope in light of the Christian gospel. Allan Hugh Cole Jr. argues that "pastoral" care is distinctive at two points: first, pastoral care is "soul-care," and second, pastoral care takes place in "the foreground of the Christian story," shaped conceptually and practically by the biblical narratives and theological principles of the faith.[13] By "soul," Cole has in mind Jürgen Moltmann's concept of "the relationship of the *whole* person to the immortal God."[14] Consequently, pastoral care is concerned with all that comprises a person's life—physically, emotionally, spiritually, relationally. And it brings that concern into conversation with the Christian story.

AFFECTION

The practice of pastoral care, because it is rooted in a relationship between persons, is fraught with ethical issues and questions that the wise pastor will think through as part of their calling. The place to begin is with the relationship between pastor and parishioner, for this is the place where care is rooted before a crisis occurs. The good shepherd cares for the sheep. Pastoral care is rooted in the pastor's genuine affection for those they serve.

Wendell Berry selects the word *affection* to describe the appropriate relationship between the farmer and the land, and also between human beings in a community. People take care of that which they hold in affection. He says, "The problem simply is that land users are using people, places, and things that cannot be well used without affection. To be well used, creatures and places must be used sympathetically, just as they must be known sympathetically to be well known."[15] In his 2012 Jefferson Lecture for the National Endowment for the Humanities, "It All Turns on Affection," Berry borrowed categories from his mentor Wallace Stegner to describe the two kinds of people who settled the frontier—"boomers" and "stickers." Stegner had described them this way: "[The indigenous Western culture] is the product not of the boomers but of the stickers, not of those who pillage and run but of those who settle, and love the life they have made and the place they have made it in."[16] Berry characterized his grandfather, who settled in Henry County, Kentucky, as a "sticker." He said, "In keeping with the sticker's commitment, he neither left behind the damage he had done nor forgot about it, but stayed to repair it, insofar as soil loss can be repaired."[17] Affection for the place and for the life lived there characterized the sticker. The boomer, on the other hand, treated the land like a mine to be exploited and then abandoned.

Affection is also a necessary practice for faithful ministry. The apostle Paul frequently and unashamedly declares his affection for his brothers and sisters in his congregations. He tells those in Philippi, "For God is my witness, how I long for all of you with the compassion of Christ Jesus" (Phil. 1:8; cf. Gal. 4:19–20; 1 Thess. 2:7–8). "Affection" is related to "pleasure" in Berry's mind. Pleasure is "affection in action."[18] The relationship between pastor and congregation, as well as between pastor and the community in which the ministry is offered, is healthiest when marked by a genuine affection for the people and the place. In this affection one finds pleasure in the work despite the challenges it may offer.

The pastor's affection for the congregation provides a healthy basis for pastoral care and ministry. Yet that same devotion can become the source of a number of ethical challenges. Pastors may become reluctant, out of affection for the congregation, to speak prophetically from the pulpit or in face-to-face conversations. That same mutual affection can prevent congregations from providing appropriate accountability for their pastors. The alternative of a detached, "professional" pastor, however, is unacceptable. Better to work at negotiating the challenges of authentic affection toward the congregation than to become the "hired hand" Jesus contrasted with good shepherds (John 10:11–13).

One might usefully think about how such affection is developed and sustained. Affection is nurtured through the personal and detailed knowledge of the people and the place over time. Martin Copenhaver served one congregation for more than twenty years. He testifies to the reality of this affection: "The affection I have for my parishioners has only grown over time. That affection extends to those members of the congregation who can be quite difficult. If I were to encounter these individuals in another setting, I might not be as devoted to them, but there is something about being entrusted with the care of someone over time than can soften the heart."[19]

Affection is somewhat the product of intimate knowledge, time, shared life and service, and the work of the Holy Spirit in the life of the minister. Praying for people, listening to people, preparing to preach God's Word to those people—all these practices and more grow such affection. The failure to engage congregational life and ministry in such a way is a form of ethical failure. Authentic Christian affection is something pastors owe their congregations ethically.

Dietrich Bonhoeffer's *Life Together* provided a rule of life for his seminary community at Finkenwalde. He called pastors to an affectionate, grateful respect for the men and women God placed in their charge. He urged them to be careful of how they spoke of their congregations: "A pastor should never complain about his congregation, certainly never to other people, but also not to God. A congregation has not been entrusted to him in order that he should become its accuser before God and men."[20] This principle stands in contrast to what one often hears in "shop-talk" conversations among pastors. Affection would lead us to speak otherwise.

The issue of affection raises the question of the pastor's having intimate friendships with those in the congregation. A previous generation of pastors sometimes warned against this, opting for a more distanced, professional relationship with their parishioners. Clearly, close friendships in the congregation can have negative consequences, such as stirring up jealousy among some or creating a conflict of interest should the pastor and the parishioner find themselves on opposite sides of some issue in the church. However, the pastor's authentic affection for the whole congregation and their own need for friendships and support may outweigh the potential negative outcomes.[21] Pastors must keep in mind, however, that these relationships remain somewhat one-sided, equivocal. In the minds of your congregational friends, you will probably always be their pastor first and their friend second. One of my close friends in the congregation introduced me to someone on the golf course as "my pastor." I asked him later, if I had been his barber, would he have done the same thing? He replied, "No, probably not." One other ethical consideration is the reality that those friendships remain when the pastor leaves, thus continuing to connect the pastor to previous congregations. Pastors must find ways to negotiate those valuable friendships without impinging on the ministry of their successors. Visits, calls, or email with one's friends should not become opportunities to listen to them critique one's successors or for the former pastor to gossip with friends about the church's life.

CONFIDENTIALITY

Pastoral care necessarily intimately connects the pastor's life with the lives of people in the congregation. Pastor John Ames, the narrator in Marilynne Robinson's novel *Gilead*, observes, "That's the strangest thing about this life, about being in the ministry. People change the subject when they see you coming. And then sometimes those very same people come into your study and tell you the most remarkable things. There's a lot under the surface of life, everyone knows that. A lot of malice and dread and guilt, and so much loneliness, where you wouldn't really expect to find it, either."[22]

Consequently, people have a proper expectation that what they speak in confidence will be held in confidence. Pastors have a responsibility to abide by that expectation, as far as is legally and ethically possible. Gaylord Noyce states this obligation succinctly: "When something is learned in true pastoral conversation, what might ordinarily be shared with others is not shared."[23]

But confidentiality as a principle presents an ethical challenge.[24] One can face a powerful urge to share with others some fact that has been divulged in confidence. The use of such pastoral conversations as fodder for sermon illustrations is a clear violation of the relationship, even if names are changed or the situations occurred in a former congregation. *Without the explicit permission of the parishioner*, the pastor holds no rights to use that conversation in any form, from the pulpit or in private conversation. Pastors may not share such moments as "prayer requests" or mention them to others they might think hold a common concern for the person's life. Such confidentiality is a sacred trust that makes such conversations possible.[25]

Pastor Jones visited Mrs. Smith in her hospital room one week and learned that the conditions that sent her there had much improved. She would likely be returning home within a few days. On Sunday the pastor mentioned this to Mrs. Smith's brother, also a member of the congregation. Mrs. Smith's brother did not know of her hospitalization and was taken by surprise. He went immediately after church to confront her about not letting him know. Mrs. Smith was furious with her pastor for passing along such information without her consent. Besides possibly violating HIPAA privacy laws, Pastor Jones had certainly ignored the confidentiality Mrs. Smith assumed was hers.[26] By simply asking her, "May I share this good news about your improvement?" the pastor could have avoided this breach of confidence.

A pastor's intent to respect confidentiality presents moral dilemmas when it clashes with other moral principles such as the duty to protect or divulge. Each situation will be handled separately as one decides based on principles, duties, and other factors, but in the end, each pastor will have to determine the best way forward ethically.[27]

Confidentiality is not absolute; it comes with legal boundaries that pastors must respect as well. Not everything spoken to a pastor in the privacy of their study is *necessarily* to be kept in confidence. The laws governing clergy communications privilege vary by state.[28] In Texas, for example, "A communication is 'confidential' if made privately and not intended for further disclosure except to other persons present in furtherance of the purpose of the communication."[29] According to the code, "A person has a privilege to refuse to disclose and to prevent another from disclosing a confidential communication by the person to a member of the clergy in the member's professional character as spiritual adviser."[30] This does not necessarily mean that something said by a parishioner to the pastor in the aisle of the local grocery store, for example, is privileged information that a pastor could refuse to offer in court without being in contempt. Clergy are sometimes summoned in cases of child custody in which both parents are members of the congregation. Not everything the pastor knows or has been told about the parties is inherently confidential. A wise pastor will consult an attorney before offering testimony or refusing to do so.[31]

On the other hand, pastors may learn things they are *required* to report to appropriate authorities.[32] These laws also differ from state to state. The Texas Family Code, for example, defines a long list of examples of abuse or neglect of a child. The law requires any person, including clergy—who are specifically mentioned with health-care professionals, attorneys, social workers, and others—to make a verbal report of *suspected* abuse within forty-eight hours. The pastor does not need definite proof in order to be obliged to report, only suspicion. The failure to report suspected child abuse or neglect is a misdemeanor in Texas, punishable by imprisonment of up to 180 days and/or a fine of up to $2,000. A later revision of the code included the requirement to report abuse or neglect of the elderly or disabled.[33] Once more, the advice of an attorney will help pastors comply with the law. Additionally, in some states pastors and religious counselors are bound by law to protect others who may be endangered by a parishioner who expresses threats or intent to harm them. In some states, self-destructive persons are to be legally protected as well.[34] Other situations may not require a breach of confidentiality legally, but may do so ethically. William W. Rankin recognizes the reality that clergy operate with values and principles that may require of them more than the law does or, in fact, something contrary to what the law does. Rankin argues,

> There is reason to suppose that professional ethics should be more rigorous than what the law allows in any given state. In other words, if clergy practices are conducted within the bounds of the law only, are these practices *therefore* being performed in accordance with a reasonable standard of ethical conduct within their profession? Or are clergy called to "higher duties," along the lines, perhaps, that proceeded from the court's minority opinion? With respect to confidentiality in particular, a professional ethic that supports such positive duties to care, refer, or prevent a (preventable) suicide will clearly entail the strong possibility of breaching confidentiality in certain cases.[35]

In such cases, acting out of conscience, a pastor may have to be willing to bear the legal liability or consequences of such action (Acts 4:19).

Donald Freeman suggests as a model of confidentiality a circle with firm boundaries, addressing the question of how one honors confidences when they cannot be kept secret. The goal is to keep the circle of confidentiality as small and as intact as possible, so as to honor the trust that confidentiality assumes while serving the best interests of the one who is confiding in the pastor.[36] For example, the circle of confidentiality may be expanded to include one's supervisor or colleagues in a supervisory group, such as those in a continuing professional education program or one's field supervisor in a counseling or social-work program. Even in these cases one usually changes the name and identifying characteristics of the people involved. One's duty to warn or protect others may require that others be taken into the circle, as in cases of abuse and neglect. Additionally, others may be included when the pastor becomes aware of information that others need to know. Freeman offers the example of a practicing professional who discloses information that those who oversee the integrity of the profession need to know. Always one must ask "Who needs to know?" and "How much do they need to know?" Freeman's model is useful to the pastor in aspects of church life that require confidentiality other than pastoral care, such as personnel matters, staff searches, and some cases of church discipline.

The issue of confidentiality in the exercise of pastoral care is a primary but not ultimate value in pastoral care. W. Dow Egerton argues, "Confidentiality is a means toward an end, not an end in itself. . . . The aim of confidentiality is to provide a certain shelter for the vulnerable—a place of safety where temptation and failure can be exposed to the light of grace, healing, empowering, and transforming. It cannot, therefore, become a mechanism for insuring impunity or an impediment to protecting others who are vulnerable."[37]

The failure to break confidence has been challenged as a form of clergy malpractice in some states.[38] However, such malpractice suits have been unsuccessful so far, for a variety of reasons. Although pastors may find themselves liable in court in areas such as invasion of privacy, breach of fiduciary duty, or outrageous conduct, malpractice charges are unlikely to stick.[39]

COUNSELING OR PASTORAL CONVERSATIONS?

Pastors frequently find themselves offering pastoral care in the form of "counseling." Christ's followers seek help from their pastor regarding questions not only of faith and spiritual practice but also about their marriages, their parenting, their jobs, their in-laws, and their failures. They come with issues around infertility, depression, abortion, sexual orientation, and moral failure. They come to talk about grief and their own impending death. They want to talk about these matters in relationship to God and faith.

A generation or two ago "pastoral care" was taught and practiced around a therapeutic model. Pastors were trained in counseling skills and techniques. Will Willimon argues that we live in a "therapeutic culture," where human ills are reduced to sickness. We want to feel better about ourselves. Willimon claims that pastors have pursued the "pastor as therapist" model because in such a secular culture it is the last socially approved role for pastors. He concludes, "The pastor is reduced to the level of the soother of anxieties brought on by the dilemmas of affluence, rather than the caller of persons to salvation."[40] Untrained, unsupervised, and without a license, pastors who purport to do "counseling" may be overstating their claims and could find themselves legally liable for the outcomes. Presenting oneself as a "counselor" in a context where that profession is licensed and regulated is ethically questionable if the pastor lacks those credentials. On the other hand, "pastoral conversations"[41] can explore the wide range of human struggles and questions with the Christian story in the background as a legitimate expression of pastoral care. Thinking and praying with one's parishioners about their life does not require a therapeutic orientation or goal. "Pastor as spiritual director" is a more authentic, honest, and ethical role to occupy than "pastor as therapist."[42]

Conducting these pastoral conversations raises a set of ethical questions for the minister. Will I meet in private with congregants of the opposite sex?

When and where will I conduct these conversations? Will others be nearby? How do I provide both privacy and accountability? What will be the purpose of these meetings? How often am I willing to meet with an individual? How will I handle feelings of transference should they emerge in the relationship?

A conversation may reveal that the congregant is dealing with more serious matters of marital conflict, parenting, or mental health than the pastor is qualified to address. Pastors need to have a set of resources in the community to which they can confidently refer their flock for help. Once a referral is made, the pastor's responsibility does not end. The church member will need to know that the pastor is not simply handing them off. The pastoral relationship to the person continues, and so follow-up around pastoral issues is necessary. Another set of questions requires attention in the case of a referral. When will I refer someone to a more qualified resource than myself or to someone who can give more time to the person? How will I vet those counselors whom I recommend to my congregation? How will I stay in touch with the person as a pastor once they have connected to a counselor or physician?

WEDDINGS

Pastors are called on to officiate at weddings as a routine part of their role in pastoral care. In the United States this has put pastors in an awkward relationship vis-à-vis the state. Signing a marriage license issued by the county effectively makes one an agent of the state. Pastors have not much thought about this hybrid role. In *Brother to a Dragonfly*, Baptist pastor Will Campbell comes face-to-face with this reality when his brother, Joe, in a drunken stupor, defines marriage as "when two people get together and give each other the right to sue each other if they ever want to."[43] Will is stunned into a new understanding of the pastor's relationship to the state in the act of conducting a wedding in Caesar's name. He never again says, "By the authority vested in me by the State of Tennessee." Instead he begins by saying, "Render unto Caesar the things that are Caesar's. If you have a license we will sign it at this time." After signing it, he tosses it aside and says, "Render unto God the things that are God's. The *wedding* begins at this point."[44]

This connection between pastors and the state was brought into focus in a fresh way in June 2015 when the US Supreme Court ruled that same-sex marriages are legal in all fifty states. Churches that desired to stick with a traditional view of marriage as between a man and a woman in their practices were advised to revisit their bylaws and to be clear that they contained a statement of belief, and in particular, a statement of belief regarding marriage. They were also advised to review their wedding policies and facility-use policies to be certain that they were worded to support the congregation's position on the matter.[45] In other words, they were encouraged to carefully think through how their practices related to Caesar's policy.[46]

The ethical questions a pastor faces regarding participation in weddings in the twenty-first century are complex. Will I perform weddings at all? Will I sign a marriage license issued by the state? Whose weddings will I perform? Church members only? Will I marry those with divorce in their past? Same-sex couples? Nonbelievers? Those of other religions? Couples who are living together? Can I as the pastor have a different answer to these questions than the congregation I serve? Where will I perform weddings? In the church's facilities only? At various secular wedding venues? What are my obligations to the couple whose wedding I officiate? Ought I require premarital sessions? How "Christian" does the wedding ceremony need to be in order for me, as a pastor, to play a part? Do I charge a fee for officiating, or do I offer my services as a gift to the couple? These are a few of the wedding questions a pastor needs to think through in order to maintain ethical integrity with the pastoral care offered in the form of a wedding ceremony. Answers to these questions will necessarily vary from one pastor to another and from one church to another, but they need to be addressed from the perspective of both the pastor's and the congregation's beliefs and values.

Ethics is essentially about managing relationships with integrity. In the context of a wedding, the opportunities to demonstrate integrity abound. The pastor will certainly be working with the bride and groom and their families. In addition, pastors also often interact with a professional wedding coordinators and their staff, sound technicians, photographers, and, depending on the context, florists and caterers. In each of these relationships the pastor has the opportunity to demonstrate Christian love and hospitality to outsiders as well as to beloved families within the congregation.

FUNERALS

Ministry during times of bereavement and grief is also a standard part of pastoral care in a Christian congregation. The ministry of comfort and hope that pastors offer is a vital part of their work, and often it is among the most meaningful expressions of pastoral care. Practices surrounding Christian funerals have shifted steadily over the past two generations. Cremation rates have doubled in the past fifteen years and are expected to exceed 50 percent by 2019.[47] Memorial services, once held in church buildings, are more regularly conducted in funeral homes. Pastors need to respect the local culture of the congregation and the community by learning which funeral practices and customs are common among them. The pastor is often at the center of helping to plan these services and has a key role to play with families and with the funeral professionals. Maintaining ethical integrity in this ministry requires a thoughtful approach.

Wise pastors will establish a relationship with local funeral directors soon after arriving on the field, since they will often be partners in this ministry during the pastor's tenure. A professional relationship with these men and women in the community can benefit the pastor and the congregation. Funeral directors who know their local pastors are usually aware of the need to contact the pastor before making concrete plans about the day and time of a service. Pastors can often be involved in meeting with the funeral director alongside the grieving family, advising about the funeral, and planning the service. In addition, funeral directors who trust local pastors may call on them occasionally to provide bereavement ministry to families that have no church connections. The pastor and the congregation are in a unique place to serve such families.

The pastor will encounter some ethical issues that orbit about funeral practices. Honesty plays a key role in the funeral service. A eulogy that all present recognize as exaggerated does not serve the pastor's reputation for integrity. Neither "preaching someone into heaven" nor "condemning them to hell" is a helpful approach when the pastor does not know about their faith. Pastors who speak as if they knew the deceased, when they did not, are less helpful to grieving family and friends. Yet pastors often are asked to conduct services for strangers. Learning all one can about the deceased is a way of honoring and serving their family, whose own words of testimony might be used in the eulogy or sermon. The funeral messages as well as private conversations with the bereaved should not presume to know exactly what their experience of grief is like. Pastors should not use their own losses as illustrations or examples.

Pastors will frequently enough be called on to conduct services for one whose death is especially traumatic, such as victims of murder, suicide, or tragic accidents. Honest pastoral care will seek to address, not avoid, the difficult reality and will attempt to do so in light of the Christian story.

Funeral practices often include a part to be played by military or fraternal organizations, usually at the graveside when there is a burial. In cases of memorial services following cremation, these groups may be present for the service at the funeral home or church. The pastor is called on to respect the family's decision to include these and to accommodate their presence.

Pastors often receive what may seem like bizarre requests for funeral services, especially when the family or the deceased does not have a connection with Christian faith or with a church. An "open mic" is sometimes suggested, which is nearly always a very bad idea. Music is frequently selected that does not contribute to the worship of God or point to Christ's death and resurrection or to our hope of eternal life. Practices such as the release of balloons or butterflies show up occasionally, which have no theological basis. How will a pastor negotiate these requests with love and care for the grieving family and yet with personal convictions about the purpose and meaning of the service? As much as possible pastors need to think through their own convictions and to have a hand in the planning of the service so that it points to hope in Christ.

Other ethical responsibilities arise in the pastor's relationship to the bereaved family and friends. Will the pastor accept an honorarium or expense check for conducting the funeral? Customs can vary across the country. How will the pastor follow up with the grieving family over the course of the next year?

Proclamation

Like the work of pastoral care, the domain of proclamation puts the pastor into relationship with others—God, the congregation, and the biblical writers, as well as other preachers and commentators who have spent time with the biblical text. Consequently, a series of ethical concerns emerge for the preacher. Raymond Bailey notes that in years of preaching, listening to preachers, and teaching preaching, he consistently observed five common violations of preaching ethics: (1) poor preparation and faulty exegesis, (2) glittering generalities, (3) loaded language and name calling, (4) emotional manipulation, and (5) misrepresentation and partial truth.[48] Ethical issues in preaching principally involve the pastor's preparation, problems related to plagiarism, personal integrity, and the content of the message.

PREPARATION

One of the chief ethical demands of a call to ministry is faithful preparation in preaching and teaching. A congregation of a hundred will collectively invest the equivalent of a week's work and ten hours of overtime listening to a thirty-minute sermon. That is not time to be squandered. Pastors may have little idea of how much effort many of their members exerted just to be present on a given Sunday morning. They come with expectations and needs and deserve the pastor's best work. A pastoral counseling center in Houston worked with our congregation to conduct a survey of life needs during a Sunday morning worship hour. Among the items in the survey was one that asked about suicidal thoughts: "I have considered taking my life during the past week." Of the nearly one thousand members present that morning, three indicated that those thoughts had been theirs during the past seven days. With no way to know who those three individuals were (and it could have been three others in another week), I was deeply impressed by how much can be on the line when a pastor steps into the pulpit. People come to that moment with needs, and the responsibility cannot be taken lightly.

The call to preach is a call to prepare. Preparation includes whatever formal training in biblical studies and preaching may be available. But it also includes the weekly engagement of the tools acquired in training to discern and deliver a message from Scripture that speaks to the life of God's people. Although pastors have many excellent tools available to help them with exegesis and illustration of truth, shortcuts are no substitute for personal listening to Scripture and to the heartbeat of the congregation.

Plagiarism

The practice of plagiarism, perhaps a subset of poor preparation, has been a temptation of preachers for centuries and has grown exponentially with the presence of the internet.[49] O. Wesley Allen Jr. cites a nineteenth-century limerick about preachers "borrowing" the work of Charles Spurgeon:

> There once was a preacher named Spurgy.
> No lover was he of liturgy.
> His sermons are fine, I use them as mine,
> And so do most of the clergy.[50]

British poet Gerard Manley Hopkins, while still a college student, wrote a couplet about his pastor, who was known to have used the work of other preachers on occasion:

> Herclot's preaching I'll no longer hear:
> They're out of date—lent sermons all the year.[51]

The Lord gave Jeremiah a word to speak against the false prophets of Judah. The oracle in Jeremiah 23 is a scathing denunciation of those who claim to preach the Word of the Lord but whose lives contradict it (23:11, 14). They have not stood in the heavenly council of the Lord; they have not listened to God. Instead they simply speak their own dreams, opinions, and agendas (23:16–18, 21–22). In addition, these prophets "steal my words from one another" (23:30). Eugene Peterson paraphrases the accusation: "I've had it with the 'prophets' who get all their sermons secondhand from each other. Yes,

I've had it with them. They make up stuff and then pretend it's a real sermon" (23:30–31 Message). Apparently plagiarism has been around for some time.

A fellow pastor in our city received a call from a college friend, now a deacon in another Baptist congregation. The caller's pastor had preached a series of sermons the previous year and a church member happened to discover the series on the internet. The deacons confronted the pastor with the fact, which he readily admitted. "Everybody does that," was his explanation. They explained to him their expectation that he should be studying and listening for God's Word to their congregation and their lives. He agreed to do so. About a year later the episode was repeated, and the pastor was asked to leave the church. This behavior is not new, but neither has it become acceptable.[52] Pastors cannot offer to a congregation a diet of canned sermons taken from the internet or lifted from their file from their previous church and popped into the microwave to be warmed up and served on Sunday morning. A call to preach is a call to prepare.[53]

The weekly sermon begins as a conversation in the pastor's study among the pastor, the Holy Spirit, the biblical writers, the voices of other commentators and preachers, and the congregation. That conversation continues when the pastor steps behind the pulpit to preach. The holy moment of preaching is preceded by holy hours of prayerful, faithful, studious preparation. Although technology can enhance this process, it cannot eliminate it. Good conversations take time. So does effective preaching.

INTEGRITY IN PREACHING

Pastors are called to stand and preach credibly in a culture where words have lost their meaning.[54] The rants of politicians are often blustery and filled with exaggerations, if not outright lies. "Fact-checking" by the media following a politician's speech or debate performance generally reveals a long list of twisted statistics, misstatements, and false claims, further undermining our confidence in both language and leaders. Preachers are not exempt from the demand to speak with integrity. Unlike politicians, pastors cannot afford to bounce their fact checks. The phrase "preacher story" has come to refer to a dubious narrative, and "ministerially speaking" means gross exaggeration of the truth. This is an indictment on ethical preaching. One cannot proclaim the truth of God and play loose and free with truth itself.

Pastors have an ethical obligation to do their own fact-checking before citing statistics, telling stories, or passing on information as illustrative material in their sermons. Email and social media have become tools for passing on the most blatant and egregious gossip, and Christians have freely participated, clicking "Share" or "Send" without ever asking, "Is this true?" Pastors can do much of the same thing in the pulpit. Part of study and research is ascertaining that you have the details right before using the information. Preachers have often felt free to tell a story about something that happened to someone else as if it were their own story. That does not pass the integrity test.

This kind of integrity applies to the pastor's biblical study as well. Exegetical fallacies are often rampant in sermons.[55] The connection between what a text says and means and what the pastor says about the text needs to be solid. American theologian Tryon Edwards remarked of the preaching in his day that "if the text had the smallpox, the sermon would never catch it."[56] To manipulate a biblical text to fit the pastor's opinion is at the same time to manipulate the listener.

Integrity in the pulpit is more than a matter of words and illustrations, however. The pastor's own life and character matter as well. Phillips Brooks is famously noted for his observation that preaching is truth communicated through personality. By "personality" Brooks certainly had in mind more than the contemporary stage or screen personality of popular preachers. He intended the person, or the character, of the preacher. "Truth through Personality," he said, "is our description of real preaching. The truth must come really through the person, not merely over his lips, not merely into his understanding and out of his pen. It must come through his character, his affections, his whole intellectual and moral being. It must come genuinely through him."[57] This is where the impact of a pastor/preacher is most profound. The care offered in the hospital room, the honesty demonstrated in the committee meeting, the shared work of ministry week after week contribute to the impact of the preaching on the listener. We cannot afford to have a "pulpit voice" on Sunday morning and another voice on Monday night. Integrity means the pastor is the same person in the pulpit as out of it.

The old adage "practice what you preach" is not yet worn out. What we are preaching as a way of faith and practice must be what we ourselves are attempting to live as well. That does not imply perfection. Nor does it mean that we can never speak about things that yet remain outside our own experience. But integrity demands that when we do, we acknowledge in some way that we ourselves stand under this Word from God and are attempting to learn it as well.

THE CONTENT OF PREACHING

The content of one's preaching and teaching also carries an ethical burden. That is, over the long haul, what does preaching contribute to the task assigned to pastors of "mak[ing] disciples" (Matt. 28:18–20 NIV) or "equip[ping] the saints for the work of ministry" (Eph. 4:11–12 NIV)? Preaching and teaching have a specific role to play in the life of the congregation, a large part of which is to lead the people of God into a maturing service in the kingdom of God.

Preaching that is merely self-help advice attractively packaged and marketed to the "felt needs" of listeners hardly qualifies as preaching. How ethical is it for a pastor to sprinkle proof texts through three points that television pop psychologists could have delivered with a straight face? Proclamation that emerges from the conversation between God, the congregation, and the pastor, and that is offered in worship as just such a conversation, will have a distinctively different tone and content from the self-help "messages" delivered to our "culture of contentment."[58]

Preaching affects the other domains of pastoral ministry. At times the pulpit is the source of pastoral care, helping men and women bring the realities of their whole embodied life into connection with the Christian narrative. We preach about marriage and family, about friendships and forgiveness, about money and generosity. We bring politics and ecology into conversation with the Christian Scriptures. This is a form of pastoral care.

Preaching also impinges on our capacity to lead. In Texas it is common to see a rancher driving his truck through a pasture, followed by a long line of cattle. They follow the truck because they have consistently had the experience of being fed from it. Jesus's words about his shepherding come to mind: "My sheep hear my voice. I know them, and they follow me" (John 10:27). Although our congregants are not mindless cattle or sheep, they are more inclined to trust a minister who has faithfully provided spiritual nourishment from the pulpit week after week. Pastors have an ethical responsibility to attend to the work of developing disciples through preaching.

The pastor who seeks to walk worthy of the calling to proclaim the gospel will think through a litany of ethical issues and questions.[59] How do I protect my time to adequately prepare to preach each week? How will I use the resources available to me electronically in a way that enhances my efforts without plagiarizing the work of others? What practices will I engage that will assure integrity in my use of illustrations and language? How will I discipline myself to provide a broad spectrum of biblical and theological truth over time? How will I preach so as to make disciples of Jesus? How will I work at increasing my competence as a biblical student and as a preacher? What practices will help me listen to the congregation's voice as I work in the study week after week?

Leadership and Administration

POWER AND AUTHORITY

Every pastor will eventually contend with the forces of power and authority. Along with money and sex, this is one of the major areas of temptation faced by Christian leaders through the generations. Richard Foster says, "To live rightly with reference to money and sex and power is to live sacramentally. To misuse and abuse these is to desecrate the holy things of God."[60] Power is unique in this triumvirate of temptation, because it often works its worst effects using the other two.

As Foster asserts, power is not inherently evil. In fact, he includes it among "the holy things of God." Power is the ability to get things done, to make things happen. It becomes perverted when combined with a selfish human heart that wants its own way and will do anything to achieve its agenda.

Authority and power are closely related. Authority is a means of acquiring or holding power. Authentic authority can be *positional*, held because of a role one has earned or has been given. Authority can be based on *expertise*. A pastor's training, education, and experience may lend authority to their opinion in a matter to which the congregation willingly yields. Authority can be *personal* as well. This is a kind of power that comes from relational trust that is earned. Those who work from such a position may not "get their way" every time, but people respect them and listen to them. Each type of authority can be a holy gift to be used to serve or a desecrated instrument used to acquire personal power.

Pastors need not shy away from authority and power. In fact, at times it needs to be accepted and claimed in order to minister effectively, and it would be a matter of ethical irresponsibility to do otherwise. When a pastor steps into a hospital room where death and grief and fear are in the air, they do so "in the name of Jesus." Unlike others who may enter the room as a friend, or a brother, sister, son, or daughter, the pastor does not simply represent oneself and one's personal relationship to those in the room. Instead, the pastor enters as a representative of Jesus Christ and Christ's church. It does not matter whether the pastor is a twenty-five-year-old newly minted from seminary or a sixty-year-old with decades of experience. The authority of Christ is present to step into that situation and to speak compassion and hope.

Neither do pastors enter the pulpit simply as themselves. They stand with an open Bible to proclaim God's Word to God's people. They stand with a pastoral authority that they need not apologize for, but must claim. Otherwise they have no business occupying that spot.

Such authority that comes with the office of pastor, especially when coupled with their perceived expertise and earned respect and trust, can put pastors in a precarious position. Forgetting their own vulnerability as sinful men or women, they can begin to abuse the power with which they have been entrusted. Over time they may soon demand privilege, manipulate people, and insist on their own way in every issue. Some would-be ministers have seen only that model of ministry and aspire to it from the beginning. A student one day asked in a pastoral ministry class, "How long were you at your church before you started installing your way of doing things?" The question implies a use of power to get one's own way that is contrary to the gospel.

The temptation is more subtle than we might think. It is natural to enter a field of ministry and to see things that you would like to have changed. Your education or previous experience tells you that things can be done better, more effectively, another way. Pastors who insist on too many changes too soon often wonder why they are receiving pushback from the congregation instead of a standing ovation. Such efforts at change may be an abuse of power that fails to respect the congregation's life, history, and culture. A colleague who once served a church in Hawaii was advised by a deacon there, "Don't change anything here until you've learned to surf." He meant that. "Get to know us and our culture and then you'll be in a position to lead changes."

How might pastors work to keep issues of power in check? Wendell Berry advises those who would care for land to ask four questions before proceeding to make changes in it: (1) What would nature be doing in a place if no one was farming there? (2) What would nature permit them to do there? (3) What could they do there with the least harm to the place and to their natural and human neighbors? (4) What would nature *help* them do there?[61] He tells of his own failed efforts that came from not respecting the uniqueness of a place. In a poem titled "Damage," Berry laments wounds he inflicted on his farm when he attempted to build a pond in the wrong place: "But a man with a machine and inadequate culture—such as I was when I made my pond—is a pestilence. He shakes more than he can hold."[62] The problem, he argues, is too much power and too little knowledge.

Pastors might do well to ask similar questions before climbing aboard a bulldozer or taking up a chain saw to change things in the congregation. What was the Spirit doing before I got here? What would the Spirit allow me to do here? What could be done with the least harm to the congregation and the community? What will the Spirit help me to do here? Listening to the congregation and the Holy Spirit for answers to those questions might mitigate an inappropriate use of power.

Richard Foster claims that the spiritual discipline of submission produces the freedom to "lay down the terrible burden of always needing to get our own way," which is "one of the greatest bondages in human society today."[63]

Henri Nouwen identifies the temptation to be powerful, which Jesus faced in the wilderness, as one of the chief temptations of leadership. He commends the practice of theological reflection as an antidote.[64]

Pastors seeking to lead in a manner worthy of their calling will ask questions about power and its use. Am I appropriately accepting the pastoral authority that is mine to minister in Jesus's name? Do I find myself thinking my way is the only way, my ideas are the only good ones, and manipulating or demanding in order to get my way? How often and how well do I listen to the voice of the congregation in order to discern God's direction? Where could I appropriately relinquish or share power in my ministry? How well do I understand the "enormous power differential" between myself and my parishioners, which can leave them vulnerable to abuse, however subtle?[65]

SERVANT LEADERSHIP

"Servant leadership" conjures up a variety of images in the minds of pastors and congregants. To some, the concept sounds weak and passive, as if the pastor is to be a doormat or an overfunctioner who attempts to do everything for the congregation. This is a misunderstanding of the concept and is itself an unsustainable approach to ministry. Robert Greenleaf, who popularized the notion of servant leadership in the corporate world in the 1970s, defined the servant leader as one whose first inclination is to serve, not to lead.[66] Servant leaders offer themselves to something higher than themselves, and they devote their gifts, abilities, time, and effort to serving. If the congregation needs someone with gifts of leadership, then leading, too, is an act of service. Servant leadership as a model calls for ethical reflection on the true needs of the congregation and on the pastor's responsibility to meet those needs or equip others to do so.

Jesus's example of washing the feet of the disciples is often cited as the model of servant leadership—he performed the tasks of a servant (John 13:1–17). As far as we know, however, washing feet was not his habit. Servant leadership took other forms as well. On occasion he confronted the disciples in their unbelief and challenged their faith (Matt. 16:8–11, 22–23). He demonstrated his servanthood in his willingness to do what was most needed to develop these disciples in their faith. In this way he served them by empowering them and sending them out (Matt. 10:1–5).

Servant leaders take responsibility for providing two vital elements necessary for congregational life: a missional focus and a clear vision.[67] The missional focus will be some concrete engagement with the Great Commission (Matt. 28:18–20) and the Great Commandments (Matt. 22:34–40). The pastor will thoughtfully engage the congregation in exploring Scripture and thinking through a clear understanding of what it means to be the church and will keep that mission before them as they worship weekly or perform the quotidian tasks of conducting church business. A missional focus creates a more faithful ministry because it keeps both pastor and congregation from being diverted from the central calling that is theirs as a church. Although the pastor may not be the one who defines the mission, as a servant leader the pastor has an ethical responsibility to see that the missional focus is identified and that it remains central to the congregation's life.

In the same way, the servant leader assumes responsibility for engaging the congregation in conversation about its future. Leadership is inherently about the future, and a leader, like a midwife, assists the congregation in giving birth to it. "Vision" may be understood as the preferred future that the congregation comes to believe God is offering them. Such a vision is not usually given to the pastor on a mountain to be brought down to the congregation waiting passively in the valley. Rather, the pastor leads the congregation to discern a shared vision under the leadership of the Holy Spirit. Such a vision, as it becomes clear, provides direction, guidance, and hope. In the absence of such a vision, congregational life can erode into conflicting individual agendas, traditionalism, or religious shopkeeping.[68] Clear vision supplies the forward direction that sustainable, faithful ministry requires. Such clarity is part of the debt the servant leader owes the congregation.

In *Leadership Is an Art*, Max Depree asserts, "The first responsibility of a leader is to define reality. The last is to say thank you. In between the two, the leader must become a servant and a debtor. That sums up the progress of an artful leader."[69] In a faithful partnership between clergy leaders and congregational members, ministers owe congregational members both a debt and service. Pastors pay down debt by sharing the privilege of ministry with the congregation, developing disciples who understand that they, too, are called to serve (Eph. 4:11–13). All of God's people have gifts to contribute to the body of Christ, and they have a part to play in its ministry. Pastors practicing faithful ministry help these believer-priests understand both theologically and practically that they are ministers—that their baptism was their ordination to serve.[70] This development of disciples is an ethical aspect of one's ministry, both in preaching and in leadership.

Faithful ministry operates out of a vision of congregational life in which church members are built up rather than depleted by the service and ministry they offer. They are developed, not abused. The congregation, like good soil, must be enriched to endure season after season of productive ministry. Church programs can easily become the end to which the congregation is the means. Some agricultural practices treat soil like dirt, regarding it merely as medium to hold plants upright while chemicals are pumped into them. Eventually the soil is depleted and is subject to erosion, becoming the "rocky soil" Jesus spoke of that does not permit the Word of God to grow and bear fruit. Conventional church practices can deplete the congregation as well, eroding or burning out the available volunteers who serve in its ministries. That is simply not ethical leadership.

Imagine a congregation member, after a challenging and tiring week of Vacation Bible School, saying, "That was the richest spiritual experience of my life. Sign me up for next year!" Envision someone coming off a three-year term on a church board confessing, "I don't know when I have grown so much spiritually. I'm sorry to be rotating off the board." What practices would make such a scenario credible? Faithful ministry, worthy of the calling, moves clergy to equip believers to serve in these necessary volunteer roles in such a way that they are spiritually formed in the process.

Equipping ministry is not a ruse for recruiting volunteers to the church's programs. Rather, it is the effort to help disciples discover a call to ministry and empowering them to engage it effectively. It is forming people as disciples and ministers of Jesus Christ. Church members do not help the pastor and staff accomplish *their* ministry; rather, the pastor and staff help church members exercise *their* ministry. Equipping ministry is a vital leadership practice for servant leaders.

Key Issues for Integrity in Ministry: Leaving the Congregation

To some degree, all pastors are interim pastors.[71] That is, eventually they will leave the congregation and will be replaced by a successor. Even in the act of departing, pastors have ethical obligations, both to their current congregation and to the prospective congregation and its search committee.[72] How well one leaves can have an impact on the congregation's ability to carry on effective ministry and on their success in receiving and adapting to a new pastor.

Perhaps the first ethical demand on pastors may be to carefully consider whether they should leave at all. A long-term ministry in a congregation may be worth the effort required to find a way to remain.[73] Lyle Schaller, a United Methodist Church church consultant, was a fan of long-tenured pastorates despite his own denomination's practice of moving ministers frequently. He told a gathering of pastors, "When you want to leave you have two choices. Go home and take a shower and take a nap. Or go home and take a nap and take a shower. Then go back to work." In addition to those of poverty, chastity, and obedience, the Benedictine tradition included a vow of stability, which encouraged the monk to commit himself to a community and stay.[74] Will

Willimon argues, "Long pastorates generally make wonderfully grounded and centered pastors, while a series of short pastorates are often an indication of a pastor who has not had to develop the resources for maturation in ministry."[75] The ethical thing to do may be to stay a bit longer.

In most congregational systems, the decision to move to a new ministry context is made in conversation with a search committee from the prospective church. The process is an awkward one ethically. One may want to be transparent with one's current congregation about the conversations with the search committee, but doing so may damage relationships and ministry, especially should the move not occur. Where it is possible to disclose the process to key persons in the church confidentially, the pastor may lessen the impact when a move is ultimately announced. Key leaders have had time to think through the process and to formulate a strategy for moving forward.

Relationships to a pastor search committee come with ethical responsibilities as well. The pastor must be as honest and transparent with the committee as possible, both on their résumé and in emails, phone conversations, and face-to-face exchanges. The pastor should be prompt in returning calls and answering electronic correspondence. Should the pastor have something in their past, such as divorce, that may be an issue with a committee, that fact should be shared with the committee chair before the group goes to the trouble of arranging the pastor's travel to a meeting. If the issue is a deal-breaker, that should be clarified as early as possible. Additionally, pastors should refrain from engaging in conversation with search committees from more than one congregation at a time without disclosing this fact. This is not fair treatment of the men and women volunteering their time to serve their churches. One congregation should not become leverage to be used with another.

When a pastor concludes that a move from one congregation to another is the right thing to do, however, they should make an intentional effort to leave well. When the time comes to announce the news, the pastor may identify those men and women who need to hear the news first face-to-face and not in a general announcement, email, or newsletter. Additionally, the news may best be shared with groups of leaders, such as deacons or elders, before it is announced to the congregation as a whole, allowing them time to think through the next steps the congregation will need to take. When leaders have such a plan already in place, the emotional impact on the congregation will be diminished.

Lawrence W. Farris offers "ten commandments" for a pastor leaving a congregation, based on his own wisdom and experience. These ten guidelines are ethical in focus and can provide a departing pastor with a rubric for thinking through their process of transition. Farris's commandments are: "Thou shalt know when it is time to go"; "Thou shalt explain thyself"; "Thou shalt not steal away"; "Thou shalt affirm thy congregation's ministry"; "Thou shalt try to mend fences"; "Thou shalt help thy successor have a good beginning"; "Thou shalt be gentle with thyself"; "Thou shalt attend to thy family"; "Thou shalt (usually) stay away once thou hast left"; and "Thou shalt grieve."[76]

In addition to Farris's wisdom, the pastor might consider other responsibilities in the transition. When the departure is more traditional, the pastor may have no more than a few weeks to wind down their work in one place, take care of real-estate issues, find a mover, and relocate. These practical needs do not relieve the pastor of taking care of relationships and responsibilities in their current congregation. When the pastor is retiring, the process of leaving may intentionally be extended over several months, especially when they have had a long tenure in the congregation.[77] The mere announcement of one's departure likely will create a level of anxiety in the congregation, and the pastor's continued calm presence and reassurance will go far in helping the congregation to confidently and calmly move through the period of transition. Edwin Friedman encourages departing pastors not to accept the "lame-duck" myth in the period following the news of their leaving. As long as the pastor is present and part of the congregation's emotional system, they can still wield an influence emotionally for good.[78]

After the transition has been made, the ethical responsibilities continue. How shall I relate to my successor? Will I accept requests from congregants to return to conduct funerals or weddings? How will I respond to congregants who complain to me about my successor? The issues of relating to this fellow pastor who is now one's successor will be taken up in chapter 5.

The day-to-day work of the pastor, immersed in relationships, is soaked in ethical obligations and responsibilities. The pastor's task is to think carefully about how these relationships and expectations are managed with integrity. The ability to embody integrity naturally and consistently will increase both the impact and the sustainability of the pastor's ministry. The various domains of pastoral work will be enhanced as they are treated with the respect and faithfulness they deserve. To do so is to walk worthy of one's calling.

Suggested Reading

Bullis, Ronald K., and Cynthia S. Mazur. *Legal Issues and Religious Counseling.* Louisville: Westminster John Knox, 1993.

Farris, Lawrence W. *Ten Commandments for Pastors Leaving a Congregation.* Grand Rapids: Eerdmans, 2006.

Foster, Richard J. *The Challenge of the Disciplined Life: Christian Reflections on Money, Sex, and Power*. San Francisco: HarperOne, 1989.

Nouwen, Henri J. M. *In the Name of Jesus: Reflections on Christian Leadership*. New York: Crossroad, 1992.

Peterson, Eugene H. *The Contemplative Pastor: Returning to the Art of Spiritual Direction*. Grand Rapids: Eerdmans, 1993.

———. *Under the Unpredictable Plant: An Exploration in Vocational Holiness*. Grand Rapids: Eerdmans, 1994.

Rankin, William W. *Confidentiality and Clergy: Churches, Ethics, and the Law*. Harrisburg, PA: Morehouse, 1990.

Stevens, R. Paul, and Phil Collins. *The Equipping Pastor: A Systems Approach to Congregational Leadership*. Washington, DC: Alban Institute, 1993.

Willimon, William H. *Pastor: The Theology and Practice of Ordained Ministry*. Nashville: Abingdon, 2016.

5

Looking at Fellow Ministers

Integrity with Your Colleagues

Reverend John Ames, a Congregationalist minister in the fictitious town of Gilead, Iowa, in the early twentieth century is the voice of the narrator in Marilynne Robinson's Pulitzer Prize–winning novel *Gilead*. Ames grew up in the area, went to seminary for theological training, and then returned to spend his entire ministry in the little town. He is an avid reader, a devout student of Scripture, and a careful and serious preacher. One of the things that made life bearable for Ames in that secluded spot was his friendship with Reverend Robert Boughton, a Presbyterian minister, whom he simply refers to as "Boughton" or "old Boughton." They had grown up together and had both gone to seminary, returning to serve in Gilead. He and Boughton shared life as friends and as colleagues in ministry. One of their practices was to meet weekly to study their preaching texts and to discuss their thinking. Ames recalls, "Boughton and I used to go through the texts we were going to preach on, word by word. He'd come here, to my house, because his house was full of children. He'd bring a nice warm supper in a basket that his wife or his daughters would fix for us."[1] The lives of these two faithful pastors and preachers intersected almost daily, with no hint of competition or jealousy. They were simply partners in the gospel in Gilead, Iowa.

This kind of collegiality among pastors is not mere fiction. Eugene Peterson tells of the "company of pastors," a weekly gathering of fifteen ministry colleagues who enriched his life and ministry in Maryland for a dozen years.

They met to talk, support, study, and to keep one another focused on the holy calling of pastoral work. Peterson recounts an event that summarizes the contribution the company of pastors made to one another:

> I had been invited to speak to a gathering of pastors later in the summer and asked the group, "What is the most important thing that we have done with one another? What of our experience has been helpful? Anything stand out that I can tell them?"
>
> Tony didn't hesitate: "To look at and understand my congregation as a holy congregation. That has revolutionized the way I have gone about my work. Treating my congregation with respect and dignity. I think 'holy' is the right word." Consensus was immediate.
>
> I reported back on the pastors' conference when we reconvened in September. "I told them what you told me to say. But I'm sorry to report that they didn't buy it. Maybe this kind of pastoral imagination can only be achieved in 'prayer and fasting' among friends."[2]

Most pastors would give anything for the opportunity to engage in such a company. But doing so requires a disciplined, deliberate focus on the priority of these relationships. And it requires a perspective that views other ministers as valued colleagues, partners in the gospel, rather than as competitors.

To engage in ministry as a vocation requires one to think carefully about how to maintain integrity in relationships with others who share that calling. Fellow staff members, one's predecessors and successors, retired ministers in the congregation, interim pastors, and neighboring pastors of the same or different denominations will inevitably be part of one's life. Relating with integrity to others who are serving Christ in vocational ministry will require a thoughtful and intentional approach.

The Challenges of Partnership in Ministry: A Calling to Collegiality

Ministry Is Not a Solo Act

Jesus never had only one disciple. From the beginning of his ministry he called together a company of followers—Peter and Andrew, James and John (Matt. 4:18–22). Others were soon added to the number. When he began engaging the Twelve in his kingdom work, he sent them out in pairs, not individually (Mark 6:7). He repeated this practice later when he sent out the Seventy-Two (Luke 10:4–12).

The story of the earliest church is about Jesus's followers partnering with each other in the work they had been commissioned to accomplish. Peter and

John minister together in the temple (Acts 3:1–10). The Twelve lead the Hellenistic Christian community in Jerusalem to select seven men to assist with the work of distributing food to the widows among them (Acts 6:1–6). Peter and John joined Philip to assist in the work he was doing in Samaria (Acts 8:14). When Barnabas saw the work of God in Antioch, he sought out Saul in Tarsus to partner with him in his ministry in that fledgling congregation (Acts 11:25–26). And when the church at Antioch sensed the leadership of the Spirit to send Saul and Barnabas to preach the gospel to the gentiles (Acts 13:1–3), they formed a team, adding John Mark, although he soon abandoned the journey (Acts 13:5, 13).

After the council in Jerusalem (Acts 15), Paul and Barnabas determined to make another journey together. A serious rift occurred between them, however, when Barnabas wanted to give John Mark another opportunity to prove himself, and Paul would not agree (Acts 15:36–39). So Barnabas and John Mark struck out in one direction, while Paul enlisted Silas to join him (Acts 15:40–41). Paul soon added Timothy to this team (Acts 16:1–3), and eventually Luke (Acts 16:10).[3] Ministry in the earliest church was done in partnerships with a variety of men and women who were engaging in the kingdom work.[4]

Paul's descriptions of these relationships point to the esteem in which he held these men and women. They are his "co-workers" [synergos] (Rom. 16:3, 9, 21; 1 Cor. 3:9; 2 Cor. 8:23; Phil. 2:25; 4:3; Col. 4:11; 1 Thess. 3:2; Philem. 1, 24), "fellow soldiers" [systratiotes] (Phil. 2:25; Philem. 2), and most of all, "brothers and sisters" (Phil. 2:25; Philem. 2). Depending on how the counting is done, eighty or ninety people are identified as Paul's coworkers in the book of Acts and Paul's Letters.[5] For the apostle, ministry was clearly not a solo act.[6]

Such camaraderie does not imply that relationships among these early Christian ministers were always harmonious. They were human beings with limited perspectives, with character flaws and moral failures, and with differences of opinion. Paul and Barnabas could not agree on the role John Mark should play on the missionary team, and so they divided the work (Acts 15:36–39). Peter's lack of moral courage in Antioch resulted in Paul's rebuking him publicly (Gal. 2:11–14). Peter himself was challenged by his fellow workers in the Jerusalem church after he baptized gentiles in Caesarea (Acts 11:1–3). Christian ministers have always had to navigate the turbulent waters of relationship with others engaging the same work, following the same calling.

At times the congregations themselves responded to their leaders in ways that could have caused unnecessary friction among the ministers. At Corinth, for example, people were contending for the priority of Apollos, Cephas (Peter), and Paul (1 Cor. 1:11–13; 3:3–4). Paul addresses the issue by identifying Cephas, Apollos, and himself as merely servants [diakonoi] through whom the Corinthian Christians had come to faith in Christ (1 Cor. 3:5). The church in Corinth is God's garden, he says. Paul planted the seed of the gospel; Apollos came along and watered it; but God was the One who caused it to grow (1 Cor. 3:6). He concludes, "So neither the one who plants nor the one who waters is anything, but only God who gives the growth. The one who plants and the one who waters have a common purpose, and each will receive wages according to the labor of each. For we are God's servants, working together" (1 Cor. 3:7–9).

Paul then shifts the metaphor to "you are . . . God's building" (1 Cor. 3:9b). Paul, like a skilled master builder, has laid the foundation with his preaching and teaching in Corinth (1 Cor. 3:10). Others, such as Apollos, have followed and built on the foundation (1 Cor. 3:11). Each one who contributes to the church's life will give an account to God for their part, but ultimately all are working toward the same goal. Together these fellow ministers are "servants" [hyperetes] of Christ and "stewards" [oikonomos] of the mysteries of God (1 Cor. 4:1).

Paul understands that a camaraderie, respect, collegiality, and a humble sense of dependence on God and interdependence with one another ought to exist among those who serve Christ's kingdom in leadership. Although he will not brook those false teachers who disturb the churches (2 Cor. 11:1–12:13; Gal. 1:6–9; 5:10–12; Phil. 3:2), he manages to affirm God's ability to work through those who disagree with him, whose motives are questionable, or who actually seem to have it in for him (Phil. 1:15–18). His love for the churches, which moves him to protect them from false teachers, is matched by a respect for those who minister the truth of Christ.

The apostle is clear that ministry in the kingdom of God is not a solo act. The first century and the twenty-first century (and all the centuries in between!) share this in common—ministry is done in relationship with others. Pastors will be called on to relate with integrity to others who share their calling and serve their King.

Ministry and the Culture of Competition

Psychologist Jim Taylor claims that "America may be the most competitive country in the world."[7] Thanks to reality TV we now *compete* in many activities people once did just for *fun*—singing, dancing, and cooking, for example. This inherent human desire to be demonstrably better than others, bigger than others, stronger than others, or faster than others rushes unrestrained into almost every aspect of our lives. Children begin to compete in sports and other activities so early in life that they will not as adults be able to recall a time when they were not competing and being compared with their peers.

This deeply embedded human lust for the top spot has invaded the church in North America as well. Perhaps it has always been there. Jesus had to rebuke his disciples on more than one occasion for wanting to have the top spot (Mark 9:33–37; 10:35–45; Luke 22:24–27; John 13:1–17). The call he issued to servanthood was one way of countering this easily corrupted desire for the power that comes through conquest. "You know that among the Gentiles," he taught them, "those whom they recognize as their rulers lord it over them, and their great ones are tyrants over them. But it is not so among you; but whoever wishes to become great among you must be your servant, and whoever wishes to be first among you must be slave of all" (Mark 10:42–44).

The church easily becomes a market-driven organization in competition for as much of its share in a community as possible, competing for members with neighboring congregations. The competitive spirit even manifests itself internally as one staff member competes with another for time on the church calendar, portions of the budget, their share of the facilities, or the senior pastor's attention and approval. Gatherings of pastors are still marked by conversations designed to demonstrate one's superiority over another, comparing church size, programs, baptisms, or whatever statistic might move one a notch above one's peers. The new pastor takes secret delight in being told that a parishioner likes their preaching much better than that of their predecessor. The predecessor relishes the conversation with a former member who says their new minister's sermons are just mediocre. Such competitive attitudes and behavior are light-years away from the words of Paul and Jesus.

A first-day-of-class learning activity in my course on leadership in ministry has students assigned to teams of five or six, each given a set of instructions, a small board, and a handful of sixteen-penny nails. They are directed to create a structure using all eleven nails in which only one nail is touching the board and the others are touching only another nail. Students are not told that the activity is competitive, but they automatically assume that it is. They carefully hide their success from their peers, they usually do not collaborate, and they do not ask questions. Eventually one of them succeeds and the others usually surrender at that point.

As we debrief, we talk about the difference between collaboration and competition. What if, instead of being about nails and boards, the project involved a way to reach a certain population in their ministry field? What if the church down the street seemed to have it figured out? How likely would it be for the pastor to approach their neighbor and ask for help? How likely would it be for the "successful" church to knock on the doors of others and share their learning? Or what if the project were internal to a congregation—the children's minister struggling to recruit additional volunteers, for example. How likely is it for the student minister to step up and offer assistance or to relinquish their own previously recruited workers? A culture of competition does not easily yield to a culture of collaboration. This culture of competition challenges the effort to live with integrity in ministry partnerships with others who share our calling.

Ministry Requires Collaboration

In the 1990s, church consultant Kennon Callahan tried to convince pastors that we no longer serve in a churched culture where our values are shared and our message is generally understood. Instead, the North American church is, and has been for some time, serving on a mission field. "The day of the churched culture is over," Callahan declared. "The day of the mission field has come."[8] This transition, he argued, did not happen suddenly. The old, churched culture disappeared quietly, and the ways of the professional minister of the 1940s and 1950s ceased to be functional on the new North American mission field of the 1980s and 1990s. He outlined the ways in which "professional pastors" need to be replaced by "missional pastors" in order to respond to the cultural shift that has occurred. He called churches to behave as if they were on a mission field in which they represented a marginal presence, because that is, in fact, increasingly the case. But in his opinion, the mission field is where the church has always done its best.[9]

Visiting overseas with a missionary friend in the early 2000s, I noticed that ecclesiastical differences did not play such a divisive role among evangelical missionaries there as they did back in the United States. These ministers were in a minority. They were marginal in the culture. They needed one another's love, support, encouragement, and prayers, and they knew it. That stood in contrast to what I had often witnessed back home. We North American pastors could go for years without speaking to our neighboring pastor—not out of animosity but simply because we and they were preoccupied with our own congregations, our own work, our own tasks. We neither bore our neighbor's burdens nor shared our own. Had we operated with a greater sense of being on a mission field, our neighboring pastor might have been held in greater esteem. We might have made time for one another. We might have seen ourselves as fellow workers, comrades-in-arms, colleagues, or fellow servants of God. Fortunately, I served in a community where pastors actually did such things.

How one relates to others who share the calling to ministry is an ethical concern. But that concern extends beyond ethics to the very nature of the kingdom itself. To live without a relationship with a fellow pastor, or to live in a competitive relationship with them, however subtle, is to live in a narrative that is contrary to the narrative of the kingdom of God.[10] This narrative must shape the way we do ministry and the way that we relate with integrity to others who share that calling. Partnership in ministry requires collaboration.

Ministry Demands Integrity

Ethics and character are not a moral buffet from which one can pick and choose. One cannot be an ethical preacher, attending to all the aspects of one's homiletical craft, and yet live in a relationship with a fellow pastor or staff member that reeks of apathy, animosity, or competition. The minister seeks a life of integrity and wholeness, where all is of one piece. Every relationship should be considered. This clearly includes our relationships with others who share our calling. The ultimate ethical commandment of Jesus is the call to love your neighbor as yourself (Luke 10:25–37 NIV). We develop moral and ethical muscles as we think through the ways this commandment shapes all our relationships in life. For ministers, that includes our relationships with others who are ministers as well—those with whom we share a partnership in the gospel (Phil. 1:5). Thinking through these important relationships will help us navigate our way with a greater sense of joy, mutual support, and integrity.

The Means to Integrity in Ministry: Partners in the Gospel

Partnering with Your Predecessor

The first church in which I served as pastor introduced me to the influence of one's predecessors in ministry. On the one hand, Leroy Pearson had been the pastor of that congregation in the 1940s. I arrived in 1979. Older church members still spoke admirably of "Brother Pearson," as if he had just left. That was easy for me to understand, because Leroy Pearson had been my pastor for eighteen years in another congregation. I loved and admired him as they did. His name on my résumé may have had something to do with their willingness to take a new seminary graduate as their pastor.

My immediate predecessor in that congregation, however, was not so beloved. I never had the opportunity to meet him. But I encountered the fallout from his ministry, often in the form of wounded church members or offended neighbors. I learned quickly that one's predecessor continues to have an impact on one's ministry. A new pastor steps into a network of emotional triangles emptied by the previous pastor. Edwin Friedman observes, "There is, of course, no guarantee that our predecessors have handled their leaving well. Even if they have, there will always be some residue. Each of us inherits the un-worked-out part of our predecessors' relationships with our congregational partner."[11] Relating to one's predecessor can be more complicated if their leaving was traumatic (forced termination or suicide, for example) or if their tenure had been lengthy.

Our predecessor is one of those "neighbors" Jesus insisted that we are to love as we love ourselves. What might that require of a minister seeking to relate to their predecessor with integrity?

Know Your Predecessor

An open, honest, one-to-one relationship with your predecessor is the place to start. Nothing substitutes for firsthand, personal knowledge when it comes to avoiding the triangles created by church members gossiping about the former pastor to the current one. Seeking to establish a personal relationship between the two of you should be a priority. This means being able to talk openly with each other, trust each other, and speak confidentially with each other. Mike Fleischmann suggests, "We may assume that from all of the second-hand accounts we already know most all there is to know about those who have led before, but honor always begins with taking interest in the person. That means picking up the phone or paying for lunch, and listening with interest about the history and the legacy of the one who has led before. Only a foolish leader assumes that their arrival ushers in a glorious new era of ministry to which all else has been prelude."[12] Besides face-to-face conversations with your predecessor at the time of your transition, occasional phone calls, visits, or correspondence can keep the relationship available as a resource.

Honor Your Predecessor

Following a beloved pastor who has served faithfully and well is both a challenge and a privilege. Their ministry has set the bar high, and, like it or not, congregants will be making the comparison. If the congregation knows that you two know and respect each other, they will find it easier to make the transition from one pastor to the next. Speaking of your predecessor and their work positively, both in public and in private, will provide a foundation for the contributions God will make to the congregation through your own ministry. Love for this neighbor forbids diminishing, critiquing, or otherwise undermining the work God has done through them. On the contrary, their work will provide a starting place for your own (1 Cor. 3:6–15).

Offering respect becomes more challenging when one's immediate predecessor has not behaved respectably. Following in the footsteps of a pastor who has been terminated for clergy sexual abuse, financial malfeasance, or other moral failure, for example, may make expressions of respect feel or sound disingenuous, and so may not be possible. In such a case, the new pastor's task remains the same—how do I love this neighbor as I love myself? Fleischmann advocates being proactive in such situations: (1) keep the former pastor in the church's story; (2) invite a process of relational healing; and (3) pray for God's best in their lives.[13] The new pastor is likely to get an earful from members about the situation. Listening to the church members' experience as objectively as possible, seeking to hear their hurt, can be an act of pastoral care. Taking sides with them against the former pastor, however, is neither necessary nor helpful.

INCLUDE YOUR PREDECESSOR

"Love is not envious," writes the apostle (1 Cor. 13:4). Envy and jealousy have no place in the relationship between ministers, especially the relationship with one's predecessor. Including them in church celebrations or welcoming them when members want them to have a part in a funeral or wedding does not diminish one's standing as a pastor. If the personal relationship between the pastor and their predecessor is healthy, they can remain partners in ministry over time. After twenty-two years of ministry in one congregation, I have enjoyed the relationship with the pastor who followed me in that role. He has been kind to invite me to preach at least once a year and welcomes me when my family is present for worship. My own predecessor in that congregation, the founding pastor, was deeply loved and found a warm reception whenever he was among us as well.

HEALTHY TRANSITIONS

In August 1981, at thirty-one years old, Ron Lyles accepted the call to be pastor of the South Main Baptist Church in Pasadena, Texas. The church had experienced the ministry of only one other pastor—B. J. Martin, who had served there twenty-six years before leaving in December 1980 to take a position with a local denominational university. B. J. and Marylyn, his second wife, remained members at South Main, although he frequently served as interim pastor for local congregations and as a supply preacher representing the university. B. J. officially retired in 1988 and was named pastor emeritus at South Main, at which time he was more frequently present for worship and other church activities. B. J. died in 2010, nearly ninety-four years old.

Although Ron's colleagues warned him about the risks involved in following a long-tenured, beloved pastor, he, B. J., and the congregation managed the transition well.

Ron and B. J. became more than predecessor/successor. B. J. became Ron's friend and mentor. They partnered in ministry regularly. When members called their former pastor about conducting a funeral, he would point them to Ron, telling them, "We work together." Ron recruited B. J. to preach when he could not. The congregation could visibly see the authentic relationship of respect and partnership the two pastors shared. When the church was about to consider relocation, Ron met with B. J. before any public announcement was made. One of the buildings in the old location had been dedicated to Ann Martin, B. J.'s first wife, who had died in 1967. B. J. was fully supportive of the decision to relocate. In 1998 one of the buildings at the new location was named for him, and a parlor, the Martin Room, was furnished with many of the former pastor's memorabilia. Ron and B. J. discussed their healthy transition and identified three key factors: (1) the predecessor relinquished their role as pastor; (2) the successor was secure as a person; (3) the church allowed the transition. Ron has now served the church for thirty-five years and is working on his own plans for succession.[14]

Bill Wilson directs the Center for Healthy Churches (chchurches.org) in Clemmons, North Carolina. A few years ago he wrote about making "a healthy handoff" by building the relationship between former and current pastors. Wilson tells the stories of two congregations that made succession work well. Brentwood Baptist Church, a congregation of more than nine thousand members, had been led for twenty years by his father, Bill Wilson Sr. Mike Glenn succeeded Wilson in 1991 and has served there for twenty-five years. Glenn says, "People loved the fact that the former and current pastors were good friends. He never missed a chance to brag on me, and I never missed a chance to say how much he meant to me. He never tolerated criticism of me from others, even when it was deserved."[15]

Wilson also recounts the successful transition at First Baptist Church of West Jefferson, North Carolina, when Ken Morris retired after thirty-three years as pastor and remained as pastor emeritus. The church called Michael Lea in 2008. Wilson interviewed both pastors and discovered a rich, intentional, ethically healthy relationship between them.[16] Wilson describes their relationship as marked by trust and open communication:

Michael says, "Ken has provided a great deal of leadership here by saying to people, 'Michael is our pastor now; let's ask him,' or 'let's look to him for leadership at this time.'" On the other hand, Michael understands that many in the church have a rich history with Ken, so they want him to be involved in funerals and weddings. The two have proactively avoided triangulation. When someone mentions Michael to Ken, Ken responds with how fortunate he is to have Michael as his pastor. When someone mentions Ken to Michael, Michael responds with a narrative description of the great pastoral leadership that has brought the church to this point. The respect between former and current pastor is clear.[17]

The emotional health and maturity of these pastors, their mutual love for Christ and the congregation, and their commitment to each other have made this transition successful.

Wilson distills some wisdom about managing the relationship with one's predecessor:

1. Do not rush the transition.
2. Recognize the principle of different gifts for different times. That allows you to bless your predecessor without reservation.
3. Be respectful of and sensitive to the history and culture of the church.
4. Honor your elders.
5. Match your territorial language. Remember that it is Christ's church, not yours or your predecessor's.
6. Leave your ego at the door.
7. Work to build trust with the former pastor and congregation.
8. Model health even if it is not reciprocated.[18]

Both the health of the congregation and the pastor's ministry will be enhanced by such a relationship during leadership transition. So many variables can complicate these situations, but the pastor seeking to serve with integrity will take responsibility for steering the relationship toward health, even "when the high road is rocky."[19]

Partnering with Your Staff Team Members

Clergy who are privileged to serve on a church staff in partnership with other like-minded ministers, pursuing a common goal, loving and supporting each other in the process, are blessed. Such church staff teams do exist. Unfortunately, however, it is possible for a church staff to be marked by division and competition, with ministers carrying on their work in a narrow silo, having little regard for the work of their colleagues. Pastors who oversee such teams bear a responsibility to develop an ethically and morally healthy environment that contributes to the experience of community shared by those who serve the congregation together. Members of the team bear responsibility for relating to their colleagues as neighbors whom they are learning to love as themselves. The law of Christ must be the ruling principle in church staff relationships (Gal. 6:2). What are the primary and necessary ethical obligations of ministers to each other as they serve together?

Understanding Staff Culture and Informal Structures

Church staff relationships can become complicated in a variety of ways. Younger staff members on a more senior staff may find themselves feeling excluded, ignored, or dismissed by their older colleagues. The reverse is also true. Older, experienced ministers serving among younger men and women can also find their opinions received dismissively. Gender can become a complicating factor. A woman serving on a staff dominated by male clergy may face the challenges of being heard, respected, and received as an equal. Ordained or seminary-trained ministers on a staff may presume more authority or privilege than some of their colleagues. These hierarchical structures that are so deeply ingrained in the wider culture can easily make their way into the culture of a church staff. The command of love for neighbor requires vigilance to assure that all who serve together are authentic partners in the ministry. Formal supervisory structures may be necessary for organizational functioning, but informal structures that relegate some to lower positions, silence their voices, or dismiss their contributions fail to measure up to love for this neighbor who serves alongside us on a church staff.

Receiving New Staff Team Members

When a minister joins the congregation's church staff team, the church and the senior pastor or supervisor bear some important ethical responsibilities to the new arrival. William Tillman observes, "Preparing for a new staff person to join the team can show a congregation how well they are following New Testament guidelines about the character traits for relationships to one another inside the membership, to those outside the membership, and to those who are chosen to lead them in staff roles."[20] If this person is going to be able to function at their best and contribute to the church's life and health, the church is obligated to do its part to make that ministry possible.

The calling to serve the church should be accompanied by clear, written expectations for the position. The supervisor and search committee should be able to articulate what success in this position would look like one year, two years, or three years down the road. The new minister should know how they will be evaluated, when, and by whom. An adequate and just salary and benefits should be provided, to the extent the church is able to do so. The new staff member should receive adequate orientation to the congregational context, the work environment, and their colleagues. If the new minister has a family, they too should be oriented to the community.[21] This process should be developed, written as policy, and followed carefully with each new addition to the staff. The ethical principle behind such policies may be found in the Christian virtue of hospitality—making space for the outsider, welcoming the stranger.

DEVELOPING STAFF MEMBERS

The task of equipping the saints (Eph. 4:12) does not simply apply to clergy equipping laity. This pastoral task can be engaged in relationship to all who serve in the church, including professional and support staff in the church. The work of the ministry can be enhanced as both ministers and administrative assistants find greater competence and satisfaction in their weekday tasks and as they understand their contributions to the kingdom. The church staff should be able to expect pastoral leadership and supervision that grounds the quotidian tasks of the church office in the greater vision of the kingdom of God. At the same time, kingdom values cannot be proclaimed from the pulpit and ignored in the intra-office relationships among those who work together. All the attributes of authentic Christian community are called for in the operation of the church's business side of things. The lay leaders who represent the congregation in personnel matters and the pastoral leaders have an ethical obligation to develop those they work with both professionally and spiritually.

AVOIDING SILOS

For almost thirty years consultants have been encouraging corporate organizations to eliminate "silos" in the workplace.[22] Typical business structures divide up responsibilities among "experts" in each area, with the result that communication between one part of the organization and another is difficult or nonexistent. At best those in one area grow indifferent to the success or struggles of those in another, and at worst an internal competition develops. Resources—human, financial, physical, and intellectual—can become tied up in one silo and unavailable to the mission of the larger organization. The greater vision is lost to the agenda of some particular segment. Corporate leaders have been working to create "boundaryless organizations" to enhance collaboration, efficiency, and better decision making.

Multistaff congregations easily adopted the corporate model of silos with "experts" over particular ministry responsibilities. Ministers of education, student ministry, children ministry, women's ministry, men's ministry, senior adults, missions, recreation, small groups, discipleship, spiritual formation—the job titles and descriptions on church staffs have multiplied over the past sixty years. These divisions of labor, although helpful and effective in many ways, easily become ministry silos, just as they do in the corporate world. Such structures may inhibit pastors and staff from working together collaboratively and congenially. The same kind of internal competition that shows up in a corporate entity can evolve among church staff members. Love of neighbor on a church staff will look like finding ways to minimize the impact of silo-like structures and strict hierarchical boundaries, rather than adhering to them. When addressing the issue of such power structures, Jesus said that pagan leaders may behave in such a way, but "it is not so among you; but whoever wishes to become great among you must be your servant, and whoever wishes to be first among you must be slave of all" (Mark 10:43–44). Where such an organizational culture exists, one may work on adjusting one's own behavior toward generosity, openness, and transparency, despite the pressure to defend one's own silo.

Communicating Clearly

Communication is a key building block to community. Serving in community with other ministers on a church staff requires us to attend to our habits, practices, and skills in communication. Several qualities characterize communication that demonstrates love of one's neighbor. We share as much information as possible with those who work alongside us. Hoarding information for the sake of power or failing to communicate out of negligence does not demonstrate ethical behavior. Competent and ethical communicators take 100 percent of the responsibility for ensuring that a message is communicated. This means working on being clear and on being understood, and looking for and responding to feedback until we are fairly certain that we have communicated. Saying "I sent an email" or "That was in the bulletin" does not free us from responsibility to communicate clearly and appropriately any message we want others to receive. Taking 100 percent of the responsibility for communicating with our colleagues also means that we read and process the written messages they send our way and that we ask questions if the messages are not clear. A failure to read and respond to communications we receive impedes the work and ministry of others.

Although we are educated in the communication tools of reading, writing, and speaking, we often receive little or no training in simply listening well. Taking 100 percent of the responsibility for communication means that we learn to listen. We attend to others who are speaking to us. We try to be truly present in meetings, not just physically occupying space in the room. Electronic devices and other distractions are put aside, and the people in the room, their ideas, problems, and needs receive our full attention. When we do not understand what another is saying, we ask for clarification. When we think we understand, we ask for confirmation to be certain. Listening is difficult work, but it is an act of love and a moral responsibility.

Ethical relationships require pastors to clearly communicate expectations to each staff member. Phil Lineberger argues, "The pastor's role as *chief communicator* enables staff members to be more effective in their calling and responsibilities. It is crucial that the pastor communicate the vision of the church and the expectations of staff members in supporting that vision."[23] Ethical communication includes responsibility for the congregation to provide clear job descriptions, fair performance evaluations, and agreed-upon indicators of success.

Demonstrating Respect and Loyalty

When the apostle Paul describes the body life of the Christian community, he recognizes that not all parts share the spotlight equally (1 Cor. 12:22–25). Nevertheless, each of those parts is indispensable, necessary for the life of the body (1 Cor. 12:15–21). Many who serve on church staff teams work behind the scenes to be sure that the church's worship and ministry take place with excellence. It is easy for those who are not visible in leadership to feel less respected than those who stand before the congregation week after week. And it is easy for those who are more visible to come to assume a greater sense of importance. Church staff teams need a sense of mutual respect that appreciates the contributions of each member. Such respect shows up in expressions of gratitude for work well done, in recognition of anniversaries each year (and special recognition at significant mile markers, such as five, ten, and fifteen years of service), in listening to the thinking of others regardless of their role on the staff, and in offering one's thinking to others as a show of support for the work they do.

Jesus concluded the parable of the dishonest manager by saying that "the children of this age are more shrewd in dealing with their own generation than are the children of light" (Luke 16:8). Jesus urges his followers to act prudently with matters of the kingdom even as unbelievers do with their dealings. Working together as part of a church staff calls for kingdom values and practices. The corporate world seeks wisdom about how people might best work together effectively in order to make a profit. The church would often benefit from their discoveries, "plundering the Egyptians," as it were,[24] learning to create effective staff teams and working relationships.[25]

For example, Google's 2012 quest to find a formula for building the most effective teams was dubbed "Project Aristotle." Intensive research on more than 180 teams and extensive data analysis yielded a set of conclusions that were both counterintuitive and commonsensical at the same time. Project Aristotle discovered that Google's most effective teams were not necessarily an assembly of the brightest or most talented employees. The team processes—the way they worked together and managed their relationships—turned out to be better predictors of how the team would perform, regardless of the task. Researchers identified two important qualities of effective teams: all members participated about equally, contributing their thinking and listening to others, and members were socially sensitive, paying attention to such things as body language, facial expressions, and tone of voice to notice when members were upset or feeling left out, for example. Less successful teams seemed to lack these qualities. These traits produced a kind of "psychological safety" where members felt comfortable speaking their minds and taking risks.[26]

The qualities described as a result of Google's research and analysis are not foreign to kingdom values and ethics that ought to show up in relationships among ministers of the gospel who serve alongside one another. Respect, appreciation, active listening, cooperation, and humility, consistently practiced, would produce teams marked by authentic Christian fellowship (*koinonia*) and love (*agape*) (1 Cor. 13:4–8; Gal. 5:22–26; Phil. 2:1–4).

Loyalty is a necessary quality for relationships among church staff teams. Congregants, intentionally or not, will occasionally approach one staff member with a complaint against another. Or one staff member might complain to a colleague about another. In any case, loyalty requires that those awkward moments be handled with love and respect. Each member of the team needs confidence that the others are engaging such encounters ethically. Those "triangles" created by complaints and gossip need to be handled in an agreed-upon, healthy manner. Taking sides against a team member rather than going to that person with concerns only destroys the effectiveness of the collaborative effort in the kingdom.[27]

Relationships on a church staff provide the opportunity for ministers to demonstrate their commitments to ethical relationships. Congregations look to their pastors as examples in Christian life and need to see them model faithful ministry with one another. When relationships among staff members evidence discord, jealousy, competition, or disloyalty, churches often pay the price in terms of ineffective ministry and congregational conflict. But when those relationships are engaged with authentic love, respect, loyalty, and collaboration, the congregation has a model for engaging their relationships with one another. When they can witness their leaders handling conflict and disagreement with respect and forgiveness, they can learn to follow that example. Ethics, like almost everything else, can be contagious—caught as much as taught.

Partnering with Your Peers

Neighboring congregations and neighboring pastors provide ministers with yet another set of relationships to engage with an ethic corresponding to the grand narrative of the kingdom of God. These fellow ministers share a common calling and seek to carry it out in a common setting. We have responsibilities toward those pastors who serve within our own denomination or tradition as well as those neighbors who work outside our denominational family. Working together in local ministerial alliances, knowing one another, and praying for and with one another are concrete expressions of a ministerial ethic grounded in love for one's neighbor. At the same time, a competitive attitude or an independent, self-sufficient spirit contradicts the nature of the kingdom in which we serve.

The loneliness that often pervades the work of ministry has at least one potential remedy available in ministerial support groups, lectionary reading groups, ministerial alliances, and local associations where pastors have opportunity to share life and struggles, thinking and learning, as well as laughter and fun, like Eugene Peterson's "company of pastors." Most pastors have their cups full on a weekly basis and need no additional responsibilities to crowd their schedules. Relationships with fellow pastors can easily be set aside, not out of animosity or competition, but simply because of a terribly crowded calendar and lengthy to-do list. As with spiritual disciplines, family responsibilities, and other important ethical demands, one must intentionally make space for relationships and obligations that matter.

The questions raised by these relationships must be answered from the perspective of love of neighbor and respect for others who are loved by Christ and created in God's image. Larry Ashlock argues, "Since we are all created in God's image, pastors will treat pastors and staff members in other congregations with respect, refusing to speak derisively about their colleagues in ministry. There is a mutuality of obligation to love other believers because all have been fashioned in Christ's image."[28] How will I respond to rumors about a neighboring pastor's struggles? How will I deal with those who frequently move from one congregation in the community to another? How will I handle the criticisms I hear from a peer's former members who are now part of the congregation I serve? What positive efforts will I make to welcome a new pastor into the community, to know the pastors who serve alongside me in the city, to collaborate with my peers and their congregations in serving our community? What will I do to be a neighbor to those men and women who serve Christ alongside me in my city?

Partnering with Your Successor

When Randy Frazee took over as senior minister at San Antonio's Oakhill Church, where prolific author Max Lucado had been serving for years, the transition was somewhat intimidating. Frazee stood before the congregation and named "the elephant in the room."

Frazee asked Lucado to come on stage. The two tried on each other's shoes, but they would not fit. Lucado is a full six inches taller than Frazee. The pastors got their point across. The congregation responded with a standing ovation. Frazee spoke: "If I come, Max is going to be Max. And I'm going to be Randy. And we are going to stand side by side and partner together in this deal."[29] One pastor cannot be expected to fill the shoes of his predecessor. The pastor who follows you will be a different person, with different gifts, for a different time in the church's life. The decision to be part of the successor's success is an ethical one, an act of loving this new neighbor as you love yourself.

KNOW YOUR SUCCESSOR

Even when we are confident that the time has come to leave a congregation for a new field of ministry or retirement, we may do so with a sense of loss or regret. Serving God's people over time develops bonds of connection and affection that do not disappear with two weeks' notice. Letting go of the former congregation may be more difficult than you think. In 2009 I left a congregation I had served for twenty-two years. I was only thirty-four years old when I arrived, and these dear people allowed me to be their pastor. Most of what I know about being a pastor, they taught me. My wife and I reared our children there, served alongside cherished friends, and found support during the deaths of our parents and a struggle with a teenage child. Leaving was a challenge, although the call to invest in the next generation of congregational ministers in a seminary was clearly a call from God.

When the transition came, I had the privilege of leaving over a period of months rather than a few weeks. It was more like a retirement than a move to another congregation. This allowed me to be as intentional about the departure as possible. I read Ed Friedman's description of his own departure from a congregation he had served for fifteen years. I found one of his realizations especially relevant: "I received my insight into the universality of all separation experiences. Until then I had been thinking of the transition as a divorce. I was leaving my 'partner' and my successor was marrying my former spouse. I realized now, however, that I felt more like a father who was turning his daughter over to a son-in-law."[30] This congregation, in whom I had invested more than two decades of my life, would soon be served by a pastor half my age. Similarly, not long after leaving the church, a young man less than half my age married my daughter, in whom I had invested two decades of life. The parallel was nearly perfect.

As I would do with my own daughter, I clearly desired to maintain a relationship with the congregation on the other side of that "marriage," but I knew it would take on a different tone. And, as with my own future son-in-law, I knew I would also want to have a relationship with my successor. This metaphor should not be pressed to imply a paternalistic relationship with the future pastor. It simply affirms that I wanted to continue to relate to the congregation in appropriate ways, not interfering in the "marriage," and that I wanted to know my successor as a person and be a resource where appropriate.

I intentionally took on that relationship, beginning with a private lunch meeting at his request when he was in the last stages of conversation with the pastor search committee. We have continued that relationship over several years now. During his first year in the church I invited him to address my "Life and Work of a Pastor" class about getting started in a new ministry context and "cleaning up after your predecessor." This connection with my successor has allowed me to maintain connections with friends in the congregation and on the church staff without posing a threat or interfering in the pastor's ministry.[31]

HONOR YOUR SUCCESSOR

The same kind of emotional triangles that come to life when one steps into a new place of ministry also light up when one steps out. The less mature among the congregation are prone to contact the former pastor with complaints about their new shepherd, flattering the departed clergy. These moments become temptations to side with the former parishioner and accept the praise. This is not an innocent move. Our successor's job becomes just a bit more difficult each time. Or a congregant may reach out to the former pastor for an opinion on a theological, ethical, or political issue, or a recent church decision. To respond to the invitation is to run the risk of undermining our successor's leadership. Such situations become excellent opportunities to affirm our confidence in our successor and to send the parishioner to their pastor for a conversation about the matters concerning them. We honor our successors when we take time to know them, when we affirm their ministry publicly and privately, and when we keep their confidence about matters they share with us.

Set and Maintain Clear Boundaries

A carefully considered relationship with appropriate boundaries with one's successor and one's former congregation is a necessary part of ministering with integrity in this partnership. Pastors who fail to fully leave a former congregation will be unable to fully cleave to the new one.[32] When the former pastor retires and remains in the community and the congregation, the difficulties of leaving the role of pastor can be compounded. If the minister has not clearly separated their identity from the role they have occupied for so many years, they may not be prepared for the challenge of waking up one morning and no longer being the pastor of the church. The successor may bear the title "pastor," but unless the former pastor has found a way to leave the role emotionally, both the congregation and the successor may struggle.[33]

Congregants who have come to love and appreciate their pastor experience anxiety at their departure. In particular, senior adults may worry about who is going to preach their funeral and may attempt to extract a promise from the departing pastor to return for the event. Young people who have grown up under a pastor's ministry may have planned for them to officiate at their wedding. These are situations that can be negotiated with the new pastor if a healthy relationship is built. In almost all cases, however, requests from family members for such things, when the event eventually occurs, should be routed first through the new pastor. A contact from a parishioner or staff member informing the former pastor about a hospitalization or death of a fellow congregant is not sufficient cause for them to move into action. Has the new pastor been informed of the situation? Have they yet spoken with the member or the family? Until it is clear that the successor has been involved, the former pastor should step back and allow people to be cared for by their pastor.

Healthy Transitions

Bill Wilson's interviews with Mike Glenn, Ken Morris, and Michael Lea about the experience of succession yielded these words of wisdom for departing pastors:

1. Work to find interests and an identity apart from pastoring that congregation.

2. Tell the congregation that you are no longer the pastor, and believe it yourself.

3. Show support and confidence in the church and in the new pastor and pastoral staff.

4. Set boundaries around funerals, weddings, and hospital visits.

5. Model health, even if it is not reciprocated.[34]

Pastors seeking to live with fidelity to their calling, their colleagues, and the congregations they serve will take seriously the power of a healthy relationship with those who follow to build on the foundation they have laid. Loving this new neighbor as yourself will require intentional efforts to know them, to establish clear boundaries with your former congregation, and to honor them and their work.

Key Issues for Partnership in Ministry

Before leaving the important issue of relating ethically to other ministers, two specific roles and relationships remain to be addressed: the ethical responsibilities of interim pastors and the role and relationship between pastors and retired ministers in their congregation.

The Interim Pastor

Many churches, especially those with congregational polity, rely on an interim pastor to preach and minister during the period of searching for a new pastor. These interim pastors are sometimes retired ministers, denominational workers, or professors from colleges and seminaries. Typically, they are expected to help stabilize the church, take on preaching responsibilities, and share pastoral care responsibilities, such as funerals, weddings, and hospital calls. They may support the work of the pastor search committee as a consultant as well. Specific training has been developed for ministers who serve as an "intentional interim©," following a program to help a congregation prepare for its next pastor.[35] Intentional interims are usually considered when a congregation finds itself in special circumstances.[36]

Whether the interim pastor is in a more traditional role or in the role of an intentional interim, they would be wise to develop an explicit written covenant with the congregation they agree to serve, outlining boundaries and expectations as well as issues of compensation.[37] The interim pastor, as well as the congregation or its representatives, needs to think through what fair compensation might be. If the interim pastor is only expected to preach on a regular basis, the congregation might consider what portion of their pastor's time would be taken up with that task each week—worship planning, sermon preparation, and worship leadership. This often occupies as much as a quarter to a third of a pastor's time. Additionally, the weekly travel time to and from the church ought to be considered, especially if the interim pastor is coming from some distance. After that, other duties expected of the interim pastor should be taken into account: weddings, funerals, pastoral care, and meetings with staff, committees, or the pastor search committee. The compensation should include travel and housing expenses paid separately.

In addition to spelling out the expectations and compensation, the interim covenant might address some ethical issues that arise in this relationship. Is the interim committed to staying in place for the duration—that is, until a new pastor is called? Some who work full time in other roles may have a time limit placed on their interim work by their "day job," which may need to be negotiated. Will the interim be considered as a candidate for the open position? Some believe it best to recuse themselves from consideration from the outset to avoid a conflict of interest and to avoid putting inappropriate pressure on the pastor search committee. (To have pressure from the congregation to "keep" the interim while the search committee is working diligently to consider a pool of candidates can place both the interim and the committee in an awkward situation.) How much influence will the interim exercise over the work of the pastor search committee? Lay leaders often appreciate some help with such aspects of their work as developing appropriate search processes, finding resources for their work, learning appropriate sources for securing résumés from potential candidates, and interpreting the various theological degrees and degree-granting institutions that appear on résumés. However, an interim may begin to step across appropriate boundaries if they attempt to push a particular candidate or veto another. It might be a solid ethical principle for the interim to serve the congregation and pastor search committee around issues of process but to avoid getting involved around particular candidates.

The interim pastor may have opportunity to consult with the candidate in the process of making a decision about the call, should the candidate desire. The interim will have to think carefully about how that relationship is treated. To "report back" to the search committee, the church staff, or congregational members with details of the conversation would violate the confidentiality that the candidate ought to be able to expect. On the other hand, the pastoral candidate ought to be able to expect an honest and candid response from the interim regarding the church and its needs from the perspective of a minister who has come to know them. Commenting to the candidate about staff problems or issues is not the responsibility of the interim pastor, however. A healthier approach would be for the search committee or personnel committee to broach such matters.

Retired Ministers in the Congregation

Many congregations are blessed to have among their members men and women who have served as ministers and who are now retired, whether from that congregation or others. Pastors seeking to relate to these retired ministers need look no further than Jesus's Golden Rule for ethical guidance (Matt. 7:12). These servants of Christ may be resources of wisdom, experience, and support that the pastor can draw on, respecting what they have contributed to the kingdom over the years. Building relationships with them creates a win-win-win situation for the pastor, the retired minister, and the congregation. Sharing ministry with retired ministers, as they are willing, allow these servants of God to continue to use their gifts, training, and experience, and provide additional ministry resources for the pastor and the congregation. Should one encounter a retired minister who seems to have difficulty letting go of their role with the congregation, extra grace, understanding, and effort may be required to build a healthier relationship. This kind of shared ministry with retired pastors requires a respect and humility on the part of the active pastor.

On the other hand, to be a retired minister in the midst of a congregation can be ethically challenging as well, especially if one retires in the congregation one has served. To continue to attempt to influence the congregation's decisions as if one were still the pastor is to fail to practice the Golden Rule with the current pastor. Should one encounter a younger pastor who seems to be insecure with the presence of the retired minister in the congregation, extra grace, understanding, and effort may be required on the part of the retiree to build a healthier relationship. Knowing when to remain silent, when to speak up, and when to be a neutral resource to the pastor behind the scenes requires a respect and humility on the part of the retired minister.

Conclusion

As you consider the ethical commitments in ministry that you are willing to sign your name to, consider long and hard the relationships you share with those who are your partners in ministry—pastors who came before you and those who will come after you, staff members you work alongside and fellow pastors in the community who are preaching the same gospel and serving the same Lord, friends in ministry across the city or around the world. The "yes" you offered to Jesus Christ in responding to a call to ministry wove your life inextricably into relationship with theirs. Consequently, the ethical responsibilities that attend those relationships must be considered if ministry is to be offered with integrity.

Suggested Reading

Nicholson, Rogers S., ed. *Temporary Shepherds: A Congregational Handbook for Interim Ministry*. Bethesda, MD: Alban Institute, 1998.

Schaller, Lyle E. *The Multiple Staff and the Larger Church*. Nashville: Abingdon, 1980.

Spooner, Bernard M., ed. *Pastor, Staff, and Congregational Relationships: Through Servant Leadership and Quality Administration*. Coppell, TX: CreateSpace, 2014.

Vanderbloemen, William, Warren Bird, and John Ortberg. *Next: Pastoral Succession That Works*. Grand Rapids: Baker Books, 2015.

6

Promoting Peace and Justice

Integrity in the Community

The work of pastoral ministry has a decidedly outward focus to it. Shepherding is about feeding and protecting God's sheep (John 10:9–11; 21:15–17; 1 Pet. 5:1–4) and about seeking those who are not yet in the fold (Luke 15:3–7; John 10:16). Church consultant Kennon Callahan tells of working with a congregation that had experienced what he called thirty-seven losing seasons. As he and those church leaders knelt at the church altar rail to pray, Callahan noticed the stained-glass window that adorned their sanctuary, depicting Christ standing in the street, knocking on a door. He observes, "In the long, lost churched culture of an earlier time, the understanding of the window was, 'Christ stands at the door knocking, hoping someone will hear the knock, and come to the door, and open the door, and invite Christ **in** to their lives.'"[1] Many preachers had used Warner Sallman's painting *Christ at Heart's Door* to illustrate this very truth, often making much of the detail that the door contained no latch or knob on the outside. It had to be opened from the inside.

That day as Callahan and congregational leaders knelt in prayer, he saw that image in the stained glass with a different meaning: "Christ stands at the door, knocking, hoping someone will hear the knock, and come to the door, and open the door so Christ can invite them **out** into his life in mission."[2] Callahan urges pastors, "Christ invites us **out into His life**. Where is Christ? In mission. Where does Christ live and die and is risen again and again? Among the human hurt and hopes God has planted all around us. Christ is in the world. When we are in the world, we are with Christ. It is not that we discover Christ, then go and serve in mission. It is in the sharing of the mission that we discover Christ."[3] Jesus said much the same thing: "Whoever serves me must follow me, and where I am, there will my servant be also" (John 12:26). His abiding presence with his church is not so much a promise that wherever *we* go, he will accompany us. His presence is promised as the church engages the world in witness following his command (Matt. 28:19–20). However, stepping out the door of the church building and into the world engages the minister in a network of ethical issues that were not found inside.

The Challenges of Community Ministry: A Call to Engagement

Biblical and Theological Basis for Community Ministry

The people of God have always had a role to play as "aliens and exiles" in the world who, rather than being separated from their context, are called to make a difference in it. Whether it was Abraham and his family living as strangers in Canaan, Moses in Egypt, or the gathered church of the New Testament, God's people have engaged the surrounding culture with an alternative narrative of God's sovereignty and promises (Heb. 11:9–10, 24–26; 1 Pet. 2:11–17).[4] The prophets of the eighth century BC confronted issues of social justice as evidence of the failure of God's people to live in covenant with Yahweh. By the seventh century BC, the people of Judah were exiles in Babylon. Although they faced the daunting task of surviving with their identity as the people of God intact, resisting the idolatrous culture of their captors, and restoring faithfulness to their covenant with Yahweh, they were asked to do more. In a letter to the exiles, the prophet Jeremiah urges them to engage the culture. He encourages them: "Build houses and live in them; plant gardens and eat what they produce. Take wives and have sons and daughters; take wives for your sons, and give your daughters in marriage, that they may bear sons and daughters; multiply there, and do not decrease. But seek the welfare of the city where I have sent you into exile, and pray to the LORD on its behalf, for in its welfare you will find your welfare" (Jer. 29:5–7).

They are in exile for their failure to live faithfully in covenant with their God. But their experience of exile also has an apostolic dimension—Yahweh has "sent" (*galah*, "to send into exile") them to the city where they now live. Their task there is not to settle into a ghetto, but to settle down into faithful living, building houses, planting gardens, rearing families. And they are to seek the welfare (*shalom*) of the city to which God has sent them. They are to pray for that city, for their own welfare will depend on the welfare of that place.

Jesus addresses those who are entering the kingdom of God at his invitation with a similar call to engagement with their world. They are to be "salt and light" to this world, penetrating it and demonstrating the life of the kingdom that is at hand (Matt. 5:13–15). He tells them to "let your light shine before others, so that they may see your good works and give glory to your Father in heaven" (Matt. 5:16). Salt and light have this in common—they bring change to any environment to which they are introduced. They penetrate their context with power to make a difference.

The kingdom narrative includes stories of apostles sent out with specific instructions to engage their world: "'The kingdom of heaven has come near.' Cure the sick, raise the dead, cleanse the lepers, cast out demons. You received without payment; give without payment" (Matt. 10:7–8). The kingdom of God is no gnostic sect, secretive and withdrawn, but an active power like salt, light, seed, or yeast that, though small, penetrates its world and changes it (Matt. 13:31–33).

Theologically, the world-changing impetus inherent to the gospel of the kingdom is rooted in hope—God's promises about the future. If God promises a future when "he will wipe every tear from their eyes," and "death will be no more; mourning and crying and pain will be no more" (Rev. 21:4), then God's people are called to live into that promise already, doing what can be done to ease the world's grief, mourning, disease, and pain. Søren Kierkegaard refers to hope as "a passion for what is possible."[5] Jürgen Moltmann shows how Christian hope is God reaching into the present from the future to bring about his promises. He says of the church, "The Christian Church has not to serve mankind in order that this world may remain what it is, or may be preserved in the state in which it is, but in order that it may transform itself and become what it is promised to be."[6]

The kingdom narrative is misunderstood and misrepresented when it produces a sectarian community that merely withdraws from the world, or a gnostic community that is interested only in the "spiritual"—saving souls for a heavenly existence "up there." The future that God declares is one in which heaven comes down to earth and "the home of God is among mortals. He will dwell with them; they will be his peoples, and God himself will be with them" (Rev. 21:3). Life in this world matters to the God who himself became flesh and dwelt among us in Jesus Christ and who promises one day to redeem this fallen world.[7]

Part of the church's engagement of the world is humble service. Another part is prophetic witness. As Stanley Hauerwas and William Willimon assert, the church is not "chartered by the Emperor."[8] The task of the church and its ministers is ultimately to bear witness through both deed and word to the alternative kingdom offered under the lordship of Christ. This will mean refusing to make God choose sides in the nation's two-party system. "God's politics," as Jim Wallis puts it, "is therefore never partisan or ideological. But it challenges everything about our politics." He explains:

> God's politics reminds us of the people our politics always neglects—the poor, the vulnerable, the left behind. God's politics challenges narrow national, ethnic, economic, or cultural self-interest, reminding us of a much wider world and the creative human diversity of all those made in the image of God. God's politics reminds us of the creation itself, a rich environment in which we are to be good stewards, not mere users, consumers, and exploiters. And God's politics pleads with us to resolve the inevitable conflicts among us, as much as is possible, without the terrible cost and consequences of war. God's politics always reminds us of the ancient prophetic prescription to "choose life, so that you and your children may live," and challenges all the selective moralities that would choose one set of lives and issues over another.[9]

For the church to be equipped to advocate for "God's politics" requires pastors who listen to Scripture, who live from the narrative of the kingdom of God, and who have the boldness and courage to bear witness to the community in which they serve with kindness, neighborliness, and love.

This kingdom narrative provides a theological basis for ministry that, though offered *through* the church, extends *beyond* the church. A pastor is called to serve the people of God in the community of faith but also to take the gospel and its implications to the civic community in which the church's ministry is carried out. The pastor is called to care for the church but also to lead the church to engage its world, both in word and deed. This will be ethically challenging territory, however, and wise pastors and congregations will engage it humbly and thoughtfully.

The Pastor as Professional Minister or Purposeful Missionary?

The North American church's fascination with the subject of leadership over the past thirty-five years has led to more spilled ink and more trees consumed than we can imagine. A Google search for the term "Christian leadership" produces more than thirty-three million hits. A search for book titles related to Christian leadership generates a list of more than twenty-three thousand. Add to that the thousands of journal and magazine articles, research papers, dissertations, and doctor of ministry projects on the subject. Koheleth's words ring true: "Of making many books there is no end, and much study is a weariness of the flesh" (Eccles. 12:12).

In the quest to help pastors become better leaders in the changing world of the twenty-first century, the pendulum may have swung too far, luring pastors away from the ancient aspects of their calling, such as the "cure of souls" and the proclamation of the Word. Mark Galli, editor of *Christianity Today*, decries the labeling of pastors who do attend to this facet of their calling as "chaplain pastors." He cites a website he had recently encountered:

> The Chaplain pastor is "wired for peace, harmony, and pastoral care. This is the type of pastor that has been produced by seminaries for several decades, though a few . . . a very few . . . seminaries are retooling. Chaplain pastors eschew change and value status quo. They don't want to stir the waters; rather, they want to bring healing to hurting souls." And if that weren't bad enough, "Chaplain pastors don't grow churches. In fact, a Chaplain pastor will hasten a congregation's demise because they tend to focus on those within the congregation rather than in bringing new converts to Jesus Christ."[10]

"The assumptions here are all too common, I'm afraid," says Galli. "So we hear in many quarters that pastors should be leaders, catalysts, and entrepreneurs, and the repeated slam about pastors who are mere chaplains."[11] The line of thinking Galli identifies continues to be argued.[12]

Besides the denigration and distortion of the good work of faithful chaplains in the kingdom of God, such arguments misrepresent the full scope of pastoral responsibilities. The domains of pastoral ministry include leadership and administration but also proclamation and pastoral care. As Jesus said of the tithing habits of the Pharisees who overlooked matters of justice, "It is these you ought to have practiced without neglecting the others" (Matt. 23:23).

Kennon Callahan's call for the church to refocus its understanding of its context from a "churched culture" to a "mission field" has implications for what it means to be a pastor in such a context.[13] Callahan invites a shift in thinking from the pastor as "professional minister" to pastor as "missionary." In making this appeal, he is by no means abandoning the significance of pastoral care or proclamation, both of which he understands to be vital to congregational life.[14] Nor is he suggesting that pastors should not work with professional standards. Instead, he is summoning pastors to focus their attention *outside* their congregation as missionaries rather than *inside* as professional ministers. In a mission field, pastors need to understand themselves as missionaries and the congregation as a mission outpost. "On a mission outpost," he says, "the leaders and pastor have an abiding compassion for the human hurts and hopes of people in the world. They invest the driving focus of their leadership and work in mission, in the world."[15]

If the ethical responsibilities of ministry are understood in terms of relationships, then what obligations does the pastor have to the civic community in which the congregation exists? What does it mean for the church to be the body of the Messiah (*Christos*) in the community?[16] The care of the congregation that is incumbent on a pastor also includes equipping them and leading them to serve and bear witness to the world about them.

Bounded Sets and Centered Sets

Missiologist Paul Hiebert borrowed a concept from mathematics to help missionaries think carefully about what it means for a person to be a "Christian."[17] He explained that we often think about such things in terms of a "bounded set," one in which an item belongs because it is like the other items in the set in identifiable ways. An item is either in or out—the middle is excluded. One might define a Christian, then, in terms of some identifiable list of beliefs or behaviors. A "centered set," on the other hand, is defined by the relationship each item in the set holds to some identifiable center. An item may be closer to the center or farther away than others. It may be moving toward the center or away from it. And while each item may differ from the others in a variety of ways, they all have a relationship to the center. This metaphor offers the possibility of defining a Christian convert in more minimalist terms. A former idol worshiper who professes faith in Jesus may not have a full-blown Chalcedonian Christology but may nevertheless, like the thief on the cross (Luke 23:42–43), be related to and moving toward the Lord Jesus Christ at the center of the set. Both types of sets, bounded and centered, can be helpful in thinking about Christian ministry and mission.[18]

The notion of bounded and centered sets may also be a useful way for a pastor to think about engagement in the issues of justice and morality in their community. With whom will you be willing to partner in the effort to feed the poor, assist in disaster recovery, or oppose an unjust law or ordinance? Will you work only with those in your own denomination? With evangelicals only? With leaders from mainline denominations? With Roman Catholic or Orthodox leaders? With Jewish leaders? Muslim leaders? Leaders of community organizations who may themselves be atheists? Using the model of bounded sets, some might most narrowly restrict their partnerships to those most like themselves. However, some might have a much larger, but still bounded, set of those who believe in the God of Abraham, Isaac, and Jacob. This concept will always look for partners who share some identifiable similarities outside of the project itself.

To approach the question from the perspective of centered sets would offer other options. What if one were committed to work with anyone, regardless of their religious or political beliefs, with whom they shared a common center of concern, such as a desire to see that the hungry in the community were adequately fed or the homeless protected from a winter storm? In this case, rather than limiting the set of potential partners by one's belief, the particular issue (hunger or homelessness) forms the center and limits the set. The shift in thinking would be, as Eric Swanson and Rick Rusaw put it, from "Do you believe what I believe?" to "Do you care about what I care about?"[19] Swanson and Rusaw assert that "churches that are transforming communities don't divide over their differences, but unite with other churches and community service organizations (faith-based or not) around their common love for the community. We can unite and work together with other churches and other groups in our communities not because we share the same theology but because we care about the same things."[20]

To choose such an approach opens one's participation in seeking the welfare (*shalom*) of the city one serves, but it also creates the possibility of being misunderstood by one's own denominational or even congregational members. Ultimately one must answer the ethical questions: How can I best love my neighbors, both those who are in need and those who are willing to join me in serving those in need? How, in this particular instance, does the church best bear witness to the kingdom of God—by collaborating or by maintaining a distinctive testimony?[21]

Community Ministry Demands Integrity

Regardless of the role the pastor assumes outside the doors of the church—missionary, prophet, servant, or priest—one thing is certain: the pastor's effectiveness in that role will depend on the degree to which the community perceives the pastor as being a person of integrity. In some ways this is no different from the reality the pastor faces inside the church. In both contexts integrity matters deeply. The pastor needs to be someone whom people trust because they see the consistency and faithfulness of the life lived among them. In other ways, community ministry can be more difficult than congregational ministry, since one may be up against the experiences and prejudices of people with a wide variety of pastors they have known or have heard about in the news. The "clerical collar" no longer automatically generates respect and trust. In fact, the pastor may have some relational work to do before the community is ready to receive their ministry at all. The groundwork for service to the community may require significant effort in building trust.

Once the pastor and congregation begin to offer their services to the community, they must be scrupulous about keeping promises, respecting confidentiality, and remaining in a servant mode. The slightest sense on the part of civic leaders or recipients of social ministries that they are being used, manipulated, or abandoned by pastors or churches can undo long-term efforts at building trust. Pastors need to be up front about their motivation to offer ministry. Is the service rendered with anticipation of making converts or gaining additional church members? Or are the recipients of the ministry respected as an end in themselves? Is service offered as genuine, humble service, or are there strings attached?

In communities that are not accustomed to pastors being active in the community or congregations being involved in service outside their own walls, pastors must be prepared to encounter skepticism, responding with humility, gentleness, and kindness. In the words of Simon Peter, "Always be ready to make your defense to anyone who demands from you an accounting for the hope that is in you; yet do it with gentleness and reverence. Keep your conscience clear, so that, when you are maligned, those who abuse you for your good conduct in Christ may be put to shame" (1 Pet. 3:15–16).

Robert Lewis was the pastor of the Fellowship Bible Church in Little Rock, Arkansas, a large and outwardly successful congregation. One day in a restaurant he overheard a conversation that changed his thinking about his and his church's relationship to the community around him. He listened as someone described their perception of Christians and churches as disconnected, judgmental, and irrelevant. Lewis began to pray and think about why that opinion was out there, whether it was accurate, and what could be done about it. He came to terms with the part he himself had played in giving credence to such a perspective. He confesses: "It began to dawn on me that my actions—no matter how sincere—were not merely ineffective, but they were, in fact, fueling an even greater hostility and alienation between our church and the community. I was *burning* bridges, not *building* them."[22]

Lewis determined to reorient the church toward service to its community, to take seriously Jesus's admonition to "let your light shine before others, so that they may see your good works and give glory to your Father in heaven" (Matt. 5:16). Eventually, Fellowship Bible Church, and its pastor, developed a reputation as people who cared for their city and who were willing to serve it. This effort required attention to the integrity of the pastor's (and church's) words and deeds.[23]

What is true of efforts to serve the community applies even more to a pastor's effort to speak into issues of morality or justice in their community. Addressing such matters will appear disingenuous and self-serving if a relationship of demonstrated love and concern for the community has not previously been established. The prophets of ancient Israel spoke to their people with broken hearts, pleading for them to choose what is just and right. Modern-day prophets frequently come across as merely judgmental or fearful. Such voices are more often scorned than heeded. Pastors who seek to engage their communities authentically as part of their calling will choose to become servants of the community before they attempt to become its prophets.

During times of crisis, pastors will want to be able to step forward and serve in more priestly roles, offering care, consolation, and comfort. Tragic deaths in the community, seismic events like the attacks of 9/11, or natural disasters provide opportunities for pastors and congregations to step forward and offer the love of God in tangible ways to people who are hurting. The capacity for such ministry is built with consistent ministry, service, and integrity in the period *before* the crisis.

Ministers known in the community for angry outbursts, financial dishonesty, broken promises, or judgmental attitudes may disqualify both themselves and their congregations from ministry to those who live around them. The warning given to Timothy about the moral qualifications of pastors still stands: "Moreover, [the pastor] must be well thought of by outsiders, so that he may not fall into disgrace and the snare of the devil" (1 Tim. 3:7). Untold damage to the church's ability to minister is done by such pastors, and it can be done quickly. When they are noisy enough to command national attention, as Fred Phelps and Topeka's Westboro Baptist Church have done, the damage is inflicted on the ministry of congregations around the country as well.[24] On the other hand, ministers who develop a reputation in the community for Christlike service and care earn the privilege of speaking both prophetically and pastorally. Such reputations are not earned quickly, but often require one's planting oneself in a ministry context for some time.

As with other aspects of ministry, Jesus sets the standard for ethical integrity in the relationship between pastors and their community with the simple commandment: "Love your neighbor as yourself" (Matt. 22:37–39). In this case the commandment applies quite literally. Our "neighbors" whom we are called to love unselfishly clearly include those about us in the communities in which we minister. Local communities deserve such neighborly love. Additionally, the neighborhood begins to expand to others about us who are not part of our congregations—those in our communities who need food, shelter, or simply justice, as well as those outside our local communities who live in our nation or in our world. Loving neighbors unselfishly will call the pastor by both word and deed to step outside the doors of the church and into the mission field that awaits.

The Means to Integrity in Community Ministry: What Should the Community Expect?

Ministry occurs in a context of relationships. And relationships always come with expressed or implied obligations. In the case of the pastor's relationship with the community, the obligations are somewhat one-sided. In one sense the community owes the pastor and the church nothing more than what is owed to every other business and organization in the area—adequate civil services, fire and police protection, and justice under the law. But pastors and churches, because of the kingdom narrative out of which they live, bear obligations to the community that the community itself may not even recognize. Ministry with integrity requires that those obligations be identified, considered prayerfully, and carried out faithfully. One way of thinking about these ethical responsibilities is to ask, "What should the community expect of God's people?" Here are five broad areas of legitimate expectation to consider in response to that question.

Good-Neighbor Practices

Pastors and congregations that determine to minister with faithfulness and integrity in their community do so by intentionally engaging good-neighbor practices. Depending on the church's location, ethical, neighborly behavior may require taking responsibility for the physical impact of the church's presence on the community. Streets that are clogged by church parking on Sunday mornings may require a more thoughtful parking plan worked out in conversation with those neighbors most affected. Church bells or carillons that may have been appreciated in a time when communities more deeply valued churches may now no longer be as welcome. Church properties, like those of any good neighbor, will need to be well-maintained and landscaped, appropriately lit at night for security or aesthetics—bright church parking lot lights shining through a neighbor's window at night is not a neighborly practice. Church signage needs to be appealing and maintained. In certain communities, such as smaller towns, relying on local small businesses for various services, even though they may be more expensive, might nevertheless be a wise investment of church resources. Goodwill is not a commodity that can be priced.

Neighbors often hear from churches only when the church wants something from them—their attendance or participation in an event, perhaps. John Beukema, pastor of Village Church in Western Springs, Illinois, suggests finding ways of taking something to them: "We had some of our people go door-to-door offering to fix, clean, paint, or haul stuff away. Recently, our junior high students stood out in the cold, handing cups of hot chocolate to commuters on their way to the train."[25]

Good-neighbor practices become especially important during construction projects. Whenever possible, neighbors might be brought in during the design phase to listen or even to contribute. Neighbors will have questions about how this permanent structure will affect their lives and their property. They will want to know what sorts of activities will be associated with the facility and when it will be operating. When the time comes for trucks to roll through the neighborhood and for the noise of construction to begin, neighbors especially need to be on the church's mind. Reasonable work hours need to be considered. Having a concrete truck backing onto the property with its loud warning sounds at six in the morning might be a problem for next door neighbors. Offering gifts of appreciation or letters from the church expressing genuine concern for those most affected during the interruption of their peace and quiet might be one way of easing the tension. An open house when the construction is done with invitations offered throughout the neighborhood might also help to build goodwill. Simply thinking about how what we do affects our neighbors and what our neighbors need is the starting point of this practice.

Vital Partnerships

Churches that are comfortable working in centered sets can take the lead in establishing vital partnerships between themselves and the local agencies in the community that are providing needed human services. Such agencies are often underfunded and in need of dependable volunteer service. A church in Houston, Texas, determined to partner with a local elementary school. The pastor met with the principal, who seemed suspicious at first. The church discovered in that school a population of children from lower-income apartment units, many from single-parent homes. The plight of these working mothers meant that the school's administrators and faculty lacked the support of a strong PTA and volunteer system. The church recruited members to help with tutoring, reading programs, judging student art shows and science fairs, and providing backpacks and school supplies. Church members became pen pals of fifth graders involved in a writing project. The congregation partnered with other local churches and gave the campus a free face-lift, adding new playground equipment and landscaping around the building at no cost to the school. After two years of dependable partnership, the church was chosen as the school's "Partner of the Year."

Another congregation was considering how best to celebrate its twenty-fifth anniversary and determined to offer twenty-five gifts to their community over the course of that year. As they began to think about the project, they invited community leaders to lunch at the church—school officials, justices of the peace, law enforcement officers, hospital administrators, business leaders, directors of nonprofit organizations. During lunch around tables, a church member facilitated a discussion around the question "What keeps you up at night?" The listening session with these leaders provided the basis for the church's formulating their plans for a year of twenty-five gifts. One of the frequently heard comments around the table was, "I've never had a church ask about these kinds of things before."

A group of Colorado pastors investigated the needs of city and community service organizations that they thought their congregations could help or partner with to meet local needs. They took what Eric Swanson calls a "Magic Bus Tour," meeting with leaders of those services to learn what they offered and to discover ways their congregations could help. Their tour included the local homeless shelter, the food bank, a day care facility, a women's safe house, a home for runaway youth, and an AIDS project. The initial skepticism they encountered eventually gave way to important relationships between those congregations and the community they serve.[26]

Vital partnerships among congregations in ministry projects also change the witness of the church in the community, expressing the faithful ministry of multiple churches.[27] Loving one's neighbor as oneself may mean joining hands with them to meet a significant need.

Dependable Responsiveness

Pastors who seek to minister faithfully in a community need a reputation for dependability and responsiveness. By making church facilities available for community association meetings, polling places, athletic practice fields, scouting programs, and other community-focused events, congregations can respond to community needs. Mobilizing to meet needs during times of community crisis is a powerful demonstration of dependability. Fires that leave neighbors homeless and without basic needs, or natural disasters such as hurricanes and tornadoes that require extensive cleanup, or tragic deaths in the community that require ministry are opportunities for a church to demonstrate its dependability and responsiveness as well as its compassion. When Hurricane Ike hit the upper Texas coastline in 2008, University Baptist Church in Clear Lake, near Houston, organized with other congregations in the community to address a wide variety of needs, from cleaning up debris, to doing mud-out work in flooded homes, to feeding people left without power. The church also opened its facility at no expense to the community and set up Camp Ike to take care of children for the two weeks in which schools were closed and parents had to return to work. They were attempting to love their neighbors and to teach them that they could depend on them to respond.[28]

Wise congregations anticipate such events and prepare a plan of response ahead of time. Additionally, churches can take initiative to know the resources available to people who come in their doors seeking help. A single congregation or pastor cannot be expected to meet every need, but it is possible to know what resources are available and to be prepared to point people to them. Communities and individuals deserve to know that they can depend on the congregation's response during times of personal or community crisis.

Community Service

Swanson recommends a move from "serve us" to "service" as one step in ethically faithful ministry to a community. Congregations that identify needs in their community and find ways to address them are far more often welcomed than resented. He cites the example of the Lighthouse Ministries of the Mariner's Church in Costa Mesa, California, which developed as a result of asking the questions "What could we do?" and "What should we do?"[29] A congregation's willingness to answer those questions with action may determine how sustainable its ministry is in that community over decades and may affect its ability to weigh in with credibility on issues of justice or public morality that inevitably surface over time.

The ethical obligation of pastors to lead the church in serving outside its own walls is matched by the ethical responsibility discussed earlier of a servant leadership that shares the work of ministry with the congregation and equips them to carry it out. In one congregation the pastor told new members that the church held "service" as one of its key values and that the pastors were committed to helping people find a place where they felt called to serve and to equipping and resourcing them to carry out that calling. One new member spoke up: "I already know what God is calling me to do. It has been in my heart for a while." She described a vision of organizing volunteers to provide transportation for cancer patients to the downtown medical center about thirty miles away. The pastor explained that, although the current church budget did not contain funds for such a ministry, he would do what he could to help her find resources. In a few months the "Driving with Care" ministry team was partnering with the local American Cancer Society office to make their services available, and a group of mostly retired men and women were spending a day or more a week driving patients to the cancer hospital, sitting with them while they waited for their treatment, praying for them while they received it, and sharing conversation on the trip downtown and back.

Providing an environment in which people are urged to listen for a call to serve and in which they are equipped to respond to the call is an ethical responsibility of pastoral leaders. Such an obligation keeps the pastor and the church stepping outside the doors to join Christ in mission and contributes to the development and formation of Jesus's followers.

Consistent Witness

In the effort to respond with integrity, service, kindness, generosity, collaboration, and dependability to their community, faithful pastors keep in mind that they and the church they lead occupy a unique niche in the ecology of that place. Although the church may offer a variety of ministries addressing crucial human needs or collaborate with others who are doing so, the church's ultimate and distinctive task is to bear witness to the love of God in Jesus Christ. Ministries of compassion and justice do not have to stand in contrast to gospel proclamation and discipleship. They were not separate in Jesus's ministry and need not be in the life of the body of Christ. Ethically faithful ministry will stay close to the heart of the church's purpose—proclaiming the good news of God's reign in Jesus Christ and helping people learn to follow him.

To do otherwise would be like a farm attending to everything but the production of food. This would obviously be unsustainable for the farmer. It would be no less so for the congregation. Ultimately, communities need to have a church among them that offers resources for the serious spiritual issues of life—meaning in this life and hope for life eternal. Learning to live this life meaningfully requires people to know how to deal practically with issues of relationships, work, politics, and money. They must know how to pray, worship, and understand Scripture. They need opportunities to serve others. They must learn to deal with a wide variety of moral and ethical issues in their lives personally and in their world. They must have resources to face suffering and death. The church has a decisive role to play in bringing Christ's gospel to bear on these real human hurts and hopes as well. Ethical faithfulness requires that the pastor and church attend to the most important issues of the life of their community in light of God's gift of grace in Jesus Christ. Although the community may never think to ask this of the church, the deepest needs of the people who live there demand it. Once more, the love of neighbor demands it.

Expressing integrity in relationship to the community in which we serve is an ethical imperative for ministry. Pastors cannot sequester themselves in their study for forty hours a week absorbed only in sermon preparation or administrative tasks. Time must be allotted to hear the knock at the door and step out into the world with Christ in the mission field. The means for making this happen are not complicated. As with other matters of priority, we handle this by managing our time well using thoughtful goals, a calendar, prayer, and the leadership of the Holy Spirit. That gets us into the world. But once there we must manage ourselves with integrity in the relationships, speaking truth with love and wisdom, keeping promises, and serving humbly.

Key Issues for Community Ministry

Evangelism

Evangelism is at the core of Christian ministry and is a central aspect of the minister's relationship to those outside the church. In the twenty-first century, in a pluralistic society, and in a postmodern culture where truth claims—particularly claims to absolute truth—are held suspect, evangelism falls on hard times.[30] In part the problem is one that the church has brought on itself by ethically questionable evangelistic practices. Stereotypes are often, unfortunately, built on some version of reality. Evangelistic motives and methods have sometimes failed to demonstrate the highest principles of love for God and love of neighbor. The methods, means, and motives of evangelism should be consistent with the good news of God's love and kingdom in Jesus Christ.

Love ought to be the first and deepest motive behind all authentic acts of ministry. This is not always the case, however. Attempts to share faith with one's neighbor can be motivated by guilt, trying to make oneself feel better about one's own Christian commitment. Evangelistic efforts can be driven by a desire to grow one's church, increase the statistical report, or achieve some church or denominational goal. Bearing witness to the gospel may take place out of a need to meet some quota that has been set by the senior pastor for staff members. Other questionable motives could be imagined. In each of these cases, the person with whom the gospel is shared has ceased to be respected as a person and has been an object, an "it" rather than a "thou," a means instead of an end. Love for neighbor gives way to love for self when our motives are skewed.

In the same way, the methods or means of evangelism must reflect the love of Christ that is being shared. Manipulating people into taking a tract, listening to a canned presentation, or assenting to a "conversion" fails the test of ethical ministry. Placing pressure on a person for a decision, using fear or threat, may result in a "decision," but it does not demonstrate the love of

Jesus. Charles Kelley insists that "ethical evangelistic methods are those methods which allow people the freedom to say no and walk away from Jesus."[31] Manipulative methods need to be especially scrutinized when working with children or recipients of social ministries. Food, clothing, shelter, or medical care should not be tied to one's "making a decision" to become a Christian.[32]

Pastors seeking to be obedient to Jesus's commission to proclaim the gospel and to make disciples can look to Jesus's summary of the Law and the Prophets—the Golden Rule—as a guide for ethical action: simply treating others the way we would want to be treated. Working with this perspective, we would approach the ministry of evangelism with what Paul Tillich called listening love: "In order to know what is just in a person-to-person encounter, love listens. It is its first task to listen."[33] Listening love does not attack the other's beliefs but seeks to understand them and then clearly states its own. We would want to comply with the instructions of Peter: "In your hearts sanctify Christ as Lord. Always be ready to make your defense to anyone who demands from you an accounting for the hope that is in you; yet do it with gentleness and reverence" (1 Pet. 3:15–16).

The apostle Paul reflects on the importance of motive in the proclamation of the good news. His opponents apparently impugned his motives, but Paul defends himself. He writes to the Corinthian believers, "We have renounced the shameful things that one hides; we refuse to practice cunning or to falsify God's word; but by the open statement of the truth we commend ourselves to the conscience of everyone in the sight of God" (2 Cor. 4:2). He insists his methods and motives are not deceitful.

In a lengthier defense to the church in Thessalonica, he explains:

> Though we had already suffered and been shamefully mistreated at Philippi, as you know, we had courage in our God to declare to you the gospel of God in spite of great opposition. For our appeal does not spring from deceit or impure motives or trickery, but just as we have been approved by God to be entrusted with the message of the gospel, even so we speak, not to please mortals, but to please God who tests our hearts. As you know and as God is our witness, we never came with words of flattery or with a pretext for greed; nor did we seek praise from mortals, whether from you or from others, though we might have made demands as apostles of Christ. But we were gentle among you, like a nurse tenderly caring for her own children. (1 Thess. 2:2–7)

Paul also exposed the motives of others who worked against him (2 Cor. 11:1–15; Gal. 6:11–13; Phil. 1:15–18). As far as Paul was concerned, motives and methods mattered. Robert Greenway concludes: "Besides living morally on a personal level, the intentions of persons engaging in evangelism must not be self-serving or self-glorifying. Nor may their methods be deceitful or manipulative. Any suggestions of reaping personal gain through evangelism should be completely ruled out. Above all else, evangelists must deliver the Word of the Gospel without change or compromise, bearing in mind that the goal of proclamation is not to please the hearers but to please God by conforming to his Word."[34] The takeaway for the contemporary pastor and congregation is clear.

All that can be said about a person-to-person proclamation of the good news of Jesus's kingdom can be applied to evangelistic ministries offered by congregations. Manipulative methods with children or youth that allow a church to record more "decisions" are ethically unacceptable. Bait-and-switch methods that lure people to a place for one reason, such as a concert or recreational event, only to trap them in a situation where they are forced to listen to a high-pressured "gospel" presentation, fail to reflect the Golden Rule. We do not like to be tricked into a dinner where friends or family then try to recruit us to sell soap in their pyramid scheme. Churches should consider how best to incorporate opportunities to share the gospel with those outside the church in ways that are authentic, honest, and respectful.

Relating to the community around us, stepping outside the doors of the church, will inevitably present us with opportunities to bear witness to our faith. Kelley argues that one ethical violation in evangelism is seen in the lack of love that *fails* to speak of Christ to our neighbor when we have opportunity.[35] Our love both for our neighbor and for Christ should compel us to bear witness. Gaylord Noyce sees authentic evangelism as flowing from "*agapaic* love rather than with the messianic triumphalism that has characterized many an American revivalist and many a 19th century missionary in their approach toward other world religions."[36] Paul writes to the Colossians: "Conduct yourselves wisely toward outsiders, making the most of the time. Let your speech always be gracious, seasoned with salt, so that you may know how you ought to answer everyone" (Col. 4:5–6). Ethical evangelism is marked by love, respect, listening, humility, and authenticity.

Public Morality

Occasionally, civic issues surface in a particular community—issues such as justice for a specific group of people, environmental concerns, economic issues, or moral issues. For the church to remain silent and distant during such times is to fail in its role as neighbor. Pastors and church leaders may need to weigh in and offer what influence they can for the protection of the community in which they serve or for the protection of the most vulnerable in the community. In Waco, Texas, recently a group of pastors raised their voices in concert with others to lessen the impact of payday lending businesses on the poor in the community.[37] Another group of pastors in a small Texas town contributed to the closing of game rooms with "eight-liners," a form of gambling that was negatively affecting their community.[38] A vital partnership between church and community requires such involvement. Communities should be able to depend on the faithful engagement of local pastors and their congregations in those matters that affect the flourishing of life in their community. To remain silent when the community is threatened in some way is to fail to love one's neighbor.

Pastors who speak out or take action on moral issues affecting the local community or the nation should be prepared to deal with the reactivity of those who have interests in the matter. Letters to the editor of the local paper may challenge the pastor's right to be involved in such issues, urging them to stick to "spiritual" matters and "saving souls." Some members of one's own congregation may be vested in the outcome of the issue or may simply be opposed to having their pastor involved in such public matters. When resistance and reactivity result, the pastor must be willing to offer a calm and Christlike response to those who lash out or accuse (Matt. 5:38–48). Guarding one's words and actions underscores the moral position the pastor is advocating.

In almost every case of becoming involved in local issues, the pastor needs to have earned the right to speak by faithful service and a demonstrable compassion for the community. It is too easy to speak to the perceived moral failings of the community from the safety of a pulpit. One's engagement in that community, outside the doors of the church, makes the prophetic word more credible to outsiders. Robert Lewis laments the approach he took to issues of public morality early in his ministry at Fellowship Bible Church: "Like so many other similarly afflicted evangelicals, I thought by hurling verbal hand grenades concerning sin and wrong-doing into the world, the shrapnel would somehow rattle sinners back to their senses. To me, jabbing and stabbing the world with the sword of what I considered impeccable logic and reasoning, backed by God's Word and a dash of holy anger, was the way to turn the world around."[39]

Lewis confesses, "The community also felt our occasional 'hot breath' concerning issues like abortion, pornography, and other specific social ills— a disembodied voice of judgment. . . . I was *burning* bridges, not *building* them."[40] Such disconnected moral opposition is unlikely to be effective. A generally recognized principle of human emotional systems is that we can only change relationships of which we are a part.[41] The ethically faithful pastor remains connected to the community and when necessary speaks prophetically from that position.

A pastor who anticipates this prophetic role can lay the groundwork for it ahead of time. Faithful service to the community builds bridges, to borrow Lewis's analogy, making clear that the pastor and the members of the congregation *belong* to the community they are addressing and do so from a posture of compassion rather than condemnation. Offering such service does not mean that the pastor will not face opposition over moral issues, but it does increase the likelihood of the pastor's voice being heard on the matter.

Faithful scriptural instruction on moral and ethical issues can also provide some groundwork by equipping a congregation to think in terms of biblical moral principles, seeing all aspects of life as falling under the reign of Christ, not just "spiritual" ones. The pastor who addresses moral issues must exercise due diligence in understanding the issue and must be careful not to rely on questionable or inadequate research. On many matters, one's denomination may have information to share that has been researched and documented. This kind of preaching and teaching also helps a congregation come to understand their pastor's commitment to aligning moral opinions with biblical ethics. When the time comes to speak into a particular local or national issue, the pastor has carved out a place to stand on such matters.

Political Involvement

Closely related to the question of a pastor's engagement in matters of public morality is the issue of a pastor's involvement in political processes, whether local, state, or national. This can be a complicated matter. In most congregations, pastors will be called on to minister to people whose political opinions differ from their own. Partisan politics have caused divisiveness among Christians for many years but have become especially contentious in the early decades of this century. Political leaders from both the left and the right have attempted to persuade the nation that their position is the "Christian" one. Additionally, Christian leaders are regularly courted by political figures, hoping for their support and the support of that group of potential voters who would take their endorsement seriously.[42]

One of the complicating factors in this tenuous relationship between the church and the state is the Johnson Amendment (1954), which prohibits tax-exempt organizations, such as churches, from endorsing or opposing political candidates.[43] Pastors and churches are free to provide nonpartisan voter guides, to encourage participation in an election by registering voters, and to host nonpartisan public forums. Pastors cross the line when they publicly endorse or oppose a particular candidate. During the 2016 presidential campaign, the Pew Research Center surveyed more than forty-six hundred adults, 40 percent of whom had attended church once or twice in the previous months. Two-thirds of those said they had heard their clergy address at least one of six political or social issues mentioned in the survey, such as homosexuality or economic inequality. This would be entirely appropriate. However, 14 percent said they had heard their clergy speak directly in support of or against a particular candidate in the previous two months.[44] One entire African-American church in Charlotte, North Carolina, made the news by publicly endorsing the Republican candidate.[45]

Ethicist David Gushee offers his personal list of guidelines for clergy during election cycles:

- Clergy should not endorse political candidates, from a pulpit or anywhere else.
- Clergy should not push out essentially partisan voter guides through their churches.
- Clergy should not offer strategic advice to candidates related to how to win a religious constituency.
- Clergy should not calibrate their preaching in order to influence the outcome of an election.
- Clergy should not invite political candidates to speak in their churches unless they invite all major candidates for a particular office.
- Clergy should not use their churches as a base of operations for partisan voter registration campaigns.
- Clergy should not identify the victory of their preferred candidate as God's will.[46]

Pastors should consider the ethical implications of political involvement. What does active Christian citizenship look like both for ministers and for their parishioners in a democratic society protected by the First Amendment? What does the narrative of the kingdom of God imply about the relationship between the kingdom of God and Caesar (Matt. 22:15–22)? How far can a pastor lead a congregation in political activism without jeopardizing its tax-exempt status? Are there circumstances in which a church might choose to abandon that status in order to have a freer voice, despite the potential impact on donations from members? How can a congregation be appropriately and effectively involved in political matters that have an impact on moral and ethical issues in society? Can a church appropriately post the American flag in its sanctuary or over its building? Does the kingdom of God or Caesar have the final decision on matters such as ministry to illegal immigrants? When is civil disobedience called for (Acts 4:17–20)? Does one's calling as a minister limit one's full involvement as an American citizen?

Rather than simply assume that the binary choices offered by partisan politics are all the options available to God and God's people, pastors might help congregations think in terms of finding a third way to address controversial political issues. Will Willimon tells of a conversation he had with a group of students in 1986. The United States had responded to a terrorist attack by bombing military and civilian targets in Libya. When asked by students about the ethics of the act, Willimon said he could not support the bombing of civilians. A student challenged him about what would be a *Christian* response. Willimon said a Christian response might be the United Methodist Church's sending a thousand missionaries to Libya. The student responded, "You can't do that. It's illegal to travel to Libya. President Reagan wouldn't give you a visa." Willimon's retort is sobering: "No! That's not right," he said. "I'll admit that we can't go to Libya, but it's not because of President Reagan. We can't go there because we no longer have a church that produces people who can do something this bold. But we once did."[47]

In 2016, a bloody civil war continued to rage in Syria. Already half a million lives had been lost. Eleven million refugees fled the country, many losing their lives in the process, hundreds drowning in the Mediterranean Sea. Europe accepted the bulk of them. Hundreds of thousands of them were taken in by Germany; tens of thousands were stranded in Greece. The United States pledged to take ten thousand. Political rhetoric and fear of terrorism kept many Christians in the United States torn between the binary choices of receiving the refugees or banning them all from entering the country. In at least one congregation, Antioch Community Church in Waco, Texas, a third way was offered. More than eighteen hundred short-term volunteers spent part of their summer, at their own expense, traveling to Germany and Greece to serve the refugees there. They logged more than one hundred thousand hours of volunteer work with more than ten thousand refugees.[48] This is a different approach to political issues than is offered in a partisan environment in which the church too often is simply swept along.

Among the ethical snares in the political realm is the ever-present danger of allowing political involvement to degenerate the gospel into a form of mere civil religion that fails to adhere to the central Christian confession: Jesus is Lord. Russell Moore warns, "By putting the kingdom first, we can speak from consciences formed by the future to know how to recognize what matters, peace, justice, righteousness, and how to recognize who matters, the vulnerable, the marginalized, the poor, the captive, the powerless. As we do, we remember, like our Lord, where we came from, and where we're going. And as we do, we render to Caesar what we ought. We pledge allegiance where we can. But we never forget how to call Jesus 'Jesus.'"[49] The primary ethical commitments—loving God wholeheartedly and loving others unselfishly— serve elegantly to help pastors keep a clear perspective on the kingdom of God and the kingdoms of this world.

Religious Services

In many contexts local pastors are asked to offer invocations at community events, civic club gatherings and banquets, high school football games, and meetings of county commissioners, city hall, state legislatures, or other governmental events. Additionally, the community sometimes sees ministers as the local providers of religious services, and people with no other contact with the church look to them to officiate weddings and funerals. Newspaper or other media may consult local clergy for a "faith-based perspective" on events in the community or in the world. In these ways and others, pastors find themselves relating to the world outside the church's doors. This aspect of the relationship to the community carries its own set of ethical concerns that are best considered ahead of time, before the requests arrive.

Pastors need a clear sense of identity in their role as ordained persons who do not simply perform these various religious tasks as individuals but as representatives of Christ and the church. In our increasingly pluralistic society, public prayers at otherwise secular events are still offered. It is likely, however, those invocations are now offered in the presence of Christians, Jews, Muslims, Hindus, Buddhists, atheists, and a wide variety of other spiritual perspectives. Weddings and funerals are no longer automatically "Christian" or even necessarily religious gatherings. Although these invitations can be opportunities for the pastor to have personal contact and ministry with those outside the congregation, the Christian minister will have to consider what it means to be called on to carry out such public roles. Will the minister be able, in the act of ministry, to adequately represent Christ and the church? Or will the pastor be restrained in ways that convert them into a kind of priest of civil religion? Will the pastor be instructed to simply offer a generic prayer at the civic event? Does the pastor's understanding of prayer allow for that kind of restriction? Does the couple who wants a wedding request that the pastor not read Scripture or pray? Does the family who asks the pastor to conduct a funeral insist on nothing "religious" being said? How will a pastor's understanding of their role affect the way they respond to these requests?

Since the US Supreme Court ruling in *Obergefell v. Hodges* in June 2015, same-sex couples have been guaranteed the right to marry in all fifty of the United States. Many congregations have struggled with the implications of that ruling on weddings performed by their clergy and in their facilities. Congregations that have taken a welcoming and affirming position have been able to receive the ruling in stride. Others, however, that have biblical or theological convictions regarding the nature of marriage as restricted to a man and a woman have had to think through their church's policies and procedures and their own practices. How does a pastor ethically respond to requests that are in conflict with their own, or the congregation's, convictions?

Pastors who find themselves invited by local or national media to speak from a faith perspective about events in their community or the world must learn to proceed with caution. It might feel heady to have a camera and a microphone pointed at them, but pastors are generally untrained in how to respond to the media. More than one pastor has had statements taken out of context, misquoted, or misused. Pastors need to remember that, as public figures, they represent Christ and the church, not themselves, in these moments. What they say will be heard as more than their own words.

Although the world outside the church's doors can be a challenging one to navigate ethically, the pastor is nevertheless compelled to do so. Relationships with those outside the church and with community and political leaders require a wise and thoughtful approach on the part of pastors and their congregations.

Conclusion

Although the work of being a good neighbor, engaging ministry partnerships, responding to needs, and bearing consistent witness for Christ may not be as glamorous as being called on to take the podium before the community, this is how a pastor builds and strengthens a relationship to the community. Because of Christ's commission to the church to make disciples and because of the nature of God's compassion for the whole world—not just the church—faithful, ethical pastors will inevitably be stepping outside the doors of their building to join Christ in mission to their world. In this way pastors are called to live fully out of the narrative of the kingdom of God, loving God wholeheartedly and loving neighbors unselfishly.

Suggested Reading

Hauerwas, Stanley, and William H. Willimon. *Resident Aliens: Life in the Christian Colony*. Nashville: Abingdon, 1989.

McKnight, Scot. *Kingdom Conspiracy: Returning to the Radical Mission of the Local Church*. Grand Rapids: Brazos, 2014.

Moore, Russell. *Onward: Engaging the Culture without Losing the Gospel*. Nashville: B&H, 2015.

Swanson, Eric, and Rick Rusaw. *The Externally Focused Quest: Becoming the Best Church for the Community*. San Francisco: Jossey-Bass, 2010.

Thiessen, Elmer John. *The Ethics of Evangelism: A Philosophical Defense of Proselytizing and Persuasion*. Downers Grove, IL: IVP Academic, 2011.

Wallis, Jim. *God's Politics: Why the Right Gets It Wrong and the Left Doesn't Get It*. San Francisco: HarperSanFrancisco, 2005.

7

Facing Clergy Sexual Abuse

The Cost of Lost Integrity

The sexual abuse of parishioners by clergy is a major ethical problem. In every one of the three congregations where I was pastor during my twenty years of full-time church ministry (1965–85), one or more of the church ministers was guilty of sexual abuse. In one suburban church, the previous pastor was forced to resign due to improper sexual relationships with several women. In addition, a full-time youth minister was sexually involved with students, and a part-time marriage counselor was guilty of sexual relations with a counselee.

Lest you assume this is rare, it is not!

When I was teaching at a seminary, a female student preparing to be a youth minister told my wife and me this story. Ann (not her real name) confided that when she was a teenager her youth minister had sexually abused her. Afraid to tell her parents, she eventually went to the pastor with her story. As he pried details from her, he too took advantage of her vulnerability and sexually molested her.

Devastated and embarrassed, she told no one and stopped attending church. Angry with all ministers and with God, as soon as she graduated she left home and began working with a hotel chain. Making a good salary, she was enjoying life and totally turned off to God, church, and everything religious.

One day in a grocery line, a lady invited her to attend her church. "No thanks," Ann replied. But one evening she thought, "I don't even have a Bible!" So the next day Ann randomly picked one of several Christian bookstores in the directory and dropped by on the way to work. As she stepped to the counter to pay for her Bible, there stood the woman she had met in the food store, who called out to her husband, "John, come here—it's the lady we met at the grocery that we have been praying for!"

"That's how I found my way back to God and why I am now in seminary, preparing to be a youth minister," said Ann. "But I have a new problem!"

Ann worked on campus as a part-time house cleaner in professors' homes. The visiting father of one professor's wife (he a minister himself) made several sexual advances. She fled before finishing her work and did not return. Afraid to share her story for fear of disbelief and expulsion from her seminary studies, Ann reluctantly confided in us.

After a lengthy conversation, Ann decided to continue her studies, graduate, and fulfill her calling as a youth minister despite these three episodes of clergy sexual abuse (CSA). To this day I marvel at her courage and strength.

Incidents such as this one have become all too common. Numerous studies during the past two decades support the early research of pastoral counselor G. Lloyd Rediger, who contends that 10 percent of clergy are guilty of sexual malfeasance and an additional 15 percent are approaching the line of misconduct.[1]

In 2002 the Religion Newswriters Association named the abuse scandal that shook the Roman Catholic Church the top story of the year and Cardinal Bernard Law the top newsmaker. He resigned following a year of controversy regarding clergy sexual abuse. The American Catholic hierarchy also received the association's "Into the Darkness Award," a designation given to organizations that try to hide information from the public.[2]

The wave of sex scandals engulfing the Roman Catholic clergy during 2002 touched nearly every American diocese and involved more than twelve hundred priests. These priests are known to have abused more than four thousand minors during the past six decades, according to an extensive *New York Times* survey of documented cases of sexual abuse by priests.[3]

The Roman Catholic sexual abuse scandal sent the public's view of clergy to its lowest point ever, twelve points lower than the previous year's Gallup rating. Asked to rate the honesty and ethics of twenty-one professions, just 52 percent of Americans gave high marks to clergy, down from 64 percent the previous year.[4]

However, the problem of clergy sexual abuse is not just a Catholic issue—the problem also extends to all Protestant denominations. An extensive study published in 2016 by the Diana R. Garland School of Social Work at Baylor University showed *no significant differences in the frequency of CSA* by denomination, region, theology, or institutional structure.[5]

In addition, Diana R. Garland also published the results of research findings from extensive sampling (for example, 3,559 in 2008) taken between 2006 and 2012.[6] This monumental study also defined "clergy sexual misconduct" as: ministers, priests, rabbis, or other clergy or religious leaders who make sexual advances or propositions to persons in the congregations they serve who are not their spouses or significant others.[7]

Mainline Protestant denominations have generally taken the earliest and most aggressive measures to prevent CSA, and fundamentalist churches the least, according to Gary Schoener, a Minneapolis psychotherapist who has handled more than two thousand cases of sexual abuse by clergy.[8] This crisis among ministers has revealed an uneven record of response that ranges from the Episcopal Church's aggressive and detailed policies to the Southern Baptist Convention's widespread lack of written standards.

The Roman Catholic response has varied dramatically, partly because each of the 195 American dioceses operates independently. Among Protestants, a landmark case in Colorado involved a woman who accused the Episcopal diocese and the presiding bishop of covering up the sexual misconduct of her priest. When the jury found the church liable and ordered church leaders to pay her $1.2 million, "that changed the Protestant game completely," says Schoener, "because it opened the door for higher-ups to be responsible." After the Colorado case, national Episcopal Church officers were told by their insurers to develop policies on misconduct and to complete initial training in sexual abuse prevention.[9]

National policies regarding clergy sexual misconduct have been adopted by most mainline denominations, including Methodists, Presbyterians, and Lutherans. Reformed and Conservative Judaism have developed policies, while Orthodox Judaism has moved more slowly. Decentralized denominations such as the Southern Baptist Convention and many evangelical bodies have no national policies, leaving each individual church to establish its own guidelines. Sexual misconduct is routinely covered up in these settings. Dee Ann Miller, a victims' advocate and author of books on the topic, has recorded complaints from victims in thirty states, half of them involving minors. Church officials largely have not been responsive.[10]

Through numerous interviews within his own profession, psychologist Peter Rutter has brought to light the power dynamic often at work in abusive relationships. This connection to power makes misconduct mainly a male problem. In his classic study, Rutter asserts that 96 percent of sexual exploitation by professionals is by a man in power who capitalizes on a woman's trust.[11] The focus of this chapter, therefore, is the sexual exploitation of females by male ministers.

Naming professional sexual abuse the "forbidden zone," Rutter defines misconduct as any sexual contact that occurs within the framework of a professional relationship of trust (such as that involving a counselor or a pastor). Thus, such abuse includes any contact or action intended to arouse erotic interest, whether there is touching or not.[12]

Seminary professors Stanley Grenz and Roy Bell assert that sexual misconduct in the pastorate is a grave betrayal of trust that operates in two directions: "It is a violation of a sacred sexual trust, marring the beautiful picture God has given of the relationship of Christ and the church. And it is a violation of a power trust, abusing the privilege of the pastoral position with which the ordained leader has been endowed by the church and its Lord."[13]

Sexual exploitation ordinarily occurs in an atmosphere of enforced silence. This silence is maintained not only by the participants but also by colluders who are unwilling to breach the dictated censorship. The director of an organization for survivors of clergy abuse writes that the initial response of church officials is to hush the victim and cover up the sexual abuse, which often continues unchecked for years.[14] Rutter insists that this "code of silence" must be broken.[15] A major step toward breaking the silence is understanding the nature and the extent of the problem.

The Scope of Clergy Sexual Abuse[16]

For the most part, congregants and the wider community assume that ministers are persons of integrity who are worthy of respect and trust. Yet clergy sexual abuse is not a new problem.

The Old Testament records the story of the sons of the priest Eli who misused their position to engage in sexual exploitation: "They slept with the women who served at the entrance to the tent of meeting" (1 Sam. 2:22 NIV). David used his divinely ordained role as king of Israel to access and rape Bathsheba (2 Sam. 11).[17] In the first century of Christianity, the apostle Paul warned church leaders about the dangers of sexual sin (1 Cor. 6:9–20; Eph. 5:3; 1 Thess. 4:3; 1 Tim. 3:2). Early church leaders such as Jerome, Tertullian, and Augustine instructed pastors about sexual misbehavior.

The sexual abuse of laypersons by the ordained continues to the present day, as church leaders and other ministers admit to sexual promiscuity. Most religious leaders begin their vocation with good intentions. Yet as they face sexual temptation and the enticement of power, some succumb. When they fall, they land hard and injure others.

Is the problem of CSA as widespread as the authorities claim? A wide variety of reputable surveys over the past three decades supports that conclusion. The most current reliable study is the perennial General Social Survey (GSS), one utilized by Garland of Baylor University in her investigations. The resource is an annual, in-person survey of a nationally representative sample of non-institutionalized English- or Spanish-speaking adults. The 2008 survey included 3,559 respondents. Several criteria ensured accuracy. This study found that 3.1 percent of women who attend religious services at least monthly reported "that at some time during their adult lives, they had been the target of a sexual advance by a clergyperson or religious leader in their own congregation."[18] Thus, one in thirty-three women who are active in a congregation has been the target of a sexually abusive minister in her congregation.

Other surveys during the past two decades have supported this study, profiling case after case of pastors, priests, televangelists, and other religious leaders who were guilty of CSA. Ethical failure in ministry has become so prevalent that insurance companies have been reevaluating their coverage of clergy, sometimes excluding coverage altogether.[19]

Today, the problem is especially acute for the Roman Catholic Church, which not only has struggled with scandal and lawsuits since 2002 but also has lost almost one-fourth of its active priests due to sexual and marital reasons.[20] Protestants are in no way immune to the problem. Therapists and some of the nation's foremost authorities, such as Gary Schoener and Ellen Leupeker of the Walk-In Counseling Center in Minneapolis, contend that Protestant victims far outnumber Catholic victims.[21]

Some years ago, the *Journal of Pastoral Care* reported the results of a survey of senior Southern Baptist pastors designed to identify factors contributing to sexual misconduct. From fifteen thousand churches in six southern states, one thousand were randomly selected. The number of individual pastors who had engaged in sexual behavior "inappropriate for a minister" (judged by the individual pastors) was 14.1 percent. Roughly 70 percent had knowledge of other ministers who had engaged in inappropriate sexual contact with members, and 24.2 percent of the group reported that they had counseled a woman who claimed to have had sexual contact with a minister.[22]

Additional surveys by religious journals and research institutes continue to support these findings. The *Journal of Psychology and Theology* reports that incidents of sexual abuse by missionaries can be found in almost every country in which missionaries are working.[23] *U.S. News & World Report* cites a nationwide study that found that "1 in 4 members of the clergy reported having some kind of sexual contact with someone other than their spouse, and more than 1 in 10 said they had committed adultery."[24]

Reports also reveal long-standing sexual liaisons, homosexual relations, abuse of children, seduction of youth, inappropriate touching, and verbal and nonverbal sexual innuendoes. Rediger identified six specifics of what he calls sexual malfeasance:

1. Sexual intercourse with persons outside a marriage covenant. This includes rape, a consenting adult, children, and incapacitated persons.
2. Oral sex with persons outside a marriage covenant.
3. Unwanted or inappropriate physical touch outside a marriage covenant. This includes genital fondling, foreplay, and any physical contact not appropriate to pastoral ministry or normal friendship.
4. Physical-sensual displays of the body or titillation of senses in ways suggestive of inappropriate sex.
5. The use of pornography, individually or with others, in ways intended to stimulate erotic fantasies of inappropriate sexual behavior.
6. Verbal and visual contact with another person that implies or demands inappropriate sexual response.[25]

The first and most important element in addressing the problem of CSA is to admit that this evil happens. To deny or minimize the sexual exploitation of parishioners by ministers is to give tacit approval.

The Nature of Clergy Sexual Abuse

Though the scope of the problem alarms us, one authority has called CSA "normal" in the sense that it is ubiquitous in religious community life, noting that "bad pastors" are no less surprising than "fleecing accountants, seducing professors, crooked cops, pilfering bankers, money-laundering corporate executive officers, and philandering therapists."[26] Though this may be generally true, most expect a higher level of morality in the lives of spiritual leaders.

To address this issue, one must first understand the basic nature of clergy sexual abuse. In most cases—well over 90 percent—sexual abuse in the Protestant church occurs between a male minister and a female parishioner.[27] When a clergyman exploits his privileged position for personal sexual satisfaction—whether by seemingly innocent innuendoes, obnoxious harassment, or actual physical contact—he has strayed into the forbidden zone. Clergy sexual misconduct is a violation of the integrity of the pastoral office, a betrayal of ordination vows. It is also a betrayal of trust between a pastor and parishioners that involves both an abuse of sexuality and an abuse of power.[28]

Betrayal of Sexual Trust

God created boundaries for sexual expression that reveal and support the intended purpose and meaning of human sexuality. Only within the context of heterosexual marriage can sexual intercourse express the proper intent of the sex act: unconditional, covenantal love. Sexual expression is meant to be both a symbol of mutual commitment and a celebration of the "one flesh" marital relationship (Matt. 19:4–6).

The sex act also carries meaning when practiced outside the context of marriage, but not the meaning God intends. Extramarital sexual relations lack unconditional commitment and all too easily become an expression of self-gratification and exploitation. Outside the boundaries of the marriage covenant, sex actually works to deny the intended meaning of the act. In such cases, sexual intercourse becomes bonding without permanency, a nonbinding covenant, and a false declaration about the depth of the relationship.[29]

For a married pastor, the basic commitment must be to marital fidelity. For a single minister, sexual faithfulness begins with an equally important commitment to sexual abstinence before marriage. Some have tried to put a positive face on certain extramarital sexual activities, but any intentional sexual contact outside the boundaries of marriage violates the marital bond and constitutes adultery (Matt. 5:27–28).

Thus, sexual misconduct by clergy is a distortion of human sexuality—a betrayal of sexual trust. For an offending pastor, whether single or married, the betrayal is a violation of God's intention for humanity from the beginning (Gen. 2:18–25).

Betrayal of Power Trust

Clergy sexual exploitation is not primarily about sex. It is an abuse of power expressed in a highly destructive sexual manner. One writer concludes that the problem "is less about sex and more about power. It has less to do with sexual misconduct such as adultery, and more to do with exploiting one's professional position for personal gain."[30] Only when the power aspect is accepted can the church stop engaging in denial and collusion and become a place of authentic power and healing.

Every minister is a symbol of religious authority. By virtue of the pastoral office, a minister interprets religious truth, the meaning of life, the way of faith, and even the reality of God. When the power of a pastor's presence through ministry is added to that status, the special influence a minister holds among his or her congregants becomes evident.

For example, in pastoral counseling a female church member brings her intimate, wounded, vulnerable, or undeveloped self. Whatever the cause of her wounds, she comes to her minister seeking acceptance, self-worth, and emotional support. Ultimately, she seeks healing. A special bond of trust develops between her and her pastor, which may lead to more openness and more vulnerability. Peter Rutter notes that "even a woman with a firm sense of sexual boundaries often stops guarding them in order that her inner self may be seen and known by this healer."[31]

Motivated by his own needs, a minister may move this relationship into the sexual sphere, seeking his own "healing." Whatever the motive, through sexual contact a pastoral counselor exploits a congregant's vulnerability, violates her trust, and meets his own needs at her expense. Karen Lebacqz and Ronald Barton accurately note that this sexual contact "revictimizes her, repeating patterns from her past, and keeps her from recognizing and claiming her own strength apart from a man."[32]

While this scenario describes a typical case of CSA, at times the sexual contact is initiated by the congregant. Or perhaps the sexual contact is by mutual consent. Most male ministers have encountered seductive behavior in unstable members, and the story of a colleague who left his spouse because of sexual involvement with a church member is not uncommon. Yet most authorities insist that any sexual contact between a minister and a congregant involves an abuse of power. Whatever the circumstances, sexual behavior by a minister (who always occupies the position of power) is inherently exploitative of a member's trust. Even a woman's advance does not excuse a minister from his responsibility to maintain boundaries.

Types of Abusive Ministers

Sexual misconduct by clergy takes many forms: voyeurism, exhibitionism, incest, child molestation (pedophiles and ephebophiles),[33] homosexual liaisons, and rape. Clergy sexual abuse usually begins with acts or statements intended to arouse erotic interest. When pastoral power is used to manipulate a congregant to engage in sexual relations, the results are devastating.

There are many ways to classify abusers. Observers of clergy abuse list as many as seven profiles.[34] Recognized authority Marie Fortune has made a major distinction between predators and wanderers, to which Grenz and Bell have added a third type: the lover.[35]

The predator is a person who actively seeks opportunities to abuse women sexually. Targeting his prey, the predator pretends to be a caring pastor but uses his power and position to manipulate his victims. The pastoral predator is "manipulative, coercive, controlling, predatory, and sometimes violent. He may also be charming, bright, competent, and charismatic. He is attracted to powerlessness and vulnerability. He is not psychotic, but is usually sociopathic; that is, he has little or no sense of conscience about his offending behaviors. He usually will minimize, lie, and deny when confronted. For those offenders, the ministry presents an ideal opportunity for access to possible victims of all ages."[36]

In contrast to the predator, the wanderer is not violent, not premeditative in his sexual abuse, and generally less successful personally and professionally. Because he is a vulnerable and inadequate person, the wanderer easily becomes emotionally and sexually involved with a congregant or counselee. According to Fortune, the wanderer "has difficulty maintaining boundaries in relationships and attempts to meet private needs in public arenas."[37] The catalyst for his sexual misbehavior is usually an equally needy woman who holds her minister in high regard, almost to the point of adoration.

The growing intimacy between pastor and parishioner usually culminates in an emotional moment when inhibitions are cast aside and the two engage in an episode of sexual intercourse. Once the passions have subsided, both begin to feel anxiety, shame, guilt, and a sense of betrayal. The two express regret and swear themselves to secrecy. Although things may seem to return to normal, a trust has been violated, and a shadow falls over their lives and relationships.

The lover is a third type of minister who enters the forbidden zone with a parishioner. This spiritual shepherd becomes infatuated with one of his flock. Though a sexual transgressor like the other two, he is motivated neither by the desire to conquer nor by the need to overcome personal inadequacies.

Although there is no stereotypical perpetrator of CSA, the distinction between predator, wanderer, and lover is insightful. The predator offender moves from conquest to conquest, leaving a trail of victims. The wanderer minister yields to temptation in a moment of crisis and immediately feels remorse over his failure. The lover minister is drawn to a church member when his passion convinces him he is in love.

Not all agree with these distinctions. Many victims of CSA believe that all ministers fall into the first category and will continue to victimize if not apprehended and removed from ministry. Perhaps these victims have never observed a wanderer, whose offense is normally a once-in-a-lifetime mistake and who ordinarily admits his failure and seeks professional help. A counselor of clergy who developed a restoration process for fallen ministers shared in a meeting that in his years of work, not once did a predator come to him for help. On the other hand, he witnessed scores of wanderers who benefited from his recovery program.

Understanding the nature of CSA raises other important questions. What is its impact on churches, victims, and the families involved? Are there ways to prevent the abuse? How should churches and denominations respond to the malady?

The Impact of Clergy Sexual Abuse

In ten years, the congregation of a middle-class church in the suburbs of a large metropolitan area grew to over one thousand members. When the only pastor most members had known accepted the call to a church in another state, the congregants were deeply distressed. Only a few lay leaders knew why Brother Jim (not his name) was leaving. He had become intimate with three married women in the church while counseling them about family problems.

Pastoral care was Jim's strong suit. He was a charismatic leader who invested much of his time in counseling members. When deacon leaders confronted the pastor with evidence of his sexual involvements, he admitted his errant behavior. The relationships were not planned, he explained. But during counseling, these needy women "fell in love" with the first man in their life who listened, cared, and gave them emotional support. He realized his sin, vowing never to let it happen again. The decision to move to another church was Jim's way of making a clean start.

Rumors that Brother Jim had been intimate with several women began to make the rounds about the time a new pastor came. The reactions of members of the congregation varied. Some believed the charges and in their anger left the church. Others disbelieved the rumors, claiming they were concocted by enemies of the former pastor or by the new pastor. Many who stayed in the church were so hurt and disappointed that they vowed never again to trust a minister.

The impact on church members was widespread and devastating. Young people who had admired their lifelong pastor were crushed. Parents struggled to explain to their children how a minister could be guilty of CSA. Families of the victims felt cut off from their church, as many blamed the abused women of being the culprits in the sexual affairs. To complicate the matter, within two years evidence surfaced that a part-time counselor and a youth minister were also guilty of sexual improprieties. For the next five years, the new pastor spent much of his ministry working to rebuild trust and credibility.[38]

Pastoral counselor Roy Woodruff, former executive director of the three-thousand-member American Association of Pastoral Counselors, is concerned about the frequency of sexual abuse among clergy. "According to informed estimates, about 15 percent either have or are violating sexual ethical boundaries. I don't think I would use the word 'epidemic' . . . but I suspect the number of incidents is increasing."[39]

Clergy sexual abuse, like the Zika virus that plagued the entire world in 2016, has a devastating impact on various victims—church denominations and congregations, the abusing minister, the perpetrator's family, and certainly the abused woman and her family.

Impact on the Church

Although sexual abuse scandals in the Roman Catholic priesthood make the headlines, no religious group has escaped the malady.[40] Leaders who work across denominational lines see no pattern. Sexual misconduct has invaded big-city megachurches and small-town pastorates, liturgical churches and charismatic congregations, and both ends of the theological spectrum.

When clergy sexual misconduct interrupts the life of a congregation, what impact does it have? As a whole, the church body tends to follow certain predictable patterns in their reaction to ministerial abuse that range from secrecy and silence to blame and excuse. The clergy perpetrator normally fails to anticipate the severe problems that descend on him and his family as a result of his transgression. Often overlooked is the effect on the abused woman and her family. The initial response of church leaders to Brother Jim's admission of clergy sexual abuse was to avoid a public scandal and to protect Jim's reputation. A "code of silence" was pledged by the few who knew the facts. However, the enforced secrecy about Jim's infidelity was a mistake.

Clergy sexual misconduct is often a secret of church life that is concealed from public scrutiny. Most people are content to deny or ignore an incident, but this is destructive. Breaches of pastoral ethics must not be dismissed. A church contributes to the conspiracy of silence when it cajoles the victims to remain silent and attempts to conceal the facts. Denominational officials often join the attempted cover-up by recommending the minister for another location without addressing his misconduct. Concealing sexual exploitation compounds the problem and augments the damage. Breaking the code of silence is a major step in dealing with the issue. Only as CSA is dealt with honestly and openly will healing, health, and safety be available to the church, the perpetrator, and the victim.

Concealment, however, continues to be the main response of churches that deal with clergy sexual abuse. If preserving the secret fails, a second strategy usually follows. Church leaders direct their energies toward protecting the church's good name and the pastor's reputation.[41] Often the victim is blamed and the pastor is excused. The only eyewitness is thus demonized, for she is "the seductress who took advantage of our pastor in a moment of human weakness!" It is also not uncommon for a church to blame the pastor's wife. If she had met his sexual needs adequately (so runs the argument), he would not have been vulnerable. Thus, the abuser (the pastor) becomes the victim, and the victims (the abused and the wife) are blamed as the real perpetrators of this tragic event.

In addition to misrepresenting the facts, this second reaction perpetuates the problem and creates additional negative responses. To excuse the pastor encourages him to deny his responsibility and to postpone confronting his behavior. Until a minister acknowledges that he is accountable for his conduct, little can be done to restore him to wholeness. Ministerial colleagues may join this charade, which pictures the pastor as the innocent victim of a seduction.

In a discussion of therapists who have sexual liaisons with their patients, psychiatrist Glen Gabbard observed: "Incest victims and those who have been sexually exploited by professionals have remarkably similar symptoms: shame, intense guilt associated with a feeling that they were somehow responsible for their victimization, feelings of isolation and forced silence, poor self-esteem, suicidal and/or self-destructive behavior and denial. Reaction of friends and family—disbelief, discounting, embarrassment—are also similar in both groups."[42]

Applying this insight to the pastorate, Marie Fortune writes that the church functions as a family. The family image, with God as Father and fellow believers as siblings, suggests a relationship of trust, intimacy, caring, commitment, and respect, which are the bases of family life. Viewed from this perspective, CSA may be likened to spiritual incest. "When the irresponsible pastor does engage in sexual activity with parishioners, the result is incest in the church family; the parallels to incestuous abuse are disturbing."[43]

One such comparison of CSA to incest by David Brubaker reveals five common traits:

1. social isolation
2. blurred boundaries
3. the paradoxical feelings of inadequacy and perfectionism
4. the "no talk" rule, which distorts communication
5. unequal power[44]

Spiritual incest is a violation of trust. Because a minister represents God and the church, to be violated by a man of the cloth is to feel violated by God and the church.

Clergy sexual misconduct impacts the church in other ways as well. In the wider society, the church's reputation is seriously marred. The pastor's misconduct will likely create public embarrassment, diminishing the credibility of the church throughout the community. In our increasingly litigious society, legal difficulties may be added to the long list of problems created by a pastor's misconduct.

Equally devastating is the turmoil created within the congregation. As news of the pastor's sexual misconduct becomes known, the event polarizes the congregation. Members of the church may feel shame, anger, resentment, or empathy. Some may become vindictive. The end result is usually strife and division within the church body. Those who were significantly helped by the pastor's ministry will be deeply hurt and confused by the sexual misconduct. People on all sides of the debate may lose faith in the church leadership.

The debilitating effect of internal strife and external embarrassment is a loss of morale. Instead of utilizing its resources for witness and service, the congregation finds itself dissipating energy on the internal crisis. Growth is stymied, attendance drops, and many families decide to join another church. Like Solomon's razed temple, once the church has been damaged by CSA, it may be unable to regain its past influence.

"Whenever a pastor is accused of inappropriate sexual conduct within a church," conclude Lebacqz and Barton, "the bonds of trust between that pastor and the congregation are stretched to the breaking point. The focus of attention within the congregation shifts from the worship of God and the mission that flows out of that worship and begins instead to concentrate on the behavior of the pastor and of church members."[45]

Inevitably, the church moves from ministry and worship to crisis management. Dealing with this problem requires the energy, time, and focus of the church. Often, outside expertise and assistance are needed. A body of literature is developing to assist churches and "after pastors" in dealing with the problems that confront a congregation for years after the abuse.[46]

Impact on the Minister

Thirty years after renowned theologian John Howard Yoder was first accused of sexual misconduct and almost twenty years after his death in 1997, the story of his abusive behavior remains painfully unresolved in the Mennonite community. With his abuse, Yoder betrayed his own theology.[47] He is not alone. A few prominent examples among many illustrate the breadth of the problem: "Ministry Leader Gothard Quits after Abuse Allegations,"[48] "Priest Firings Climbed in '11–12,"[49] "Ex-Pastor Gets 12 Years,"[50] and "Ex-Youth Minister Gets 22 Years for Sex Abuse."[51] Church and legal sanctions are just a small part of the impact of CSA on the minister.

Sexually abusive behavior also has devastating consequences for the professional life of the abuser. The sexual misconduct undermines the integrity of his ministry, for it is a denial of all he has claimed to be and all he has taught others to be. Once reputation and credibility are lost, a minister's vocation is in serious jeopardy. Legal liabilities and financial pressures add to the turmoil. Equally serious is the collateral damage done to the minister's colleagues, his church, and his denomination. Like waves from the wake of a passing ship, CSA washes muddy waters across the reputation of ministry at large. An incident of clergy sexual misconduct breeds a loss of faith in all ministers and ministry.

Impact on the Perpetrator's Family

The impact of CSA moves beyond the pastor and the congregation. The transgression also touches the minister's spouse (normally the wife) and family. An immediate reality is the loss of income. A common reaction by church leaders to a pastor's sexual misconduct is to demand an immediate resignation. At best, this usually means no more than two to four weeks of severance pay. If the family is living in the church parsonage, it is not abnormal for the church to request that the manse be vacated within a few weeks. In their haste to deal with a difficult situation, church leaders often overlook the financial effect of their decisions on the pastor's wife and family.

Financial instability is a serious reality, but it is not the most devastating issue faced by the minister's spouse. Her husband is guilty of marital infidelity. If the sexual misconduct went on for months without her knowledge, the deceit is devastating. The emotional pain and confusion felt by the spouse are captured in the comment of one minister's wife: "It is impossible to describe the mental and physical pain—if he dies before me, he will have died twice."[52]

Along with an immediate loss of trust and intimacy, the minister's wife often begins to feel a sense of shame, guilt, and personal inadequacy. The incident raises in her mind typical questions about her adequacy as a sex partner, a marital companion, a mother, and a pastor's wife. Whatever the outcome of the clergy sexual misconduct for her husband, she will face profound changes in her entire way of life. She is denied her sense of calling as a pastor's wife. Most of her church friends will disappear. Often the job of explaining "Daddy's problem" to the children will fall on her shoulders. If the couple decides to rebuild their relationship, it will take years of hard work.

The losses faced by the children are similar to those confronting their mother. They too will be cut off from church friends, lose face among their peers, and feel the financial pinch of a family lacking reliable employment. Should their father's sexual misconduct lead to a divorce, the children will experience the trauma of separation.

In the aftermath of clergy sexual abuse, the family members of the minister are innocent bystanders, immediately affected and most often overlooked. Disillusionment at the deepest level often permanently alienates the spouse and children from the church and fellow Christians. Family members may wonder whether God also has left them.

Impact on the Abused Woman and Her Family

None of these consequences seem to equal the havoc experienced by the victim of CSA. Most victims never come forward. Generally, the vulnerable survivor who does bring allegations disappears from the story early on, as few people truly care about her or reach out to her.

Grenz and Bell observe that a woman exploited during counseling (about one in five of those abused) often faces triple jeopardy. In the beginning, personal problems led her to seek her pastor's care. Needing personal healing, she found instead sexual violation from a man she trusted. Once the incident is public, her church rejects and abandons her. In this wounded condition, the victim who sought help instead found further injury from her family, her pastor, and her church family.[53]

The personal repercussions of CSA on a woman are similar to those experienced by abuse victims of other caregiving professionals. Often they are caused not by the abuse but by the collusion that comes later. Physical disorders are common. Health problems ranging from back pain to nervous disorders appear. Emotionally, the victims of CSA may experience anxiety, fear, panic, depression, mood changes, guilt, anger, loss of trust, problems with sexual intimacy, and thoughts or attempts of suicide. Socially, the victim may find it difficult to maintain close relationships, which may lead to social withdrawal and alcohol and drug abuse.[54]

The impact on the abused woman's family is just as devastating as on the perpetrator's. Marriages often end in divorce. Children may become rebellious and turn to antisocial behavior such as drugs, crime, and illicit sex.

Once the victim realizes she has been led into sexual abuse by a trusted caregiver, this awareness can cause grave damage to her view of herself as a woman. Coming to her pastor for healing from former hurts (sometimes incurred in earlier abusive relationships), she found instead someone who violated and used her, like a commodity to be exploited.

Pamela Cooper-White summarizes the impact of clergy abuse on the victim: "The pastoral relationship can and should be a sacred trust, a place where a parishioner can come with the deepest wounds and vulnerabilities. . . . By modeling appropriate boundaries and healthy responses, the pastor can begin to empower her to heal those wounds. The harm done when this is exploited is no less than a violation of sacred space, which further ruptures and destroys the woman's boundaries, devastating her mental health and her sense of self."[55]

Thus, abandoned by her church, betrayed by her pastoral counselor, unaided by her dysfunctional family, and devastated by physical and emotional disorders, the abused woman suffers from guilt, isolation, and humiliation. Her mood deepens from shame and self-blame to despair and desperation. She may ponder or even act on thoughts of suicide. Inevitably, she faces a crisis of faith. If all those who represent God have betrayed her, she may feel betrayed by God also.

Prevention of Clergy Sexual Abuse

If three decades of research is accurate, 10 to 12 percent of ministers engage in sexual relations with members of their church, and 25 to 35 percent of clergy admit to sexually inappropriate behavior with parishioners. Clergy sexual abuse is seldom an isolated action. Rather, it is a complex problem involving a confluence of circumstances and motivations, especially the twin dynamics of sexuality and power.

What can be done to prevent this destructive behavior? Why do some clergy fall and others do not? Are there protective measures that can help ministers and churches avoid this breach of power and trust? Some offer a straightforward solution to the problem: the church should weed out those who are likely to harass or abuse. Certainly, ordination and ministerial placement should be limited to persons of the highest spiritual maturity and moral integrity (1 Tim. 3:1–13). No one disagrees with that principle.

However, clergy sexual misconduct is very difficult to predict. As Christian psychologists Jack Balswick and John Thoburn confirm, "No one factor in and of itself can be identified as the reason why a given minister succumbs to a sexual temptation. In most cases, a combination of factors contributes to their behavior."[56] Adding to the difficulty of predicting abuse is the fact that comparatively little has been written about the factors that make a person vulnerable to victimization. Even less is available on what makes an individual in the institutional church vulnerable to colluding.[57]

A better approach for preventing clergy sexual misconduct is to equip ministers and churches to understand negative influences and to encourage positive resistance. Clergy and churches must refuse to succumb to the demons of denial, ignorance, and minimization, which usually foster secrecy and collusion.[58] Research indicates that ministers who withstand sexual temptation understand their own personal susceptibility, recognize the danger signals, and build strong support systems. Churches assist in prevention by perceiving the dynamics of the clergy role, encouraging methods of accountability for ministers, and developing wise policies.[59]

Personal Awareness

For perpetrators, victims, and colluders, the first step in the prevention of clergy abuse is a personal recognition of the problem. An inadequate approach is to ask "Who's at fault?" The blame game usually misreads the situation and offers little help for prevention. Some blame the minister who profanes his calling by taking advantage of a vulnerable church member. Some blame the church that puts its pastor under pressure to perform. Some identify the culprit as a seductive female or an inadequate wife.

Sex abuse expert Fortune insists that most offending ministers violate ethical sexual boundaries long before they commit vocational suicide. However, it is not about sex. It is a misuse of power. Fortune observes that church members want to excuse the pastor and often slip into denial, but it is not fair to the pastor or the congregation to ignore the real problem. "We need to say, 'Look, it was wrong. It was unethical behavior.'"[60]

The ministry is an attractive profession for anyone who is looking to exploit vulnerable people, claims Roy Woodruff. "The average parish pastor has no one he reports to or is supervised by. And he has a lot of needy people coming for help. A pastor who could be needy himself can exploit the needs of others."[61]

Awareness of the dynamics of CSA is basic to all prevention strategies. Every minister needs to realize that he is at risk of crossing the boundary into the forbidden zone every day. The male pastor is not exempt from sexual attraction to congregants. He must be aware of his feelings and honestly acknowledge the sexual urges he senses.

In addition, as a professional caregiver a minister may have difficulty accepting his limitations, especially in counseling members of the opposite gender. Pastors who see themselves as rescuers may create a codependent relationship that is dangerous. A rescuer-healer minister is susceptible to sexual misconduct because he may cross healthy boundaries to fulfill his own personal needs.[62]

A minister must be aware of personal susceptibilities that make him more prone to sexual abuse. Deep-seated insecurities, which easily surface as sexual and power needs, often fuel misconduct. Unresolved questions relating to a pastor's own sexuality, especially destructive experiences from the past, can contribute to the exploitation of others. Sexual addiction has a critical influence on some abusers.

Pastoral counselor Woodruff contends that sexually abusive ministers usually fit one of two profiles: the prima donna or the depressed pastor.[63] The prima donna pastor operates out of a desire for power and control, loses touch with boundaries, overdirects people's lives, and develops a sense of "I can do no wrong." Central to this person is the idea of entitlement—that he is entitled to certain behaviors that others are not. The highly publicized televangelist scandals and the sexual failure of many contemporary megachurch pastors illustrate this type. At the other extreme is the depressed pastor whose judgment becomes cloudy because of low self-esteem and a growing inability to function as a minister or as a man. Thus, he becomes vulnerable to relationships that provide gratification. The prima donna pastor and the depressed minister share one fatal weakness: isolation.

What lessons can be learned from this summary of factors related to clergy sexual misconduct? First, male ministers who are inclined to harass or abuse urgently need personal therapy. For them, the personal and professional risk of ministering to women is too great. For pastors who do not sense a vulnerability toward abusing parishioners but do recognize the reality of sexual temptation, the dynamics of the pastor/congregant relationship may offer another lesson. Peter Rutter observes, "Every forbidden-zone relationship in which sexual tension appears also presents an opportunity to heal."[64] The male minister holds the power to move the arousal of sexual feelings from temptation to an opportunity for the healing of deeper wounds. He alone can turn an impending disaster into a life-giving moment.

Warning Signs

Knowing the warning signs of CSA can aid in the prevention of it. Ministers should be aware of their boundaries and always seek to maintain them. "Even if the boundaries for sexual intimacy are the same for pastor and lay person, the responsibility for maintaining those boundaries falls to the professional person."[65]

Ministers need a warning system that will alert them when they are approaching unacceptable levels of intimacy with parishioners. Lebacqz and Barton have proposed a checklist of signals that warn ministers when they are headed for trouble:

- the publicity test: what would others think?
- physical arousal—one's own or the other's
- inordinate sexual fantasy
- sexual gestures or body language
- intuition, instinct, or not feeling right
- wanting to share intimacies that are not called for
- a parishioner wanting too much time or attention
- wanting to shift the focus to sexual subjects[66]

Clergy sexual abuse expert Fortune has developed a list of questions to which affirmative answers suggest the possibility of sexual misconduct:

- Is the minister doing a lot of counseling beyond his or her scope of responsibility?
- Is the minister not taking care of himself or herself, canceling vacations, neglecting time with family?
- Does the pastor tend to sexualize conversations?
- Are mechanisms of accountability being ignored?
- Is lay leadership discouraged?
- Does everything in the church focus on the pastor?[67]

Grenz and Bell offer six warning signs that indicate boundaries are being violated:

1. The conversation becomes increasingly personal, as the pastor talks unduly about himself.
2. The pastor's physical contact has moved beyond greetings to inappropriate pats and hugs.
3. The pastor fantasizes about a sexual relationship with the congregant.
4. The pastor offers to drive the congregant home.
5. The pastor arranges meetings with the congregant outside the normal counseling time.

6. The pastor increasingly hides his feelings for the parishioner and his meetings with her from his accountability systems, especially his wife.[68]

Support Systems

One of the best ways to ensure responsible sexual behavior is for a minister to build strong support systems. Accountability relationships offer a crucial antidote for misconduct.

A good marriage reinforces sexual faithfulness in many ways. It provides the context for wholesome sexual expression. Marital intimacy also facilitates honest communication while reminding the married church leader that he is accountable to his partner. The research of Balswick and Thoburn reveals, "Over one-fourth of the pastors cite their relationship with their wife as the most important reason for sexual fidelity." The study concludes, "Marital dissatisfaction coupled with work boredom is the kind of situation that has been conducive to the most fantasy and openness to actual liaisons."[69]

In her monumental study of CSA, Diana R. Garland highlights the work of "support groups such as The Hope of Survivors, an online support network for survivors of clergy sexual abuse (http://www.thehopeofsurvivors .com)."[70] Colleagues and personal counselors provide another support group. A pastor should not hesitate to seek personal counsel from trusted friends or professional advice from a qualified therapist when he needs inner healing and emotional health. Another important support group is composed of models and mentors. Many pastors belong to accountability groups whose members meet regularly to develop trust, offer encouragement, and hold one another morally accountable.[71] One group of ministers in Phoenix meets weekly, and members ask one another a series of questions, beginning with, "Have you had any sexual thoughts about women in your congregation since we last met?"

The greatest role model for ministers is Jesus, who ministered to women without moral compromise. He viewed each woman he encountered through God's eyes, not as objects for selfish gratification or pawns to be controlled but as persons with deep needs and spiritual aspirations. As disciples of Christ, pastors are to minister to women as Jesus did.

Professional Safeguards

Ideally, prevention safeguards for ministers should be established during preparation for ministry. Seminary students and new ministers need information about and clarification of ethical standards for ministry. Many denominations have begun developing educational and training resources for their clergy and laity.[72]

> [Ministers] need to understand the nature of the power and authority of their role and the responsibility that goes with it. They need to learn how to maintain boundaries in relationships with parishioners and counselees. They need to learn to care for their own emotional and sexual needs in appropriate ways.[73]

Seminaries may be the first line of defense in protecting church members from sexual abusers. Although there is no reliable test for identifying abusive applicants, seminaries do rely on essays, recommendations, applications, and psychological tests to screen prospective students.[74]

Individual churches share some responsibility for prevention. Churches should have policies about standards of conduct, screening procedures, supervision guidelines, adequate insurance coverage, honest pastoral references, and procedures for handling allegations of sexual misconduct by ministers.[75]

Safeguarding potential victims from perpetrators is made more difficult by the common practice of abusers moving from one state to another, one institution to another, and one denomination to another. The structure and practice of autonomous churches make them more vulnerable to traveling abusers. As a result, these churches need to do a thorough background check on every potential minister.

How can churches escape the trap of recycling sex abusers? Even among activists and experts, there is no consensus. A survey by a church journalist compiled these priorities:

- a ministerial code of ethics
- seminary training
- church-approved policies
- outside help
- reporting abuse
- abuser database[76]

Should denominations bear some responsibility for unethical clergy? In 2002, one denominational group (for the first time in its 118-year history) recognized its obligation to assist congregations in identifying past abusers (even though their churches are autonomous) by maintaining a file of clergy sexual misconduct. The file was based on convictions, confessions, and reports from congregational officials, who believed that if a past history of sexual abuse is discovered in a candidate, the church body should be informed.[77] Regrettably, in 2016 the executive board of this Baptist convention decided to eliminate its file of clergy charged with CSA, mainly because in the previous two years, no church had requested information.[78]

It is worth noting that most other professionals (such as doctors and lawyers) operate under an accepted code of ethics developed and enforced by their peers. However, clergy face three major problems in writing a code of ethics: authorship, instruction, and enforcement.[79] In addition (as previously noted), congregational-type churches have been reluctant to accept a standard code of ethics for all ministers. However, in June 2016 the Cooperative Baptist Fellowship Governing Board approved a task force on clergy sexual misconduct.[80] The CBF will collaborate with Baptist Women in Ministry in a task force formed to focus on prevention of clergy sexual misconduct, creating and distributing policies, education, and after-care for survivors of CSA.

People need to know their church is a safe place. Denial is deadly. As long as a church ignores the problem of sexual misconduct or cajoles victims to remain silent, the problem persists. Ignorance compounds the issue and augments the damage sexual abuse perpetrates. To ignore clergy sexual misconduct is to become a colluder, one who joins the perpetrator in victimizing the vulnerable and their families. Prevention, therefore, is the responsibility of everyone.

Responding to Clergy Sexual Abuse

The phone rings. With anguish, a female victim of CSA tells you her story and then asks the question, "What can we do?" A second call comes from a lay leader in the church of the minister abuser and his victim. He confirms the allegations and then asks the same question: "What can we do?"

When a minister is accused of sexual misconduct, those involved are perplexed about how to respond. Victims are embarrassed and ashamed. Should they keep quiet or report the incident? Family members cope with several levels of disruption. Where do they turn for help? Not knowing what else to do, church leaders may join the perpetrator in a denial of the accusation.

A common scenario is as follows: Secrecy is urged by church leaders for the sake of the church and the families involved. As news of the incident spreads, many blame the female victim, assuming she is guilty of seducing the minister. Others suggest that the pastor's wife may be at fault—if she had been an adequate partner, he would not have strayed. Whether the allegations are true or not, church leaders usually choose one of two options: they either support the pastor and try to keep the charges undercover, or they force the pastor to leave through resignation or termination.

Why do most churches and their members fail to respond appropriately to reported clergy sexual abuse? Two major reasons emerge: (1) a lack of understanding of the nature of the problem and (2) a failure to have well-defined policies and procedures in place. The first reason was addressed above by defining the nature of CSA, its impact, and various prevention strategies. Addressing the second reason involves outlining appropriate and practical ways the church and other entities involved can respond to pastoral sexual misconduct.

Ensuring Justice

When allegations of sexual abuse by a minister come forth, protecting the good name of the church or salvaging the pastor's ministry may become the highest priority. If that is the case, the victims of clergy abuse suffer injustice. True concern for the victimized congregant and her family means the church, first and foremost, must ensure justice through due process.[81]

Justice means just treatment of all persons involved. Justice means no cover-up or whitewashing of evil. Justice means giving a fair and impartial hearing to the allegations of the congregant and to the response of the accused. Justice means refusing to make assumptions or reach conclusions before all the evidence is presented. Justice means launching a formal accountability process immediately. If the charges prove to be true, justice may include removing the abusive pastor from office so that he cannot victimize others. Fortune explains why this is crucial: "When a minister like Donovan [the guilty pastor in her story] behaves unethically and the authorities merely express concern and issue a warning, he is likely to be more discreet in the future but not likely to change his behavior."[82]

The process of ensuring justice is often difficult and painful. The goal of the process is not to resolve a conflict between two persons but to advocate for those who have been harmed and to hold the offending party accountable.[83] Therefore, when it becomes clear that CSA has occurred, the attention and energy of those in charge must be directed toward ensuring justice.

Interpersonal Resolution

The 2002 Southern Baptist Convention adopted a resolution calling for churches and civil authorities to hold ministers guilty of sexual abuse accountable. Thus, the largest non-Catholic flock acknowledged that sexual misconduct among spiritual leaders is a problem that Baptists face. The resolution, however, contained a fatal flaw: It "called for Southern Baptist churches to discipline those guilty of sexual abuse by the pattern provided in Matthew 18."[84]

Some in the church argue that any dispute between two Christians should be resolved between them. Did Jesus not provide detailed instructions that apply to every interpersonal problem in the church, including sexual misconduct (Matt. 18:15–17)? Indeed, the first step outlined by Jesus is a face-to-face encounter between the accused and the accuser (18:15).

At first this approach seems reasonable and biblical. However, a closer examination of the text reveals that the situations involved were private, personal matters. The sexual exploitation of a parishioner by a minister, though personal, is never merely a private matter. Furthermore, this passage describes two people who have a peer relationship. Two believers are advised about reconstructing a marred relationship between equals. Sexual abuse by a minister does not fit this description. In addition, requiring a victimized congregant to confront her abuser privately could actually work against Jesus's intent that victims receive justice. An offending pastor could use the confrontation to silence his victim or even to persuade her that she is responsible for the event.

A study of women who attempted to confront their offender revealed: (1) they were met with strong denials; (2) church members and leaders were reticent to believe their story; and (3) when the victims were heard, they were under intense pressure to bypass the biblical mandate calling for public confrontation ("tell it to the church" [Matt. 18:17]).[85] The call of church leaders "to forgive" replaced the clear call to bring the matter to the congregation. To dispense with justice in the name of forgiveness becomes a simple way for churches to resolve a "messy problem."

Response of the Church

In her lead story about an abusing minister, Fortune raises the question, "How could a credentialed, highly regarded, well-liked pastor in a mainline, middle-class Protestant church do such things and get away with it for so long?" The abuse expert identifies three primary factors that leave churches unprotected against pastoral offenders:

1. The church is myopic about the problem of abuse by clergy.
2. The power of the pastoral role is seldom acknowledged, especially in denominations with a strong congregational polity.

3. The familial model of congregational life is assumed, which makes incest a possibility.[86]

Acceptance of responsibility is the necessary first step in dealing with clergy sexual abuse. Since the church called the minister, the church must hold the minister accountable. At the same time, the church must also accept its share of responsibility.[87]

The first responsibility of a church is to develop guidelines for ministry to victims and their families. The previous discussion under the heading "The Impact of Clergy Sexual Abuse" explains the needs of those victimized by abuse and makes suggestions for responding and ministering to their unique needs.

The second responsibility of a congregation is to develop policies and procedures for responding to accusations of clergy sexual abuse. If a church waits until an allegation occurs before developing procedures, it will be too late. Policies need to be in place to ensure justice and due process. When a report of sexual misconduct by a minister is received, a church must respond immediately. A fair hearing of the victim's account of the abuse needs to be witnessed by an appropriate group without delay, followed by an immediate investigation. Established policies make a speedy response possible. Every report of clergy sexual abuse must be taken seriously. Church leaders must never be guilty of sweeping charges under the rug or denying their significance. Claiming that the matter is a personal problem between two people or practicing a code of secrecy compounds the problem and escalates the damage. Wise policies and procedures will ensure that a church's response is fair, sensitive, and serious. A procedure for responding to charges of clergy sexual abuse may be found in appendix A.

The third responsibility of a church is to develop sound procedures for minister search committees. When a church seeks a minister, it has the responsibility to check a candidate's background and references thoroughly. The editor of the largest Baptist state paper challenged search committees to ask serious questions of people giving references such as "Would you consider calling this person as pastor of your church?" or "Is there any reason why you would be hesitant to hire this person to serve your church?" He added, "If you get any hesitancy, check further."[88]

Although there is always a first time for crossing the ethical boundaries into the forbidden zone, research indicates that a large percentage of incidents involve a pattern of sexual abuse. Failing to check thoroughly the background and references of every potential minister invites tragedy.

Ultimately, church leaders and church members must acknowledge the reality of ministerial sexual misconduct, understand the nature of this behavior, and develop a response that ensures justice through due process and ministry to victims. Anything less than this is less than Christ would have us do.

Suggested Reading

Fortune, M. M. *Is Nothing Sacred? When Sex Invades the Pastoral Relationship*. New York: Harper & Row, 1989.

Gaede, Beth Ann, ed. *When a Congregation Is Betrayed: Responding to Clergy Misconduct*. Hampton, VA: Alban Institute, 2005.

Garland, Diane R. "Clergy Sexual Misconduct: Don't Call It an Affair." *Journal for Family and Community Ministries* 26 (2013): 66–95.

Grenz, Stanley J., and Roy D. Bell. *Betrayal of Trust: Confronting and Preventing Clergy Sexual Misconduct*. 2nd ed. Grand Rapids: Baker Books, 2001.

McClintock, Karen A. *Preventing Sexual Abuse in Congregations*. Hampton, VA: Alban Institute, 2004.

8

Developing a Personal Code of Ethics

A Plan for Integrity in Ministry

In a large church, a complex situation erupted that raised several ethical questions. Over a period of many months, a single college student made advances to several church youth, all under sixteen years of age. To further complicate the matter, the college student also served as a part-time minister on the church staff.

After one young person told his parents of an episode, the family confided in an associate minister. Other incidents soon came to light. Finally, two staff ministers went to the student minister with the accusations. When confronted with the facts, he broke down emotionally and admitted his guilt. Although he expressed deep sorrow over the pain he had caused, he refused to accept advice or seek counseling, stating again and again that his problem was "insurable." He immediately moved to a distant city, where he soon found employment as a student minister in another church.

This crisis posed several questions in regard to ministerial ethics. First, there was the issue of confidentiality. One youth confided in an associate minister, who was unsure how to handle the situation. Should he tell the parents? The pastor? The youth minister? How far does confidentiality extend, and under what conditions can a promise of confidentiality be broken?

A second question concerned obligations to colleagues. What responsibility does one minister have to another, especially if that other is his or her supervisor? A difficult decision came in relation to the student after he moved. After much discussion, the church ministers decided to inform the student minister's new pastor of the incidents, both to protect against recurrences and to open the door for ministry to the student.

Another ministerial ethics question concerned the congregation. How much information should be shared? How would it affect the parents of the youth? Should anything be shared with the church youth, especially since some of them knew of the encounters? Certainly, there were legal obligations to the community at large. The laws of most states require that any act of sexual abuse involving minors be reported.

Most ministers have never reasoned through a professional dilemma such as this one or developed guiding principles. Ordinarily, church leaders simply respond to problems as they arise, hoping their ability to think clearly will carry them through. This approach sometimes works, particularly if the minister is mature, experienced, and well trained. Too often, however, tragic mistakes are made that create vocational headaches and personal heartaches.

Is there a way for clergy to be prepared for the ethical questions inherent to their profession? Are there obligations that are basic to the role of the ordained? Can a code of ethics for ministers be developed that guides and motivates them as they make decisions in their professional life?

Chapter 1 noted that almost all functional definitions of *professional* include self-regulation, usually in the form of a code such as the Hippocratic oath or the Code of Professional Responsibility of the American Bar Association.[1] Virtually every profession has a written code of ethics to guarantee moral performance in the marketplace.

Previously I have stated my conviction that church professionals should follow "mutually accepted rules of conduct" (chap. 2). It seems enigmatic that in the one profession expected to model morality, very few codes of ethics can be found. Although some religious denominations have written codes for their clergy, the number of codes decreased in the last century. Nolan Harmon's classic text on ministerial ethics contains sample codes adopted by five major denominations between 1926 and 1944, but none of these is in current use.[2] A search among these same five denominations uncovered only two with contemporary standards: the Disciples of Christ and the Unitarian Universalist. Occasionally, a smaller group of ministers will develop a written code.[3]

As shown in earlier chapters, the call to Christian ministry leads to many ethical dilemmas. The complex role of the modern minister and the structure of the contemporary church make it difficult for clergy to maintain ethical consistency. The contemporary cleric often feels like a person driving through a large city who makes one wrong turn on the freeway and gets horribly lost. After several detours and dead-end streets, the traveling minister searches for a map.

One possible road map to assist clergy in their professional conduct is a code of ethics. Although such codes by themselves cannot create an ethical person, they can give guidance and warn of dangers. Codes promote personal responsibility by encouraging a minister to think seriously about ethical obligations in ministry. At his daughter's graduation ceremony, Arthur Becker heard the class of veterinarians pledge compliance to a code of ethics. The Lutheran teacher wondered why something similar does not exist for ministers. "I think we need to have underscored for us the fact that being a professional in large part means being accountable to a set of values which guide our behavior as ministers."[4]

The credibility of church shepherds is contingent on their ability to control their own ethical conduct. James Allen Reasons, in his thorough study on the role of codes in ministerial ethics, states, "It is crucial that the minister be able to discern the ethical difficulties unique to his profession and act on them in a biblical manner."[5] In a book dealing with sexual exploitation in the pastoral relationship, Marie Fortune calls for "the establishment of clear ethical guidelines concerning clergy misconduct by each denominational body" and urges church leaders to develop "unequivocal policies and procedural safeguards."[6]

Yet the question remains: Is a ministerial code of ethics a help or a hindrance? A second question follows: Is it possible to write such a code for ministers? Some clergy oppose a written code for theoretical and practical reasons. Some clergy may feel that the strong deontological bent of professional codes inevitably leads to legalism.[7] Other clerics may fear that a denominational hierarchy will use the code as a club to keep disloyal ministers in line and out of significant churches. Ministers of every stripe are nervous about a document that could threaten their pastoral autonomy.

Developing a code of ethics for any professional group poses three major problems: authorship, instruction, and enforcement.[8] First, who should write the code: the professionals, the clients, or third parties? Second, who should teach the code: someone outside the profession or a colleague from within? Third, who should enforce the code: the professionals themselves or others?

There are lesser problems.[9] What subjects should be addressed in a code? Should the document consist of rules, principles, or both? How should the code be distributed? What sanctions are fair? What process should be used to enforce the code? To lead a group of ministers through that wilderness of questions might require another Moses!

Although developing and implementing a code of ethics for ministers is an arduous task with many risks, it is a worthwhile endeavor. It will not be a panacea for every ministerial problem, nor will it automatically ensure safe passage through the moral maze of ministry. Nevertheless, a written code of ethics can serve as a guide and a goal; it can both teach and inspire.

Let us now explore that possibility. First, we want to look at how codes function in the secular professions. The way doctors, lawyers, and other professionals utilize codes can reveal their potential for ministers. This overview will prepare us to address the heart of this chapter: the value of a ministerial code of ethics. A related task—how to write a code of ethics—is a third major concern. One practical result of this study can be for you, the reader, to write your own personal code of ethics.

Codes in the Professions

Visiting professor Amitai Etzioni thought he was overprepared to teach ethics to a group of MBAs at Harvard Business School. He had just completed a book on ethics after thirty years of teaching at Columbia University, the University of California at Berkeley, and George Washington University. He soon discovered, however, that these business-leaders-to-be were not easily swayed. In one class period, after presenting a case study, the professor asked, "Is that ethical?" One student responded, "I'm not sure there is such a thing as the subconscious."

Later the subject of binding moral duties was introduced with the sentence, "I would *like* to go to a movie but *ought* to visit a friend in the hospital." The students challenged the ethical dilemma, saying, "The real reason for your moral quandary is that you are just trying to impress your friends." In the minds of the students, there were no noble acts in human behavior; moral goodness was always a result of baser motives, such as self-interest.

The teacher noted that these MBAs were joining an age-old tradition called reductionism by denying the existence of morality. In so doing, they were also diluting its significance. While indicating that his teaching was not a complete failure, Etzioni did confess that he "had not found a way to help classes full of MBAs see that there is more to life than money, power, fame and self-interest."[10]

For the last two decades, there has been a growing concern about the ethical values of professionals. Blatant moral misbehavior has erupted at the New York Stock Exchange, among corporate CEOs, in Congress and the White House, throughout the health-care system, and among religious leaders.

As noted in chapter 1, this crisis in professional life has been caused primarily by a loss of common values. Alasdair MacIntyre thinks discussing professional ethics in a pluralistic society is impossible because of this lack of shared moral values.[11] Three major movements in Western culture have precipitated the crisis: secularization, pluralism, and relativism. Like an infestation of termites, these cultural trends have eaten away the foundation of professionalism.

Many professionals today lean in the direction of self-interest and away from altruistic service and moral commitments. However, countering this tide are two positive trends: a surge of interest in professional ethics and the reintroduction of ethics studies in schools of law, medicine, business, and other professional institutions.[12]

Not everyone is convinced this will help. When it comes to the use of professional codes, many professionals are skeptical, believing codes are basically self-serving and contribute to unethical conduct. Michael Bayles strongly disagrees, stating that professionals engage in unethical behavior for the same reasons others do: financial gain, fame, the desire to benefit clients or employers, and the simple failure to reflect on the ethical import of one's conduct.[13]

The Purposes of Professional Codes

Why should professionals have codes of ethics? In the broad sense, these codes specify the moral role of the professional and the special obligations understood by the profession. "They tell professionals how to act *as a professional*, as understood by the professional group."[14]

Specifically, written codes of professional ethics have four major purposes. First, they spell out guidelines accepted collectively by peers. "The ethic of the professional is to be found in the dialectical interaction between the conscience of the individual professional and the collective conclusions of the profession as a whole, and the formulations of the 'Professional Code,' always provisional and continually being revised."[15] Having guidelines protects professionals from possible errors and "keeps us from reinventing the wheel every time we make a decision."[16]

Second, codes of ethics protect a profession from incompetent practitioners. Standards are established to protect the medical profession from quacks and the legal profession from shysters. "Although it is not a virtue, competence is probably the most crucial of a professional's characteristics. Professionals have an ethical responsibility not to hold themselves out to do or accept work they are not competent to handle."[17]

Third, codes support and protect individual members.[18] The existence of a code protects a professional from social pressures to violate the code. An engineer can refuse to reveal corporate information simply by saying, "Sorry, my professional code of ethics forbids such disclosures." It also reminds a professional that personal actions represent to society the ethical convictions of colleagues and of the entire profession.[19]

Finally, a professional code defines the nature of a profession.[20] Codes help to define the moral values of a group. Individuals considering entrance into a profession know from its written code what the ethical tone of that particular vocation is.

Karen Lebacqz has observed that if codes are simply guidelines for specific behavior in certain circumstances, then they rapidly become either too vague to be helpful or too rigid to adapt to change. She makes this proposal: "Rather than looking for specific guidelines for *action* in professional codes, they might be better understood as statements about the *image* of the profession and the *character* of professionals."[21] Understood this way, codes are not simply rules for action. They identify the moral stress points within a profession and present a model of a "good" professional.

The Nature of Professional Codes

Professional ethics usually takes the form of a code, contract, or covenant.[22] A contract involves a promise between people in which an obligation to perform is expected, followed by a reward when the action is accomplished. The covenant approach involves both codal and contractual elements but is based on a gift between two parties, resulting in a covenant promise and a change in the covenanted people because of this relationship (Gen. 17:1–22). The code approach is the most common for evaluating professions, professionals, and their conduct. It involves listing the obligations a professional has in regard to clients, colleagues, and the community.

In their classic study of the professions, A. M. Carr-Saunders and P. A. Wilson note that most professional codes are characterized by positive prescriptions and negative sanctions.[23] These codes usually try to balance the ethical concerns of the professionals, their clients, and the general public.

Do professionals live by different moral standards from the rest of society? Some say that they do, believing that higher standards give professionals a sense of mission to act appropriately. Others just as vigorously contend that they do not. Two sets of standards breed elitism, confuse the public, increase distrust of professionals, and put nonprofessionals in a vulnerable position.

A better understanding involves a combination of these two points of view. Ordinary morality governs all members of society, including professionals, but a profession's special ethical obligations are reflected in a professional code. These codes do not promote a unique system for an elite group "but rather . . . utilize societal values to give the professional useful, specific direction."[24]

The Structure of Professional Codes

Professional codes have a long history. The earliest known code is a medical code found on a stone pillar dated 2250 BC. Attributed to Hammurabi, the code contains a diverse set of laws with a section dealing specifically with the physician-patient relationship. Hippocrates of Greece (350 BC) wrote the most famous medical oath (which bears his name) to separate medicine from magic. Also called the doctor's oath, it established a formal code of conduct for physicians who treated disease. In the Middle Ages, Maimonides, an Egyptian who practiced medicine (AD 1135–1204), wrote ethical guidelines that obligated a physician to treat any patient needing care regardless of financial status.

Codes of ethics vary considerably in content and structure. The majority tend to include certain basic categories of duties. The key ingredients of professional codes are:

- private or personal obligations
- responsibilities to clients and special interest groups
- obligations to colleagues and to the profession
- responsibilities to the community or society as a whole

C. S. Calian surveyed eight codes from various professions and developed a list of fifteen items of commonality. Six of the fifteen items are personal obligations the professional assumes: a sense of calling, the value of knowledge and skill, the need for continuing education, the derivation of primary income from the profession, the need to reduce conflicts of interest, and the need to maintain good health.[25]

A second major area covered by professional codes of ethics relates to obligations between the professional and the client. Calian's list includes questions about confidentiality, the primacy of service over remuneration, the duty to know one's limits and consult others, and the attitude of respect for the worth of every individual.

A third area of responsibility contained in most professional codes concerns obligations individual professionals have in regard to their profession and their colleagues. In the eight codes Calian reviewed, one item relating to fellow professionals made his list of fifteen: the need to cooperate with colleagues. Three specific obligations professionals have in regard to one another are to offer respect, to provide information concerning the competence and character of applicants to the profession, and to bear their fair share of the work in the profession's social role.[26]

Finally, what are the obligations professionals have in regard to their community or society at large? Calian listed three: to be sensitive to consumers' rights and well-being, to be discrete in publications and solicitations, and to exemplify good citizenship.

A professional's responsibility for public good has at least three other facets. First, there is the role of social leadership, such as service to charitable organizations or governmental boards and agencies. A second facet of responsibility for public good is the improvement of professional knowledge and skills. A third facet is to preserve and enhance the social role of the profession, which ultimately benefits society.[27]

This brief overview of the structure of professional codes reveals something important for the formation of a ministerial code of ethics. Secular codes typically outline the kinds of ethical dilemmas professionals encounter, the loyalties expected of them, the duties they perform, and the conflicts their role creates. These obligations are not simply codes for action but statements that project the character of the professional.[28]

The Enforcement of Professional Codes

Before we leave the subject of professional codes of ethics, it is necessary to explore one other issue: enforcement. Historically, professional groups have been self-regulating, which most believe is the best approach. The traditional method for ensuring compliance has been selective admission and discipline of members, mainly through sanctions. Some ethicists believe a focus on sanctions is a mistake because there is no evidence that adequate sanctions (whether blame or loss of license) deter misconduct by others.[29] William May strongly denounces using a code to solve the problem of professional discipline, preferring an approach that seeks to be remedial and inclusive rather than codal and exclusive.[30]

The enforcement of codes of ethics poses many problems.[31] The basic problem of distribution is often overlooked. The regular distribution of a written code to members is not sufficient to ensure compliance. On the other hand, simply posting an organization's code on a bulletin board will almost certainly encourage noncompliance. The assignment of accountability is also vital to enforcement. Experts contend that enforcement committees should be composed of both professionals and laypersons to prevent in-house protectionism.

The enforcement of codes of ethics is chiefly dependent on the willingness of colleagues and the public to report violations. Once guilt has been determined, disciplinary action usually takes one of three forms: censure, suspension, or termination.

The Limitations of Professional Codes

What then can be said about professional codes of ethics as they apply to ministerial ethics? Do they benefit the professions today?

Many people feel uncomfortable with a rules approach to morality, which professional codes appear to be. This deontological bent seems to downplay the role of character and overlook the complex question of motives and consequences. As many note, the inner integrity of a professional may be assumed, but it is seldom encouraged in the codal approach to professional ethics.

Another concern regarding traditional professional ethics is the failure to consider the nature of social roles. Codes of ethics fail to recognize the "power gap" between professional and client. It is also difficult to translate the ethical ideals of justice and liberation into codes of ethics.[32]

A third concern could be labeled self-interest. Lisa Newton attacks professional codes as "a code of Professional Manners oriented toward a Professional Image for the protection of Professional Compensation."[33] Her scathing critique notes that codes limit advertising, suppress competition, and forbid contradiction of professional judgments, which she calls "gentlemanly etiquette." Yale professor Gaylord Noyce agrees, stating that the codes of professional groups "are shot through with collusive self-interest."[34]

No doubt, codes also have a serious problem with accountability. Because the authorship, instruction, and enforcement of codes generally take place within each professional organization, the perception is that professionals are more concerned with self-interest than with ethical conduct. This obstacle is best overcome by including nonprofessionals who have no vested interests in all aspects of the code process.

Despite these limitations, professional organizations continue to depend on codes of ethics to ensure standardized behavior. A report by the Business Roundtable found that 84 percent of Fortune 500 companies have a code of ethics.[35] Professional codes communicate the basic ethical expectations within an association of professionals. Codes of ethics will serve professionals, their clients, and society at large for some time to come.

A Ministerial Code of Ethics

According to some, a code of ethics for ministers seems about as necessary as running shoes for a jaguar. "After all, ministers live and breathe morality, don't they? Their job is *upholding* a community's ethics, isn't it? So why a code for pastors?"[36]

In the earliest days of the settlement of Texas, a historian wrote of the organization of a "Committee of Vigilance" in May 1837. It was composed of six Protestant ministers "to prevent imposters from securing the confidence of the people, in the exercise of ministerial functions."[37] This must have been one of the earliest attempts to codify ministerial ethics.

A discussion of standards for ministers appeared in 1928 titled *Ministerial Ethics and Etiquette: The Minister's Own Manual of Conduct—Practical Guidance for Specific Situations*. Like so many early ministerial codes, "it is interesting as a period piece—but it is minimalism in ethics."[38] The book contains some discussion about relationships with colleagues, a denomination, and a community, but most of the lengthy admonitions concern personal life, finances, conducting worship, appropriate dress, and professional etiquette.[39]

Since these words were penned, expectations for an ethical ministry have increased greatly. Moral lapses among the clergy have alarmed parishioners and aroused the public. Church leaders in every denomination are calling for a thorough study of ethical issues involving the clergy and seeking ways to increase moral accountability in the ministry. Concerned that denominations and local churches are not holding pastors to high moral standards, Focus on the Family in 2003 asked fifty thousand pastors to adopt a "Shepherd's Covenant" for greater accountability.[40] In 2012, the National Association of Evangelicals (NAE) urged pastors to seek a common moral ground by uniting under a consistent code of ethics. NAE leaders said the new code will provide uniform guidance to church leaders across the forty denominations that compose the nation's largest evangelical group.[41]

After a Colorado district court awarded $1.2 million in damages to a woman who had an affair with an Episcopal cleric, Bishop Peter Lee of Virginia warned his priests: "Laity and others who turn to the clergy for pastoral counsel and prayer have every right to expect their most painful secrets to be safe, their most confusing thoughts to be heard, their hopes and their aspirations to be received with respectful concern. But some persons expect their clergy to provide the permanent tenderness of intimacy they missed as children or that eludes them now as spouses."[42] His letter also cautioned priests against offering themselves as "substitute objects" for the longings of their parishioners.

Absent from the bishop's communiqué, however, was any acknowledgment of clergy vulnerability or any plan for prevention.

This episode highlights one of the difficulties ministers share with the secular professions. They are self-protective. Jürgen Moltmann reminds us that clergy protect the status quo. We fear we have much to lose if we examine our practice as clergy in the context of new understandings about our responsibilities; if we find ourselves wanting, we will have to change. We may have to give up established ways.[43]

As already observed, professional groups have traditionally regulated themselves (though not always with success), utilizing codes of ethics and disciplining boards. The professions regularly examine their responsibilities to their constituencies, evaluate their behavior, compare codes, and work to improve ethical practice. Should there be equivalent accountability among the clergy? It is indeed startling that these concerns are so seldom raised by the ordained. Some believe ministers do not need ethical reflection because ministry is a moral work and therefore self-correcting. Others claim it is demeaning to approach ministry as one would a secular profession.

A major reason codes of ethics for ministers are so rare, claims Paul Camenisch, is the clergy's dedication to "atypical moral commitment." Such a commitment is a significant part of the self-image of the minister and the public's expectations. "I would suggest that one reason the clergy has been slower than the other major professions to develop its own distinctive ethic is that this atypical moral commitment was assumed to be so central to the profession that many thought it insulting to suggest that specific rules and guidelines were needed to require it."[44]

Because of the separation of church and state in the United States, the public sector ordinarily does not regulate the standards of clergy as they do those of other professionals, except in two areas: performing marriage ceremonies and counseling.[45] From an ethical perspective, this should be no problem. Clergy standards should always be higher than legal codes, which are only society's baselines. In spite of this or any other variation, the question remains, "Does this difference free us from the accountability we expect of sisters and brothers working in other vineyards?"[46] We cannot presume that just because preachers proclaim justice, righteousness, and morality that they will be just, righteous, and moral.

Ministers are accountable for their behavior not only because of professional expectations but also because of their commitment to Christian ethics. Being a moral example in ministry is a biblical expectation.[47] Ethical conduct based on theological convictions is the very soil in which the clergy work. A ministerial code of ethics is supported by biblical principles, theological conclusions, professional standards, and practical considerations. That is why a clergy code of ethics, properly developed, clearly written, and appropriately enforced, is needed.

Unlike other professionals, ministers will probably never be driven by outside forces to begin this task, nor should they be. Their own moral convictions and vocational expectations should motivate them to seek the highest ethical standards for ministry. Their calling from God, personal character, and commitment to Christian ministry will allow them to do no less.

The Purposes of a Ministerial Code

The overarching purpose of a ministerial code of ethics is accountability. Ministers sometimes resist codes and regulations because they want to be answerable to no one except God. When questioned about financial accountability, televangelist Paul Crouch of Trinity Broadcasting Network declared publicly that "the Almighty [was] his only watchdog." An editorial in *Christianity Today* responded that eventually we all get what is coming to us, but "in the meantime it helps to have structures that encourage us to behave."[48]

Professional codes are usually written to specify the moral obligations of the professional, as understood by the professional group. Likewise, a code of ethics for ministers should reflect how the ordained of God should conduct their ministry, as understood by their fellow ministers. In other words, a Christian minister is accountable not only to God but also to other members of the clergy. Codes are usually developed over many years and represent the combined experience of many people. Writing an adequate code, therefore, is more than a personal enterprise.

The four major purposes of professional codes also apply to clergy codes. The first purpose of a ministerial code is to provide guidelines that reflect the values of ministry. Clergy ethics affirms that to be a Christian minister means assuming certain basic obligations common to all clergy. These norms guide those called to serve toward an ethical ministry and stress the areas in which ministers are uniquely vulnerable.

Archibald Hart of Fuller Seminary describes a strange paradox in Christian ministry: "We can be supersensitive to sin and immoral behaviors, but we are often oblivious to the need for ethical boundaries. This partially accounts for the fall of upright, spiritual, and well-intentioned pastors."[49] Hart concludes that the underlying problem is not so much a lack of morality as a lack of broad ethical guidelines to govern the practice of ministry.

Guidelines for ministers serve three functions.[50] First, they articulate personal ethical standards that are significant. Such standards relate to financial and family responsibilities and classic labor-management issues such as work schedules, study habits, vacations, and sabbaticals. Second, guidelines govern expectations regarding a minister's conduct in relation to colleagues, the congregation, and the community. Third, guidelines express ministerial ideals. Like the best examples from professional codes, clergy norms should stretch toward a higher standard of behavior than is currently being practiced. The Disciples Code reads, "I will seek to be Christlike in my personal attitudes and conduct toward all people regardless of race, class, or creed."[51]

The second purpose of a ministerial code relates to competency. At first we may think this trait applies more to the secular professions than to the ministry. Doctors need to be well trained and to keep up with the latest medical discoveries. People confide in lawyers to protect their legal rights. Physicians and lawyers possess "threatening knowledge" that, if used carelessly or improperly, could be harmful. Yet ministers also have threatening knowledge in the form of confidential information and the knowledge they possess about God. For a pastor to be competent in the use of this knowledge requires at least two essentials: ministry skills and mental and spiritual health. Most ministerial codes require ministers to grow "through comprehensive reading and careful study and by attending . . . conferences" and to cultivate their personal devotional lives.[52]

Third, a code of ethics can support and protect an individual minister. Under the topic "financial matters," a 1990 Presbyterian code states, "Ministers and church professionals shall not use church funds, accounts, and/or resources . . . [or] parishioner funds, accounts, and/or resources for personal or private advantage."[53] Codified statements such as this one can protect a pastor from behavior that could lead to serious personal or congregational problems. Hart views morality as the edge of a precipice. On one side is safe ground (non-sin); on the other there is disaster (sin). "It's only one step from safety to falling off the cliff. A code of ethics is like a fence erected well back from the precipice edge. It warns all those who come close that this is dangerous territory: CAUTION! PASS HERE AT YOUR OWN RISK."[54]

A final purpose of an ethical code for ministers is to define the moral necessities of the ministerial profession. For the person planning to become a minister, as well as for the layperson, a written code explains the ethical expectations of the pastoral vocation. For example, an association of ministers in the United Church of Christ has completed a policy on sexual ethics for their group. The document begins by explicitly defining sexual misconduct:

- sexual advances, welcomed or unwelcomed
- requests for sexual favors

- inappropriate affection such as kissing, touching, bumping, patting
- any sexual contact related to terms of employment
- any sexual contact that exploits the vulnerability of a parishioner, client, or employee
- dating of parishioners by religious professionals is a gray area filled with ambiguity; in such situations, consultation with colleagues is essential[55]

There should be no doubt among this group of ministers or their congregations what is construed as sexual misconduct.

These four purposes of ministerial codes should not mislead a person to view them as a collection of moral rules to keep ministers out of trouble. In a sense, "a professional code of ethics is simply an intensification of the ethical concerns of normal life, but an intensification needed because of the more specialized role, the intense knowledge in human situations of high risk and vulnerability, which are a part of functioning as an ordained pastor."[56] As such, codes are not merely guidelines for how ministers are to act in certain situations. If so, they would always be too specific or too general to be helpful.

As Karen Lebacqz has so well explained, codes of ethics for ministers are better understood and utilized as statements about the "image of the profession and the character of the professionals."[57] Clergy codes of ethics reflect the virtues and values of the person called to minister in Christ's name. Simply put, a code paints the portrait of a good minister.

The Structure of a Ministerial Code

A growing concern about the spiritual formation of seminary students and their readiness for ministry led the Association of Theological Schools (ATS) to conduct intensive research in the late twentieth century. To develop a profile for ministry, the study group surveyed over four thousand clergy and laity representing all denominations affiliated with the ATS. The results, along with recommendations, were published in the document *Clergy Assessment and Career Development*. One section of the report reveals some serious deficiencies in ministerial morality, which leads the researchers to make three proposals: (1) that a more formal code of ethics be established to help regulate ministry relationships, (2) that a pastor set up an accountability system as a prevention strategy, and (3) that a minister know his or her personal limits and vulnerabilities.[58]

Let us assume that a group of ministers took the first charge seriously. What topics should they address in a code? Should the document be composed of principles or specific obligations? In particular, what categories should be covered in a ministerial code?

As a result of a renewed interest in clergy ethics, a host of publications have appeared. A survey of the literature reveals several recurring themes, many focusing on the moral character of the cleric. According to these writers, an ethical minister should possess certain fundamental virtues: trustworthiness, prudence, faithfulness, truthfulness, and integrity.

When the conduct of the ordained is specifically described, certain issues rise to the surface. Presbyterian professors Walter Wiest and Elwyn Smith are most concerned with truth telling, especially in relation to plagiarism, letters of recommendation, and theological differences. A philosophy professor writing about "Professional Ethics and the Practice of Religion" suggests that any discussion of the clergy/parishioner relationship should deal with clerical roles, truth telling, confidentiality, paternalism, and behavior control.[59]

Another text analyzes organized religion from a critical point of view. The book begins by looking at three central ethical issues: confidentiality, "risk taking," and "convert seeking." The author seems most concerned with religious groups that endanger the life and health of members or use coercive conversion techniques.[60]

Studies such as these do pinpoint some of the more obvious and crucial issues in ministerial ethics. As might be expected, however, one of the best ways to analyze the structure of clergy codes is to study existing ones.

During the early part of the last century, several mainline denominations developed formal codes of ethics for their ministers (app. B). In comparison to these early examples, the few denominational codes in use today appear to be extensively updated (app. C). The present trend is away from denominational documents and toward codes constructed by smaller associations of ministers, usually covering only one area of responsibility, such as clergy sexual ethics or counseling ethics.

An analysis of these statements reveals a certain common structure and great similarity in content. One thing that is not apparent is the kind of language that best fits a clergy code. One Christian psychologist acknowledges that "some of the unique roles of the pastor don't easily lend themselves to ethical codes"; therefore, he prefers basic principles.[61] However, if a primary purpose of a code is to serve as a guideline, then specific obligations should be spelled out in addition to guiding principles.

Another purpose of codes is ensuring competency. This intent does not surface in many of the present or past documents. Theological, pastoral, and spiritual qualifications for ministers need to be clearly defined to endorse skills in ministry.

The practice of ministry also involves many unique roles and responsibilities. Most written codes address the major areas of ministerial vulnerability (such as sex, money, and power), as well as unique pressure points (such as family, confidentiality, and plagiarism). Codal statements that cover these topics serve to support and protect a minister by clearly defining ethical boundaries.

Sometimes a code begins with an introductory paragraph, a preamble affirming a minister's sense of calling to the ministry and commitment to ethical integrity. The Disciples Code begins: "I am a minister of the Lord Jesus Christ, called of God to proclaim the unsearchable riches of His love. Therefore, I voluntarily adopt the following principles in order that through dedication and self-discipline I may set a more worthy example for those whom I seek to lead and serve" (see app. C).

As already shown in this book, a clear definition of pastoral ethics can be given by addressing four areas of obligation in a minister's life: to self and family, to the congregation, to colleagues, and to the community. Most clergy codes follow this format in one way or another. To lay the groundwork for a code of our own, let us look at each of these four worlds of the minister.

Normally overlooked in other professional codes are the personal and family responsibilities of the professional. Not so in codes of ethics for ministers. The personal integrity of a servant of God is at the heart of ministry. Guarding that integrity involves such obvious matters as lifestyle, which is why most denominations have written and unwritten codes defining conduct unbecoming of a minister. The codes cited in appendixes B and C are quite specific: They require a minister to keep physically fit, avoid debts, be scrupulously honest, pay bills before moving, and give ample time to family life. When pastoral needs collide with family needs, a minister must be sure that church duties do not become an idol before which the spouse and children are sacrificed.

The personal integrity of a pastor is important because it affects credibility. As the "medium of the message," the life of the prophet of God must point to the truth of the gospel. Credibility in ministry includes such basic matters as a minister's covenant to cultivate a devotional life, reserve study time, refuse to plagiarize sermons, and keep in touch with the best religious thought.

Ministers are forever pulled by weekly necessities (sermon preparation, newsletter articles, committee meetings), unanticipated ministries (funerals, counseling, visiting the ill), and the need and desire for spiritual development (reading, conferences, spiritual disciplines). Meanwhile, the family waits at the dinner table. The busy church leader desperately wants to keep work and family life in proper balance. A well-written code can help a minister establish priorities and stick to them.

The second area addressed in a ministerial code is the congregation. Most difficult problems for professionals appear in relation to parishioners. Although the member of a congregation is a "client," several important differences exist between a typical professional-client association and a minister-parishioner relationship.[62] For one thing, the distinction between laity and clergy is not as well defined as it is for the client and other professionals. The authority of the minister is perceived differently from that of a professional (and it should be). Another major disparity is that a minister's "clients" are an organized group; in fact, in many denominations the vote of the congregation determines employment, termination, and salary.

This reality imposes a vulnerability on a minister. No doctor worries about a disgruntled patient starting a campaign among clients to have his or her salary frozen. Yet every time a pastor serves an individual member, possible repercussions in the flock must be considered. Why? Misperceptions could erupt into church conflict and cause the pastor's dismissal.

With all this in mind, what ethical obligations do pastors have regarding parishioners? One shepherding sin is almost universal in codes for ministers. It is "the unethical aspect of what we call 'sheep stealing' or proselytizing members from another community of faith."[63] This practice, perhaps influenced by the competitive nature of American business, undercuts the credibility of the pastoral office. Other responsibilities involving congregations that are covered in codes include service rather than salary as the primary motivation for ministry, integrity in preaching, fairness in dealing with factions, impartiality in administrative decisions, and the basic obligation to nurture the believing community.

The limits of confidentiality are another issue with which all professionals wrestle. Many states now have legal codes that carefully prescribe "confessional privilege." Beyond what is legally required, a pastor must carefully consider obligations regarding confidentiality. A minister's obligation is often stated in codes as an absolute principle: "The confidential statements made to a minister by his parishioners are sacred and not to be divulged" (Presbyterian Code). It would be better to word the standard in a way that allows each minister to define the rare circumstances in which information may be divulged.[64]

Although ministers have a community of colleagues, they often lack structural unity. Ministry can be a lonely profession. Most ministers confess that they need support from their colleagues, including moral discernment, empathetic understanding, encouragement, ministry resources, and general camaraderie. Too often the relationships among ministers are characterized by competition and conspiracy rather than mutual blessing. Clergy can find many positive ways to build healthy relationships with other ministers and still uphold ethical standards. Almost all codes emphasize four basic obligations ministers have regarding one another:

> I will not speak scornfully or in derogation of any colleague in public. In any private conversation critical of a colleague, I will speak responsibly and temperately. [Unitarian Universalist Ministers Association (UUMA) Code]

> It is unethical for a minister to interfere directly or indirectly with the parish work of another minister. [Methodist Code]

> Except in emergencies, ministerial service should not be rendered to the members of another parish without the knowledge of the minister of the parish. [Presbyterian Code]

> If I am to share the ministry of a church with (an)other minister(s), I will earnestly seek clear delineation of responsibility, accountability, and channels of communication before responsibilities are assumed. [UUMA Code]

A variety of other collegial responsibilities appear in some current codes (app. C). The Disciples Code adds a number of pledges: not to compete with other ministers for pulpits or honors; not to embarrass successors by "meddling in the affairs" of a former church; to show courtesy to predecessors; to show loyal support to a pastor after retirement; and to show respect toward all ministers, regardless of the size or nature of their field.

The Eastern Oklahoma Presbytery Code (EOP) is thorough—twenty-five pages written in a narrative style. Under "Colleague Relationships" the authors present forty-four imperatives in nine categories. Most of these obligations cover the common ground of staff relationships, denominational duties, treatment of predecessors and successors, and the role of retired pastors. The document does plow some virgin soil, however, in two important areas overlooked in other codes: the responsibilities of the "minister-without-pastoral-charge" and proper relationships with other professionals.[65]

Are there limits to clergy collegiality? We all know ministers who destroy healthy congregations. Some are on the way out of ministry. Others are truly incompetent. A few have serious spiritual, moral, and emotional problems that will not change until they receive help. When such pastors fail and are forced to move on, do ministers close ranks behind the flawed colleagues and try to find them another place of service? Herein is a major ministerial dilemma. How can ministers be supportive of a comrade in the ministry and at the same time honestly fulfill their responsibilities to other congregations? Truthfulness in letters of recommendation and "truth in love" to the guilty colleague are a starting point.[66] One current code reads, "Should I know that a colleague is engaged in practices that are damaging . . . I will speak openly and frankly to her/him and endeavor to be of help" (UUMA Code).

The final statement of the Congregational Code is a principle that summarizes for ministers the responsibility they owe one another: "As members of the same profession and brothers in the service of a common Master, the relation between ministers should be one of frankness, of comradeship, and of cooperation."

The final area usually covered by traditional ministerial codes is a minister's responsibility to the community. This appears to be one of the weaker sections of most written codes. Three of the four early codes were silent on this subject. Only the Unitarian Code spoke to community obligations: The minister is "not under obligations to marry every couple that comes to him to be married," and as a citizen "he should, therefore, be faithful to his public obligations and should respond to reasonable requests for assistance in community work."

More recent codes have more to say on the subject, but most of the counsel centers on the self-interests of the church rather than on service to the community. The concern of the Disciples Code seems to be a fear that the church or its ministers might be corrupted by the world; thus, it warns ministers "to be human . . . but . . . never lower [your] ideals in order to appear 'a good fellow.'" It further cautions its clergy to avoid "funeral or marriage rackets" and to beware of consuming the time of business and professional people with "unimportant matters."

A more positive word about church and community as it relates to the ministerial profession comes from three denominational groups. First is an obligation to be a moral and spiritual leader in the community: "I will maintain a prophetic pulpit, offering to the community religious and ethical leadership" (UUMA Code).

Second is a charge to remember that one's primary calling is to be the pastor of a congregation, a minister's primary community. This means, on the one hand, "I consider that my first duty to my community is to be a conscientious pastor and leader of my own congregation" (Disciples Code). On the other hand, "Ministers may assume outside commitments that do not detract from their pastoral responsibilities" (EOP Code). The Disciples document adds that this primary responsibility to the church should never be used "as an easy excuse to escape reasonable responsibilities that the community calls upon me to assume."

Only rarely do codes direct pastors to step into the community to render beneficial service. Whereas professional codes emphasize that doctors, lawyers, and engineers have an obligation to be social leaders, assume community responsibilities, and work for the betterment of society, this concept is glaringly absent from ministerial codes.

One clergy code prohibits accepting "fees or gifts as payment for business or professional referrals" (EOP Code). Another encourages "sympathetic support to neighboring ministers or other religious bodies" (UUMA Code). The only time the codes of ethics for ministers focus on the needs of the community is when they say, "I will encourage members' participation in efforts to solve community problems" (UUMA Code), and "Ministers shall support efforts to better that community" (EOP Code). Obviously, this area of a minister's responsibility needs serious thought. If the church is to be salt and light to the world (Matt. 5:13–16), then the moral leaders of the Christian community surely have significant obligations to society.

What have we discovered then about the structure of ministerial codes? First, the language of the codes is dualistic: Both specific norms and general principles are declared. Second, certain key issues, such as confidentiality and truthfulness, appear in most codes. Third, the points at which a minister is most vulnerable ethically, such as sexual temptation and imbalanced work habits, receive a great deal of attention. Finally, most codes for ministers focus on the four major categories outlined above: self and family, the congregation, colleagues, and the community.

The Enforcement of a Ministerial Code

Earlier we noted three major difficulties in developing a code of ethics: authorship, instruction, and enforcement. The first two problems will be discussed when we consider how to write a code. Before us now is the issue of enforcement.

When the National Religious Broadcasters formally established its ethics and financial accountability code in January 1989, the organization told members to comply within three months or they would be dismissed. Before the year ended, officials admitted they had been overly optimistic about implementation and enforcement.[67] The variety of ways church groups have enforced their codes, or failed to do so, indicates the complexity of this issue for ministers as well.

By assumption of the role, a minister vows to abide by certain codes of conduct, whether written or not. Formal clergy codes are based on this accountability. A ministerial code of ethics, by its very nature, assumes the acceptance of personal responsibility, the reporting of violations, and effective enforcement. Yet this last matter of disciplining code breakers has long troubled churches and denominations.

A minister who chairs an ethics guidelines committee in his religious body told of a dilemma. One of the denomination's prominent pastors became sexually involved with a married parishioner. After he expressed repentance for his failure, the erring cleric's church voted to restore him. Pastoral colleagues in the Ministers Association felt they also had an obligation to respond, as the group's code of ethics had been violated. After investigation by the association, the group sent a letter of admonition to the clergyman.

When church shepherds break their covenants to God and fail to fulfill their responsibilities to their congregation, what should be done? Should a minister report the sexual abuse of a parishioner by another pastor in the name of collegial support? What enforcement procedures should churches or denominations follow? What sanctions, if any, are appropriate? How should the laity and clergy relate to a fallen minister who needs healing and restoration?

As noted earlier, professional groups historically have been self-regulating. The importance of including both professionals and laypersons on enforcement committees, say experts, cannot be overstressed. Another essential ingredient is the willingness of colleagues and the public to report problems. Key components in effective enforcement by committees are confidentiality, fair and just representation, and the release of committee members from legal liability. The most common practice of most groups is to have an ethics committee that decides on all aspects of ethical behavior. As one regulatory board said, "We are the police, we are the prosecution, we are the grand jury, and the petit jury."[68]

Studying the practices of churches and denominational groups in response to ministers accused of unethical behavior is indeed a frustrating exercise. Most congregations have no established procedure, church groups act in an informal way; they simply deal with offenses as they arise. When a pastor or other staff member is charged with a transgression, an established church authority (deacons, elders, or a committee) usually investigates the accusation. They then either exonerate the falsely accused or sanction the guilty.

There is no end to the ways religious bodies respond to ministerial misconduct. This obvious inconsistency among churches cannot help but diminish ministerial accountability. Why should the ordained seriously reflect on their ethical obligations if church and denominational expectations are lax or nonexistent? The ministerial codes written during the first half of the twentieth century (app. B) contain no instructions about enforcement. The documents seem to assume, with unrealistic optimism, that the ethical ideals contained in the codes would so motivate ministers that no enforcement would be necessary.

The more recent pastoral codes (app. C) are not so naive. "A profession that will not police itself runs the danger of being policed by others," states the EOP Code. Although the newer documents evidence a great deal of diversity, they all contain a procedure for compliance. At the same time, none of them outlines a method of distribution of the code, and only one of them addresses the vital responsibility of reporting infractions.

Two documents that model a more complete procedure for enforcement are the EOP Code and the UUMA *Guidelines*.[69] They are also helpful because of the church traditions they represent—the limited hierarchical structure of the Presbyterians and the congregational ecclesiology of the Unitarian Universalists.

In the EOP Code, a great deal of space is given to defining the responsibility of the governing authorities of the church. Briefly described, the process follows this order:

1. Allegations are brought to an elder.
2. The accused is confronted.
3. The elder takes the accusation to session.
4. The session confronts the pastor and investigates.
5. If the charge is false, the accuser is disciplined.
6. If the allegation is true, the Committee on Ministry (COM) is contacted.
7. The COM may address the problem or assign it to a committee.
8. The investigation is done by a special disciplinary committee, which decides on sanctions.
9. The presbytery may initiate its own investigation without a request.

The EOP report also includes a policy regarding the immoral or unethical behavior of "Potential Members of Presbytery." This "front door" regulation determines the moral fitness of ministers who seek membership in the presbytery.

Although the doctrines of the Unitarian Universalist denomination are significantly different from those of most Christian churches, its government is basically congregational, which is similar to that of Baptist and Congregational denominations, as well as that of many evangelical churches. UUMA ministers are called and ordained by a local congregation. If they plan to move to another church, they need to receive ministerial credentials from the Fellowship Committee, which is the gateway to membership in the Ministers Association.

An accusation against a UUMA minister is first handled by the local church. The *Guidelines* explain procedures for dismissing a minister by vote of the congregation and the conditions of termination. Charges of immoral behavior can be taken to the Fellowship Committee, which can investigate the allegations. The Ministers Association may also initiate investigation, usually at the request of colleagues. A minister determined to be guilty by either group faces six possible sanctions: three levels of censure (caution, admonition, or reprimand) and three severe sanctions (probation, suspension, or removal from UUMA membership).[70]

A major problem in ministerial ethics in the twenty-first century is the proliferation of large, nondenominational churches led by a charismatic pastor (who usually has dictatorial control over the church). Through television ministry and high-powered advertising, these "contemporary churches" gather a large following and, it seems, the twenty-first-century church member is attracted to the anonymity of these congregations, especially the lack of responsibility other than occasionally attending and giving financial support. With no denominational ties and with church authority vested in the pastor (sometimes along with a handpicked group of "elders"), ordinarily ministerial ethics are defined by the "man at the top."

To their credit, professional codes of ethics over the years have developed carefully worded procedures that prescribe enforcement of their standards. To their detriment, ministerial codes of ethics seldom deal with compliance. With rare exception, the few that do will seldom go beyond a few words of counsel about the censure or termination of ministers. Parachurch group codes are only slightly better.

What lessons can we learn from these limited attempts at enforcement of ethical standards by denominations, associations of ministers, and other Christian groups? Obviously, ensuring compliance to a code is a difficult task with many risks. Perhaps that is why enforcement procedures are so rare among clergy codes. Nevertheless, since ministerial codes are based on accountability, there must be some group to which a minister is accountable.

This brief overview also reveals the importance of having a system for reporting violations that is free from intimidation or coercion. Perhaps the most difficult aspect of enforcement is the one assigned to an authoritative group: the responsibility to investigate charges, determine actions, and apply sanctions. A committee adequate for this task must represent all involved, both laity and clergy.

To make certain that enforcement procedures are just and complete, a well-thought-out and clearly written policy is imperative. Of course, the church polity of a person's denomination will significantly influence the entire process.

This discussion of a ministerial code of ethics has made known the purpose, nature, and structure of codes, as well as their enforcement. Other professional ethics models have revealed the strengths and the weaknesses of clergy codes in general. Now the discussion becomes more specific. As we approach the final assignment, that of writing a code of ethics suitable for today's minister, we will seek to apply what we have learned thus far.

How to Write a Code of Ethics

Voices from many sectors of the religious community are calling for a recon-
sideration of the value of a written code of ethics for ministers. "Many groups,
especially mainline Protestants, have elaborate books of order or discipline
governing the conduct of their clergy. Even evangelicals have come to realize
in recent years that there must be some way to guide ministerial conduct in
matters that are not made explicit in Scripture."[71]

Recently, the National Association of Evangelicals (NAE) urged pastors
to find a common moral ground by uniting under a consistent code of ethics.
An NAE survey claimed that seven in ten evangelical leaders are not required
by their congregations to sign a formal code of ethics.[72] A study by the Association of Theological Schools attempted to assess the correlation between
readiness for ministry and seminary training. The published report contained
many recommendations. In a section stressing the importance of personal
growth for clergy, the authors noted with regret that ministers are "currently
only loosely bound by a moral code that is subject to differing interpretations."
Therefore, they proposed that "a more formal code of ethics be established
to help regulate ministry relationships."[73]

More than two decades ago, the growing problem of pastoral abuse of
women was the subject of an article in the *Christian Century*. One solution
suggested by the alarmed author was the creation of "a new ethical code that
accurately names and recognizes the problem."[74]

Another voice supporting codes of ethics for ministers is that of a psychology professor. H. Newton Maloney observes that clergy malpractice issues are increasing, and ministers have no agreed-upon statement of ethics to
which they can subscribe and by which they can be judged. He adds: "A recent
national survey concluded that there is a dearth of concern for professional
ethics among church bodies. . . . This lack of overt concern, coupled with
denominational protectionism and the separation of church and state, leads
me to say that the statement that there is no agreed upon code of ethics for
clergy across denominations is not an exaggeration."[75]

Ministers, unlike other professionals, have no central organization or single
code of ethics to which they can turn for support. Even among religious
denominations, as we have just seen, there are relatively few statements of
ethical guidelines for clergy. It is alarming that in the two major sources that
contain more than two hundred professional codes, not a single code for
ministers can be found.[76]

This void may be due partly to the nature of the ministerial profession and
partly to the existence of religious pluralism in the United States. American

religious diversity, however, does not prevent religious denominations or groups of ministers from creating a code for their own constituency. Most certainly it does not hinder individual ministers from reflecting on their own moral obligations and writing a personal code as a guide for ethics in ministry.

Certainly, a written code of ethics by itself does not guarantee satisfactory moral performance. Notre Dame law professor Thomas Schaffer notes, "Such guiding codes are thus at one and the same time absolutely necessary as a first level in establishing the ethics of the profession and also a serious, if unrecognized danger when they serve to reduce moral inquiry and wrestling to a merely literal conformity devoid of moral argument."[77] Nonetheless, a clear statement of ministerial ethical standards, adequately authored, properly developed, and appropriately implemented, can go a long way toward strengthening ministerial integrity.

Authorship—the "Who" Question

Who should author codes—individuals or groups? Should authorship come from within the profession or from without? As late as the nineteenth century, leaders in professions did serve as the sole authors of codes. Today, virtually no professional code has a single author; "codes by committee" is the norm.[78]

The most common practice is for the members of a profession to write a code themselves. This is the pattern used for most medical, legal, and business codes. The obvious problem with this method is that the document may be written in the self-interest of the members with little regard for the clientele or society.[79] Proponents of internal authorship believe, however, that members of a profession can best determine what policies are in society's best interest and that members are in a better position to relate them to society than a third party.

Those who argue for external authorship do so from one of two perspectives. One group believes that codes should be written entirely by outside sources. Since professions depend on society's willingness to promote them, only society can "provide a sufficient moral foundation."[80]

A second perspective, and one that seems to be the best option, is that professionals should write codes in conjunction with laypersons. To do otherwise is to place too much importance on the work of either group. This cooperative effort also provides credibility later if people question certain practices.

How do these trends apply to the ministerial profession? The best code, the most comprehensive code, and the one most free from self-interest is undoubtedly the one produced by a committee composed of both laypersons and clergy. Since parishioners are the ones most affected by ministries, they should be included in defining ethical standards and supervising implementation. The committee chosen to author a clergy code should also be inclusive, representing male and female, young and old, and all ethnic groups within the larger body.

Does this mean a personal code authored by an individual minister is obsolete? Not at all. Writing a personal code of ethics is a good exercise in developing one's own ethical standards in ministry. Every minister should at some time think through their own ethical conduct in ministry. What better way to do so than by writing a personal code of ethics? Such a document should allow for evaluation and updating. As ministers grow in ethical sensitivity, they should expand and adjust their moral guidelines. A personal code of ethics written by a minister could also be shared with the cleric's own congregation. Most churches would be pleased to learn of their spiritual leader's ethical standards. Shared codes serve two main purposes: they support ministers in clearly defining ethical intentions, and they hold ministers ethically accountable to a larger group, which is a central purpose of all ethical codes.

Procedure—the "How" Question

When a denomination, a church, or a group of ministers decides it needs a code of ethics, how should those involved proceed? A typical approach might be as follows. A church approves a resolution authorizing a code committee to go to work. A representative committee is selected and begins by reviewing past and present clergy codes, comparing the recent codes of similar organizations, and studying helpful resources in the field of ministerial ethics. A preliminary draft of the new code is circulated to all members for feedback. When the responses have been assimilated, the committee puts the code in final form and sends it to the entire membership for study. The church then ratifies and adopts the document, and implementation begins.

A minister who is writing a personal code of ethics would follow a similar procedure. After wrestling with the key questions of ministerial ethics, the pastor would reflect on the basic areas of clergy ethics to be covered by the code (see the worksheet following this chapter). After writing a preamble, the pastor would compose statements of obligation regarding self and family, the congregation, colleagues, and the community. The first draft could be reviewed by another minister and a layperson to provide perspective, as well as to prevent serious oversights. The final draft would become a working document as the pastor matures in ministry.

Content—the "What" Question

We have come now to the "meat and potatoes" of a clergy code, the content. What subjects and statements should be included in an ethical code for ministers? Before we can unravel that question, a preliminary distinction must be made.

Professional ethics scholars have called attention to differences between present and older codes. Modern Generation I codes, products of the early twentieth century, dealt with the etiquette of relationships—"Do not speak ill of a colleague." Since the 1980s, complex ethical questions have led to the era of Modern Generation II codes, which "deal with dilemmas rising out of new knowledge, new technology, and new social attitudes."[81]

In like manner, the older clergy codes in appendix B reflect Modern Generation I codes. The content of contemporary codes (app. C) reveals a more complex ministry in an increasingly complicated world—Modern Generation II codes.

One way to address the "what" question of ministerial codes is to use a threefold division first introduced by Christian apologist C. S. Lewis. His approach focuses on the major areas of the moral life itself: What do the codes say about the inner moral life of the practitioner, the relationships between individuals, and the purpose of human life as a whole?[82]

Whereas other professional codes pay scant attention to the inner life of the practitioner, ministerial codes focus on the moral character of the clergy, as well they should. Clergy codes are not just talmudic collections of rules to guide action. Laws will do little to promote ethical conduct unless the ministers to be guided are persons of character. Integrity is central to ministry; it is not an option. A car may lack air conditioning and still be a good car. Not so for a minister and moral character. "Losing integrity is like having your lungs cave in," writes Lewis Smedes. "Everything else goes out with them."[83]

Those composing guidelines for ethics in ministry must underscore the centrality of character. Ministerial codes of conduct should point to the inner life of the one called of God to be an overseer of the church. Paul reminds Timothy that a pastoral overseer must be "blameless" (1 Tim. 3:2 NKJV). In personal life, family relationships, and spiritual leadership, the person set apart to minister must be "above reproach" (1 Tim. 3:1–7). Solomon, possibly reflecting on his father's thumbprint on his own life, writes, "The righteous walk in integrity—happy are the children who follow them!" (Prov. 20:7).

The shortcoming of most codes is that a set of rules fails to instill internal character. Many professional codes assume the integrity of their members and do not attempt to develop the inner life, which is the Achilles' heel of professionalism. Writers of codes for ministers must not make this mistake. Though all pastors should be persons of good character, a code should contain statements that harmonize the inner life of church ministers with their personal ethical standards.

Far more coverage is given in the ministerial codes to the second area of the moral life: relationships between individuals. The codes in the appendixes discuss duties regarding parishioners, fellow ministers, and people in the community. Insofar as the clergy codes spell out in detail a cleric's obligations to others, they encourage enablement and discourage exploitative relationships.[84] Writers of codes need to pay serious attention to stress points in the congregation, between colleagues, and among persons in the community in relation to the church minister.

Self-interest is often overlooked. Ministers are no different from other professionals, who often use their power to promote their own interests. One illustration of this is seen in procedures outlined for reporting ministerial misconduct (EOP Code). A layperson is immediately disciplined if the accusation cannot be substantiated; a minister rightly charged is given numerous levels of appeal and a wide assortment of lesser sanctions. The system is weighted against the lay accuser.

In the third area of ethics outlined by C. S. Lewis, that of the purpose of human life, most codes receive a low score. Many older codes, from that of Hippocrates in the fourth century BC to that of Florence Nightingale in the nineteenth century, were explicitly religious. Modern American pluralism and secularism have put an end to that.

Codes of ethics for ministers should express in clear language a worldview based on Christian belief. The preamble is an appropriate place to state basic convictions about God, Jesus Christ, the church, the world, and the cleric's call and commitment to ministry. The code should also contain statements of ministerial ideals, which represent a higher standard of behavior than most are practicing.[85] These ethical principles point to the moral will of God and provide a theological framework for clergy ethics.

The word that sums up the content of a ministerial code is the same word that characterizes ministerial ethics: *integrity*. A clergy code envisions an integrated moral life. The Hebrew word for integrity is *tom* and means "whole," "sound," "unimpaired." Modern dictionaries define *integrity* as "soundness," "adherence to a code of values," "the quality or state of being complete or undivided."

In reality, no human being has arrived at wholeness. The important thing, however, is direction, not destination. A code of ethics for ministers is intended to guide them on that journey. As Smedes states: "We have to check our intentions regularly and see whether we are still moving on the journey or whether, at some shadowed station, we left the train and went off to nowhere. For without integrity, anywhere is nowhere."[86]

Implementation—the "When" and "Where" Questions

The mere existence of a professional code is no guarantee of ethical performance. Darrell Reeck observes that the code of the American Bar Association did not prevent lawyers surrounding President Nixon from committing unethical and illegal acts.[87] The question now raised is this: What programs for implementing the code will make a difference?

A primary component of implementation is distribution. The first responsibility of any group producing a clergy code is to get copies printed and into the hands of every member. Simply publishing the code in a denominational journal is not enough. Every minister in the group must personally receive a copy.

A lack of instruction is a common weakness in all professions. A ministerial code of ethics is merely a document to frame and hang on the wall unless responsible leaders provide training. Either someone within the group who worked with the code committee or, better, an ethics authority from outside the profession could serve as a teacher. Immediately after a code is ratified, instructional meetings should be scheduled. From that point forward, regular training sessions should be provided, both to teach new ministers about the code and to help longtime clergy maintain a working knowledge of their ethical guidelines. These regular gatherings also provide a forum for dialogue, updating, and adaptation of the guidelines to changing needs.

A third responsibility of implementation is organization. Once the code is approved, what ongoing structure is needed to ensure distribution, instruction, reporting, and enforcement? By assumption of the ministerial role, church shepherds obligate themselves to abide by the group's code of ethics. This first means personal responsibility, but it also means accountability to all members of the ministerial association, for misbehavior brings criticism to the entire body.

The best insights from other professions reveal that a ministerial group should elect or appoint a standing committee to oversee enforcement, instruction, and other organizational responsibilities. As was true of the original code committee, this board should evidence gender, age, and ethnic diversity.

Concerning reporting and enforcement, the standing committee should develop methods that encourage both colleagues and the public to share information about violations. Enforcement is dependent chiefly on the willingness of people to report infractions. As discussed at length in the previous section, the enforcement of a code is one of three major difficulties in developing a code. The enforcement committee could be a separate council, but for several practical reasons one standing committee would probably be adequate for most ministerial groups.

The toughest problem any denomination or association of ministers faces is prescribing disciplinary action that is appropriate, fair, legal, and redemptive. The three most common options are censure, suspension, and termination, although the latter two may have to be enforced by a local congregation in denominations with autonomous churches.

The Value of a Ministerial Code of Ethics

In sum, then, does the writing of a clergy code of ethics, along with its implementation, enhance ministerial behavior? This limited survey of past and present efforts suggests that the clergy profession has much work to do to make codes a vital part of daily practice. Compared to ethical guidelines of other professions, codes for church leaders suffer many deficiencies in authorship, procedure, content, and implementation.

Despite this apparent failure, a code of ethics for ministers has many positive values. The mere existence of a ministerial code radiates an unseen influence. The fact that a church minister receives a copy and reads it at least once, and perhaps in times of crisis refers to it for guidance, suggests a subtle but real influence.[88]

At the beginning of this chapter, two questions were raised: Is a code of ethics for ministers a help or a hindrance? Is it possible to write such a document? By now it should be clear that the answer to both questions is positive. Writing such a code is not only possible but also imperative! Ministers need the guidance and support a code gives. Laypersons need to understand the ethical commitments of their clergy. Ministers need to be accountable to one another.

Addressing the serious problem of sexual misconduct among the clergy, an associate minister concludes her appeal with several suggestions: "The most efficacious approach is clearly to work at prevention. Churches should encourage mutually supportive clergy marriages; develop clear professional ethical guidelines spelling out procedures and consequences for sexual misconduct; set limits on time, place, and circumstances of pastoral visits and counseling sessions; decrease pastoral stress factors . . . ; and put into place ministerial accountability (to the congregation, to denominational officials, and primarily, to God)."[89]

We share this conviction about the need for guidelines and accountability. We also share a dream that reaches beyond this book. From our perspective, the purpose of this book is not fulfilled until its readers possess an ethical code to guide them in ministry. At the primary level, this means developing a personal code of ethics. That is the reason for the worksheet following this chapter. At a second level, it means initiating a code of ethics for a group of ministers to which they belong, such as a local ministerial association.

The denominational level is admittedly the most difficult. This is especially true in ecclesiastical groups with strong convictions about congregational government and local church autonomy. The largest Protestant denomination, the Southern Baptist Convention (which has historically opposed any hint of control over individual churches), recently published a lengthy article with numerous alarming statistics on clergy misconduct, followed by specific advice to churches. Though the insightful article stops short of suggesting codes of conduct for Southern Baptist ministers or churches, the statement leaves no doubt that the response of church leaders to clergy malfeasance must be swift, wise, and informed.[90]

At the same time, is it not possible for such bodies that traditionally have produced confessions of faith that are accepted as doctrinal guides (although they may have no binding authority on the churches) to develop a code of ethics for ministers? Further, could not each local church in those denominations adopt and support a denominationally approved code or write one of its own?[91]

Why do we dream such dreams and see such visions? We believe, as the biblical prophets did, that such hope for integrity in ministry is not in vain. We pray that others agree. Phillips Brooks, the renowned pastor of Holy Trinity Church in Boston, lived an exemplary and contagious Christian life. There was a saying that on gloomy days in Boston, when Brooks appeared in public, the sun came out. One day Josiah Royce, a Harvard philosopher, was asked by a student, "What is your definition of a Christian?" Royce walked to the window, peered over the campus, and pondered the question. After a moment of silence, he replied to the freshman, "I do not know what is the definition of a Christian, but there goes Phillips Brooks."[92] Brooks preached by example, and so do ministers. May their codes be their lives, and may their lives illustrate their codes.

Suggested Reading

Allen, Ronald J. "A Code of Ethics for Preachers." *Encounter* 66, no. 4 (Autumn 2005): 343–48.

Bayles, Michael D. *Professional Ethics*. 2nd ed. Belmont, CA: Wadsworth, 1989.

Reasons, James Allen. "The Biblical Concept of Integrity and Professional Codes of Ethics in Ministerial Ethics." PhD diss., Southwestern Baptist Theological Seminary, 1990.

Reeck, Darrell. *Ethics for the Professions: A Christian Perspective*. Minneapolis: Augsburg, 1982.

Theology Today 59 (October 2002): 329–450.

Ministerial Code of Ethics Worksheet

Preamble

_____

_____

_____

_____

_____

_____

_____

Section 1: Personal and Family Relationships (see chap. 3)

_____

_____

_____

_____

_____

_____

_____

_____

Section 2: Congregational Relationships (see chap. 4)

_____

_____

_____

_____

_____

_____

_____

Section 3: Collegial Relationships (see chap. 5)

_____

_____

_____

_____

_____

_____

Section 4: Community Relationships (see chap. 6)

_____

_____

_____

_____

_____

_____

_____

Appendix A

A Procedure for Responding to Charges of Clergy Sexual Abuse

Constructing a deliberate and methodical response to allegations of ministerial sexual abuse is a serious task.[1] A clearly stated process is needed to ensure that everyone involved is fully heard, adequately defended, and justly treated. Once an acceptable procedure is approved, a church must instruct its ministers and the congregation about the process and provide a clear definition of clergy sexual abuse. In addition, churches must be aware of all legal requirements, such as reporting any sexual abuse involving minors. The following is a broad outline that may serve as a guide for churches. Each church will have to adapt it in light of church policies.

Step 1: Hearing the Accusation

1. The church appoints and trains a specific committee, containing both men and women, to hear all complaints of clergy sexual misconduct. People on this committee must be trustworthy, compassionate, and spiritually mature. Since this committee investigates and possibly charges ministerial staff, staff members should not serve on this committee. Also, staff could be prone to a prejudicial view and may be needed as witnesses.

2. A complaint from a congregant is heard immediately by the committee, which assesses the veracity and the seriousness of the alleged offense.

3. A written summary of the charges is recorded and outlined in a clear, specific, and reasonably documented manner. Both the complainant and the accused should have access to this document and be given an opportunity to respond orally or in writing.

4. The committee explains the process to the complainant, stressing the intent of the church to address the charges without delay.

5. All parties maintain strict confidentiality.

Step 2: Confronting the Accused Minister

1. A meeting between the accused minister and the committee follows immediately. Since public trust is at stake, consideration should be given to placing the minister on administrative leave at the conclusion of this meeting. Suspension in no way assumes guilt.

2. Before this meeting, the committee prepares by: (1) reviewing the factual details of the complainant's story, (2) understanding the dynamics of the minister's possible responses (disbelief, anger, denial, evasion, panic, shame, or even confession), and (3) committing themselves to the same fairness and compassion as was given to the complainant.

3. The committee explains the purposes of the meeting to the accused minister: (1) to hear the allegation of clergy sexual abuse, (2) to assure the minister of the committee's intent to ensure justice through fair and impartial hearings, and (3) to allow the minister to respond to the charges.

4. If the minister denies the charges, the committee determines whether further investigation is needed, whether the members can reach a decision concerning guilt or innocence, or whether the complaint should be taken to the church.

5. If the minister admits the truth of the accusation, the committee must resist the temptation to accept his resignation and avoid scandal by keeping the incident from the church. This hasty "solution" derails the process designed to remove offenders from leadership and to bring healing into the lives of all persons involved, including the church membership. If the pastor resigns, the committee should still complete its investigation and report to the church.

6. The committee outlines for the minister the process that follows.

7. A written summary of the meeting is recorded, focusing on factual information. As before, the minister and the complainant may read the document and respond to it.

8. After deciding whether further investigation is needed, the committee composes its report and recommendation to the adjudicating body (for autonomous churches, the congregation).

Step 3: Preparing for the Formal Hearing

1. If the church follows congregational polity, the committee calls a meeting of the membership to inform the church of the charges and to explain the hearing process.

2. The church must follow due process in accordance with the church's code of ethics (written or assumed) and its procedure for dealing with disciplinary matters.

3. A formal hearing is scheduled immediately following the conclusion of the investigation. Public access to this meeting supports the church's quest for justice in both the hearings and the verdict.

4. The congregation may consult someone who has expertise in clergy sexual abuse to assist in the process.

5. The church may consider getting legal advice concerning specific matters.

Step 4: Conducting the Formal Hearing

1. Church leaders such as elders, deacons, or members of a personnel committee appoint a moderator who is highly respected and fair-minded and is capable of maintaining order, decorum, and a spirit of mutual respect.

2. The committee reads to the church the charges brought against the minister, a summary of the interviews with the complainant and the minister, and any additional relevant information discovered by the committee.

3. The committee answers appropriate questions from the congregation.

4. The committee recommends to the church one of the following actions:

   a. If the charge is considered false, the minister is exonerated and the church acts to restore the minister's reputation. The complainant receives appropriate discipline and/or counseling and ministry from the church.

b. If the accusation is considered true, the committee recommends possible sanctions according to the nature of the offense. Levels of censure can range from admonition to severe sanctions such as probation, suspension, or termination of employment.

5. If the minister is a sexual predator who refuses to admit wrongdoing and evidences a pattern of manipulation, coercion, and control, the church takes whatever action is necessary to keep him from doing further harm to the membership, other churches, and the community at large.

6. If the minister is a first-time offender, acknowledges his abuse, and is genuinely remorseful, the church assists the minister in enrolling in a supervised program of professional counseling designed for clergy sexual abusers.

Step 5: Ministering to the Victims of Clergy Sexual Abuse

1. The church offers support to the complainant and their family. This may include providing counseling, emotional support, financial assistance, and pastoral care to enable them to deal with the personal and family problems resulting from the clergy sexual abuse.

2. The church reaches out to members of the minister's family, who feel isolated and rejected as they deal with vocational, relational, and marital disruptions. They may need professional counseling, financial assistance, emotional support, and pastoral care.

3. Denominational leaders and officials are notified of the church's action so that a perpetrator is not able to continue victimizing the vulnerable in other churches or institutions.

4. A final action of the committee may be to recommend that the church employ a consultant or an interim minister who can help church members deal with the internal turmoil (hurt, confusion, anger, resentment, shame, or even empathy) experienced in the aftermath.

An allegation of sexual misconduct by a minister is a serious matter. If the charge proves to be true, the consequences can be enormous. Marriages may be severed, homes divided, children hurt, churches split, and ministries ruined. The lives of those involved are never the same again. Chronic depression and even suicide attempts are not unusual. A healthy response to clergy sexual abuse can aid the healing of both the church and individuals.

Appendix B

Early Denominational Codes of Ethics

The Congregational Code

I. *The Minister and His Work*

1. As a minister controls his own time, he should make it a point of honor to give full service to his parish.
2. Part of the minister's service as a leader of his people is to reserve sufficient time for serious study in order thoroughly to apprehend his message, keep abreast of current thought, and develop his intellectual and spiritual capacities.
3. It is equally the minister's duty to keep physically fit. A weekly holiday and an annual vacation should be taken and used for rest and improvement.
4. As a public interpreter of divine revelation and human duty, the minister should tell the truth as he sees it and present it tactfully and constructively.
5. It is unethical for the minister to use sermon material prepared by another without acknowledging the source from which it comes.
6. As an ethical leader in the community, it is incumbent on the minister to be scrupulously honest, avoid debts, and meet his bills promptly.

7. The minister should be careful not to bring reproach on his calling by joining in marriage improper persons.

II. *The Minister's Relations with His Parish*

1. It is unethical for a minister to break his contract made with the church.
2. As a professional man the minister should make his service primary and the remuneration secondary. His efficiency, however, demands that he should receive a salary adequate to the work he is expected to do and commensurate with scale of living in that parish which he serves.
3. It is unethical for the minister to engage in other lines of remunerative work without the knowledge and consent of the church or its official board.
4. The confidential statements made to a minister by his parishioners are privileged and should never be divulged without the consent of those making them.
5. It is unethical for a minister to take sides with factions in his parish.
6. The minister recognizes himself to be the servant of the community in which he resides. Fees which are offered should be accepted only in the light of this principle.

III. *The Minister's Relations with the Profession*

1. It is unethical for a minister to interfere directly or indirectly with the parish work of another minister; especially should he be careful to avoid the charge of proselytizing.
2. Ministerial service should not be rendered to the members of another parish without consulting the minister of that parish.
3. It is unethical for a minister to make overtures to or consider overtures from a church whose pastor has not yet resigned.
4. It is unethical for a minister to speak ill of the character or work of another minister, especially of his predecessor or successor. It is the duty of a minister, however, in flagrant cases of unethical conduct, to bring the matter before the proper body.
5. As members of the same profession and brothers in the service of a common Master, the relation between ministers should be one of frankness and cooperation.[1]

Methodist Ministers' Ethical Code

When a Methodist minister becomes a member of the conference he promises to employ all of his time in the work of God. We again call attention to the fact that he is thus honor bound to give full service to his parish.

Part of the minister's service as a leader of his people is to reserve sufficient time for serious study in order thoroughly to appreciate his message, keep abreast of current thought, and develop his intellectual and spiritual capacities.

It is equally the minister's duty to keep physically fit. A weekly holiday and an annual vacation should be taken and used for rest and improvement.

As a public interpreter of divine revelation and human duty, the minister should tell the truth as he sees it and present it tactfully and constructively.

It is unethical for the minister to use sermon material prepared by another without acknowledging the source from which it comes.

As an ethical leader in the community, it is incumbent on the minister to be scrupulously honest, avoid debts, and meet his bills promptly.

The minister should be careful not to bring reproach upon his calling by joining in marriage improper persons.

As a professional man the minister should make his service primary and the remuneration secondary. This implies a salary, paid regularly, and adequate to the work he is expected to do and commensurate with scale of living in that parish where he serves.

The confidential statements made to a minister by his parishioners are privileged and should never be divulged without the consent of those making them.

In the making of conference reports, it is unethical for a minister to report other than the actual salary received.

The minister recognizes himself to be the servant of the community in which he resides. Fees which are offered should be accepted only in the light of this principle.

It is unethical for a minister to interfere directly or indirectly with the parish work of another minister; especially should he be careful to avoid the charge of proselytizing.

Ministerial service should not be rendered to the members of another parish without consulting the minister of the parish, or by invitation from him.

It is unethical for a minister to speak ill of the character or work of another minister, especially of his predecessor or successor. It is the duty of a minister, however, in flagrant cases of unethical conduct, to bring the matter before the proper body.

It is unethical for a minister on leaving a charge to leave the parsonage property in other than first-class condition, with all dirt, rubbish, etc. removed.

Common courtesy to his successor demands the observance of the Golden Rule.

As members of the same profession and brothers in the service of a common Master, the relation between ministers should be one of frankness, of comradeship, and of cooperation.[2]

The Presbyterian Code

I. Personal Standards

1. As a minister controls his own time, he should make it a point of honor to give full service to his parish.
2. Part of a minister's service as a leader of his people is to reserve sufficient time for serious study in order to thoroughly apprehend his message, keep abreast of current thought, and develop his intellectual and spiritual capacities.
3. It is equally the minister's duty to keep physically fit. A weekly holiday and an annual vacation should be taken and used for rest and improvement.
4. It is unethical for a minister to use sermon material prepared by another, without acknowledging the source from which it comes.
5. As an ethical leader in the community, it is incumbent on the minister to be scrupulously honest, avoid debts, and meet his bills promptly.

II. Relations with the Parish

1. In accepting a pastorate, a minister assumes obligations which he should faithfully perform until released in the constitutional manner.
2. As a professional man, the minister should make his service primary and the remuneration secondary.
3. A minister should not regularly engage in other kinds of remunerative work, except with the knowledge and consent of the official board of the church.
4. The confidential statements made to a minister by his parishioners are sacred and not to be divulged.
5. As a minister is especially charged to study the peace and unity of the church, it is unwise as well as unethical for a minister to take sides with any faction in his church, in any but exceptional cases.

6. The minister is the servant of the community and not only of his church and should find in the opportunity for general ministerial service a means of evidencing the Christian spirit.

III. Relations with the Profession

1. It is unethical for a minister to interfere directly or indirectly with the parish work of another minister; especially should he be careful to avoid the charge of proselytizing from a sister church.
2. Except in emergencies, ministerial service should not be rendered to the members of another parish without the knowledge of the minister of the parish.
3. A minister should not make overtures to or consider overtures from a church whose pastor has not yet resigned.
4. It is unethical for a minister to speak ill of the character or work of another minister, especially of his predecessor or successor. It is the duty of a minister, however, in cases of flagrant misconduct to bring the matter before the proper body.
5. A minister should be very careful to protect his brother ministers from imposition by unworthy applicants for aid and should refer such cases to established charitable agencies rather than send them to other churches.
6. A minister should be scrupulously careful in giving endorsements to agencies or individuals unless he has a thorough knowledge and approval of their work lest such endorsements be used to influence others unduly.
7. As members of the same profession and brothers in the service of a common Master, the relation between ministers should be one of frankness and cooperation.[3]

Unitarian Ministers' Code of Ethics

I. The Minister and His Task

1. The minister should always place service above profit, avoiding the suspicion of an inordinate love of money, and never measuring his work by his salary.
2. He should be conscientious in giving full time and strength to the work of his church, engaging in avocations and other occupations in such a way and to such a degree as not to infringe unduly upon that work unless some definite arrangement for part-time service is made with his church.

3. The minister should count it a most important part of his work to keep in touch with the best religious thought of his day and should make it a point of honor to set aside sufficient time for reading and study.

4. It is the minister's duty to keep himself in as good physical condition as possible.

5. The minister should set a high moral standard of speech and conduct. He should be scrupulous in the prompt payment of bills and careful in the incurring of financial obligations.

6. The minister should never speak disparagingly of his church or his profession.

II. *The Minister and His Church Officials*

1. The minister's relation to his parish is a sacred contract, which should not be terminated by him, or broken by his resignation, without at least three months' notice, except by special agreement.

2. The minister is the recognized leader of the parish, but he should not assume authority in church affairs which is not expressly granted to him by the terms of his contract, or the usage of his office, or the vote of his church.

3. The minister rightfully controls his own pulpit, but he should not invite persons into it who are not generally acceptable to the parish, and he should be ready to accede to all reasonable requests by responsible church officials for its use.

III. *The Minister and His Parishioners*

1. The minister should remember that he is pastor of all his people. He should avoid the display of preferences and the cultivation of intimacies within the parish which may be construed as evidence of partiality. He should not attach himself to any social set either in the church or in the community. He should not allow personal feelings to interfere with the impartial nature of his ministrations.

2. In the case of parish controversy, the minister should maintain an attitude of good will to all, even when he himself is the subject of controversy.

3. It is unethical to divulge the confidences of parishioners without their consent.

4. Professional service should be gladly rendered to all, without regard to compensation, except for necessary expenses incurred.

IV. The Minister and His Brother Ministers

1. It is unethical for a minister to render professional service within the parish of another minister, or to occupy another minister's pulpit, without the consent of that minister, whenever obtainable, and this consent should be given readily.

2. He should be very careful not to proselytize among the members of another church.

3. He should discourage all overtures from a church whose minister has not yet resigned.

4. He should always speak with good will of another minister, especially of the minister who has preceded or followed him in a parish. It may be his duty, however, to bring to the attention of the responsible officials of the fellowship any instance of gross professional or personal misconduct that may injure the good name of the ministry.

5. The minister should be very generous in responding to reasonable requests for assistance from his brother ministers and his denominational officials, remembering that he is one of a larger fellowship.

6. It is his duty to show a friendly and cooperative interest in his brethren, attending the group meetings of the ministers, assisting his brother ministers with labors of love, defending them against injustice, and following them with kindly concern in their hours of need or distress.

7. He should never accept from a brother minister fees for professional services at christenings, weddings, and funerals.

V. The Minister and His Community

1. The minister is not under obligations to marry every couple that comes to him to be married. The power of refusal, however, should be exercised with great discretion.

2. The minister's responsibility to the state is that of a citizen. He should, therefore, be faithful to his public obligations and should respond to reasonable requests for assistance in community work.[1]

Appendix C

Contemporary Denominational Codes of Ethics

The Disciples Code

My Ministerial Code of Ethics

I am a minister of the Lord Jesus Christ, called of God to proclaim the unsearchable riches of His love. Therefore, I voluntarily adopt the following principles in order that through dedication and self-discipline I may set a more worthy example for those whom I seek to lead and serve.

I. My Personal Conduct

I will cultivate my devotional life, continuing steadfastly in reading the Bible, meditation, and prayer.

I will endeavor to keep physically and emotionally fit for my work.

I will be fair to my family and will endeavor to give them the time and consideration to which they are entitled.

I will endeavor to live within my income and will not carelessly leave unpaid debts behind me.

I will strive to grow in my work through comprehensive reading and careful study and by attending conventions and conferences.

I will be honest in my stewardship of money.

I will not plagiarize.

I will seek to be Christlike in my personal attitudes and conduct toward all people regardless of race, class, or creed.

II. My Relationship to the Church I Serve

I will dedicate my time and energy to my Christian ministry and will maintain strict standards of discipline.

In my preaching I will exalt the Bible and will be true to my convictions, proclaiming the same in love.

I will maintain a Christian attitude toward other members of the church staff and will not expect the unreasonable of them.

I will not seek special gratuities.

In my pastoral calling I will have respect for every home I enter, for I am a representative of Christ and the Church.

In my administrative and pastoral duties I will be impartial so no one can truthfully say that I am pastor of only one group in the church.

I will strive with evangelistic zeal to build up my church but will maintain a Christian attitude at all times toward members of other religious bodies.

I will under no circumstance violate confidences that come to me as a minister.

I will strive to strengthen the congregation when leaving a pastorate regardless of the circumstances.

III. My Relationship to Fellow Ministers

I will refuse to enter into unfair competition with other ministers in order to secure a pulpit or place of honor.

I will seek to serve my fellow ministers and their families in every way possible and in no instance will I accept fees for such services.

I will refrain from speaking disparagingly about the work of either my predecessor or my successor.

I will refrain from frequent visits to a former field and if, in exceptional cases, I am called back for a funeral or a wedding, I will request that the resident minister be invited to participate in the service.

I will never embarrass my successor by meddling in the affairs of the church I formerly served.

I will be courteous to any predecessor of mine when he returns to the field and will be thoughtful of any retired minister.

I will, upon my retirement from the active ministry, give my pastor loyal support.

I will not gossip about other ministers.

I will hold in sincere respect any minister whose work is well done, regardless of the size or the nature of the field he serves.

I will consider all ministers my co-laborers in the work of Christ and even though I may differ from them I shall respect their Christian earnestness and sincerity.

IV. My Relationship to the Community

I will strive to be human in all my relationships to the community but will never lower my ideals in order to appear "a good fellow."

I will not be a party to funeral or marriage rackets.

I will be considerate of the working hours of business and professional men and will not consume their time with unimportant matters.

I consider that my first duty to my community is to be a conscientious pastor and leader of my own congregation, but I will not use this fact as an easy excuse to escape reasonable responsibilities that the community calls upon me to assume.

V. My Relationship to My Communion

I will at all times recognize that I am a part of a fellowship that has made large contributions to my church, my education, and my ministry. In view of this fact I acknowledge a debt of loyalty to my communion and will strive to fulfill my obligations by cooperating in its efforts to extend the Realm of God.[1]

VI. My Relationship to the Church Universal

I will give attention, sympathy and, when possible, support to the Ecumenical Church, recognizing that my church is a part of the Church Universal.[2]

Code of Professional Practice as Revised at the Unitarian Universalist Ministers Association Annual Meetings of June 1987 and June 1988

Statement of Purpose

We, the members of the Unitarian Universalist Ministers Association, give full assent to this code of professional life as a statement of our serious intent and as an expression of the lines and directions that bind us in a life of common concern, shared hopes, and firm loyalties.

1. Self

Because the religious life is a growing life, I will respect and protect my own needs for spiritual growth, ethical integrity, and continuing education in order to deepen and strengthen myself and my ministry.

I commit myself to honest work, believing that the honor of my profession begins with the honest use of my own mind and skills.

I will sustain a respect for the ministry. Because my private life is woven into my practice of the ministry, I will refrain from private as well as public words or actions degrading to the ministry or destructive of congregational life.

As a sexual being, I will recognize the power that ministry gives me and refrain from practices which are harmful to others and which endanger my integrity or my professional effectiveness. Such practices include sexual activity with any child or with an unwilling adult, with a counselee, with the spouse or partner of a person in the congregation, with interns, or any other such exploitive relationship.

Because the demands of others upon me will be many and unceasing, I will try to keep especially aware of the rights and needs of my family and my relation to them as spouse, parent, and friend.

2. Colleagues

I will stand in a supportive relation to my colleagues and keep for them an open mind and heart.

I will strictly respect confidences given me by colleagues and expect them to keep mine.

Should I know that a colleague is engaged in practices that are damaging, as defined in our Code of Professional Practice, I will speak openly and frankly to her/him and endeavor to be of help. If necessary, I will bring such matters to the attention of the UUMA Board.

I will not speak scornfully or in derogation of any colleague in public. In any private conversation critical of a colleague, I will speak responsibly and temperately.

I will inform my colleague in advance of any public engagement I may accept in his or her community or church, which might bear upon local issues or policies. I will accept no request for my services in the office of the ministry within my colleague's congregation without his or her explicit invitation or permission. I will inform my colleague of any request for advice or counsel from members of his or her congregation, and I will consider with respect any objection to my meeting such a request. When in doubt I will err on the side of deference to the prerogatives of my colleague's call.

If I am to share the ministry of a church with (an)other minister(s), I will earnestly seek clear delineation of responsibility, accountability, and channels of communication before responsibilities are assumed. I will thereafter work in cooperation and consultation with them, taking care that changing roles and relations are renegotiated with clarity, respect, and honesty.

If I am a member of a colleague's congregation, I will in all ways honor the priority of his or her call to the ministry of that congregation, and I will carefully shun inappropriate influence which other members may tend to yield to me. I will be generous toward a colleague who is a member of my congregation.

I will share and support the concerns of the Unitarian Universalist Ministers Association, especially as reflected in these Guidelines.

I will keep my collegial relationships alive by attending UUMA Chapter meetings whenever possible and by thoughtfully considering matters of mutual professional interest.

3. Congregation

I will uphold the practices of congregational polity including both those of local self-government and those of counsel and cooperation within our Association. I will only serve regularly a congregation(s) issuing a call in the manner prescribed by the Bylaws of the congregation(s) or under a program instituted by the UUA or its member groups. Throughout my ministry I will teach the history, meaning, and methods of congregational polity, recognizing informed and faithful adherence to these practices as the bond preserving and reforming our free corporate religious life.

I will respect the traditions of the congregation, enriching and improving these in consultation with the members.

I will hold to a single standard of respect and help for all members of the church community of whatever age or position.

I will respect absolutely the confidentiality of private communications of members.

I will remember that a congregation places special trust in its professional leadership and that the members of the congregation allow a minister to become a part of their lives on the basis of that trust. I will not abuse or exploit that trust for my own gratification.

I will not invade the private and intimate bonds of others' lives, nor will I trespass on those bonds for my own advantage or need when they are disturbed. In any relationship of intimate confidentiality, I will not exploit the needs of another person for my own.

I will not engage in sexual activities with a member of the congregation who is not my spouse or partner, if I am married or in a committed relationship. If I am single, before becoming sexually involved with a person in the congregation, I will take special care to examine my commitment, motives, intentionality, and the nature of such activity and its consequence for myself, the other person, and the congregation.

I will exercise a responsible freedom of the pulpit with respect for all persons, including those who may disagree with me.

I will encourage by my example an inclusive, loyal, generous, and critical church leadership.

I will take responsibility for encouraging clear delineation of responsibility, accountability, and channels of communication for the minister(s) and other staff.

I will take responsibility for encouraging adequate and sensible standards of financial and other support for minister and staff.

Prior to sabbatical or other leave, I will clearly negotiate a minimum amount of time to serve as minister to the congregation upon my return before making myself available as a candidate for another pulpit.

I will inform the Board of the congregation immediately when I have accepted a call to another position.

4. Movement and Association

I will encourage the growth of our congregations and the spread of the ideals of the Unitarian Universalist tradition and fellowship.

I will participate and encourage lay participation in meetings and activities of our Association.

I will encourage financial support of the Unitarian Universalist Association and its associated programs.

I will inform myself of the established candidating procedures of the Unitarian Universalist Association, and I will strictly observe them.

I will make myself a candidate for a pulpit only with serious intent.

5. Community

In word and deed I will live and speak in ways representing the best Unitarian Universalist tradition and leadership in the larger community.

I will maintain a prophetic pulpit, offering to the community religious and ethical leadership.

I will encourage members' participation in efforts to solve community problems.

I will offer sympathetic support to neighboring ministers of other religious bodies.[3]

The Pastor's Code of Ethics (United Church of Christ)

As a minister of the Lord Jesus Christ, called by God to proclaim the Gospel of his love, I subscribe to the following principles in order that I may set a more worthy example for those whom I seek to lead and serve:

My Personal Conduct

I will observe times of quietness for reading the Scriptures, meditation, and prayer.

I will endeavor to keep physically and emotionally fit.

I will remember my obligations to the members of my family to give them the time and consideration to which they are entitled.

I will endeavor to be a student at all times, through comprehensive reading and study and attendance at conferences and institutes.

I will be honest and responsible in my stewardship of money.

I will seek to be Christlike in my attitudes and conduct toward all people.

My Relationship to the Church I Serve

I will remember that a minister is also a servant. I will love the people I serve with the love of Christ, exercising conviction with patience, guidance with understanding.

In preaching, I will be diligent in my preparation, scriptural in my presentation, speaking the truth in love.

I will be diligent in the discharge of my responsibilities as pastor, preacher, and teacher, observing proper work habits and responsible schedules.

I will strive with evangelistic zeal to build up the church I serve but will not proselytize the members of other religious groups.

I will not violate confidences which come to me as a minister.

I will not seek special gratuities or privileges as a clergyman.

My Relationship to My Fellow Ministers

I will endeavor to be a brother in Christ to my fellow ministers and to offer and receive counsel in times of difficulty.

I will not speak disparagingly about the work of either my predecessor or my successor, nor encourage members in their real or imagined grievances.

I will refrain from visits to a former field for professional services, such as baptisms, weddings, funerals, and anniversaries, except upon invitation of the resident pastor.

I will, upon retirement from the active ministry, give my pastor my loyal support.

My Relationship to the Community

I will consider my primary duty to be the pastor but will also accept reasonable responsibilities which the community may call upon me to assume.

I will not set aside convictions and ideals to win popular favor.

My Relationship to My Denomination

I will recognize that I am a part of the larger fellowship which is the United Church of Christ and will strive to fulfill my obligations to it, accepting my responsibility both to support and to constructively criticize its efforts to extend the Kingdom of God.

My Relationship to the Church Universal

Recognizing that the United Church of Christ is a part of the Church Universal, I will participate in the work of the Ecumenical Church, supporting, as my convictions and energy permit, whatever measures may be proposed toward the strengthening of the fellowship of Christians everywhere.[4]

The Covenant and Code of Ethics for Professional Church Leaders of the American Baptist Churches in the U.S.A.

Having accepted God's call to leadership in Christ's Church, I covenant with God to serve Christ and the Church with God's help, to deepen my obedience to the Two Great Commandments; to love the Lord our God with all my heart, soul, mind, and strength, and to love my neighbor as myself.

In affirmation of this commitment, I will abide by the Code of Ethics of the Ministers Council of the American Baptist Churches and I will faithfully support its purposes and ideals. As further affirmation of my commitment, I covenant with my colleagues in ministry that we will hold one another accountable for fulfillment of all the public actions set forth in our Code of Ethics.

- I will hold in trust the traditions and practices of our American Baptist Churches; I will not accept a position in the American Baptist family unless I am in accord with those traditions and practices; nor will I use my influence to alienate my congregation/constituents or any part thereof from its relationship and support of the denomination. If my convictions change, I will resign my position.

- I will respect and recognize the variety of calls to ministry among my American Baptist colleagues and other Christians.
- I will seek to support all colleagues in ministry by building constructive relationships wherever I serve, both with the staff where I work and with colleagues in neighboring churches.
- I will advocate adequate compensation for my profession. I will help lay persons and colleagues to understand that professional church leaders should not expect or require fees for pastoral services from constituents they serve, when these constituents are helping pay their salaries.
- I will not seek personal favors or discounts on the basis of my professional status.
- I will maintain a disciplined ministry in such ways as keeping hours of prayer and devotion, endeavoring to maintain wholesome family relationships, sexual integrity, financial responsibility, regularly engaging in educational and recreational activities for professional and personal development. I will seek to maintain good health habits.
- I will recognize my primary obligation to the church or employing group to which I have been called and will accept added responsibilities only if they do not interfere with the overall effectiveness of my ministry.
- I will personally and publicly support my colleagues who experience discrimination on the basis of gender, race, age, marital status, national origin, physical impairment, or disability.
- I will, upon my resignation or retirement, sever my professional church leadership relations with my former constituents and will not make professional contacts in the field of another professional's church without his/her request and/or consent.
- I will hold in confidence any privileged communication received by me during the conduct of my ministry. I will not disclose confidential communications in private or public except when in my practice of ministry I am convinced that the sanctity of confidentiality is outweighed by my well-founded belief that the parishioner/client will cause imminent, life-threatening, or substantial harm to self or others, or unless the privilege is waived by those giving the information.
- I will not proselytize from other Christian churches.

- I will show my personal love for God as revealed in Jesus Christ in my life and ministry, as I strive together with my colleagues to preserve the dignity, maintain the discipline, and promote the integrity of the vocation to which we have been called.[5]

Signed _____

Code of Ethics for Ordained and Licensed Ministers and Lay Speakers in the Church of the Brethren

We believe that we have been called by God, through the church, to the set-apart ministry in the Church of the Brethren. It is our calling, and our function, to lead and facilitate the church in its mission to obey and serve Christ and to witness to the good news of the gospel. We are committed to fulfilling the trust the church has placed in us by maintaining a high standard of Christian conviction, by sincerity of purpose, by nurturing and sharing our gifts, and by integrity of our character. We are dedicated to upholding the dignity and worth of every person who seeks or is reached by our care and proclamation. In order to uphold our standards we, as ministers in the Church of the Brethren, covenant to accept the following disciplines:

1. We will be true to the Judeo-Christian Scriptures in our preaching, teaching, and conversation.
2. We will be true to Christian convictions as revealed in the Bible and interpreted, taught to, and nurtured in us by the church under the guidance of the Holy Spirit.
3. We will live lives of integrity, upholding the commitments we make to God, to others, to the church, and to ourselves.
4. We will exercise lifestyles consistent with the teachings of Christ, giving serious attention to relevant Annual Conference statements.
5. We will treat members of our family with Christian love and respect.
6. We will not misuse the trust placed in us and the unique power inherent in our function by exploiting in any way those who seek our help or care. We will guard against violating the emotional, spiritual, and physical well-being of people who come to us for help or over whom we have any kind of authority. We will not use our authority to defame, manipulate either individual or congregational decisions, or to create or cultivate dependencies. We will avoid situations and relationships which could impair our professional judgment, compromise the

integrity of our ministry, and/or use the situation or relationship for our own gain.

7. We will avoid all forms of sexual exploitation or harassment in our professional and social relationships, even when others invite such behavior or involvement.[6] We will not seek sexual favors from volunteers or employees of the church as a condition of their participation or employment.

8. We will not engage in any form of child abuse, sexual, physical, or emotional.

9. We will not use our office or authority to apply influence upon a parishioner or others in order to get bequests, gifts, or loans that would personally benefit us.

10. We will act with financial integrity in all our dealings, professionally and personally.

11. We will endeavor to manage our affairs in order to live within our income and neither expect nor specify financial favors, fees, or gratuities because of our position.

12. We will be responsible and honest in the management of all resources and funds entrusted to our care in the course of our employment.

13. We will give credit for all sources quoted or extensively paraphrased in sermons and prepared papers. We will honor all copyrights.

14. We will respect the privacy of individuals and will not divulge information obtained in confidence. We will share confidences revealed by others without their consent only where such information may need to be revealed for legal reasons or for professional consultations.

15. We will neither exchange nor tolerate scandalous, malicious, or inaccurate information with or about other persons.

16. We will, wherever possible, maintain a friendly, courteous, and cooperative relationship with other ministers, both within our denomination and in the larger Christian community. We will not proselytize people from other churches. We will not render professional service in the congregation being served by another pastor without the knowledge and consent of that pastor, except in emergencies

17. We will not perform professional services in former parishes, unless invited to do so by the present pastor. We consider it unethical to be involved in the pastoral affairs of a congregation after leaving it or upon retirement, or to cultivate such relationships with former parishioners as may hinder the ministry of the new pastor.

18. We will assume responsibility for our physical and emotional health and for our spiritual growth and enrichment. We will strive to maintain

reasonable expectations for ourselves and not allow others' unreasonable expectations for us to endanger our well-being.[7]

Note: Richard M. Gula concludes his *Ethics in Pastoral Ministry* by noting that pastoral ministers in the Roman Catholic Church have no formal code of ethics; nevertheless, he then proposes a "tentative and limited one, open to revision."[8] Two other contemporary codes that are quite lengthy are the Eastern Oklahoma Presbytery Code (adopted February 13, 1990)[9] and the National Capital Presbytery Code of Ethics for Clergy and Other Church Professionals (approved January 24, 1995).[10]

Appendix D

Sample Codes of Ethics

Pastor or Senior Minister Code

[Includes basic obligations for all ministers][1]

Preamble

As a minister of Jesus Christ, called by God to proclaim the gospel and gifted by the Spirit to pastor the church, I dedicate myself to conduct my ministry according to the ethical guidelines and principles set forth in this code of ethics, in order that my ministry may be acceptable to God, my service beneficial to the Christian community, and my life a witness to the world.

Responsibilities to Self

1. I will maintain my physical and emotional health through regular exercise, good eating habits, and the proper care of my body.
2. I will nurture my devotional life through a regular time of prayer, reading of Scripture, and meditation.
3. I will continue to grow intellectually through personal study, comprehensive reading, and attending growth conferences.
4. I will manage my time well by properly balancing personal obligations, church duties, and family responsibilities, and by observing a weekly day off and an annual vacation.

5. I will be honest and responsible in my finances by paying all debts on time, never seeking special gratuities or privileges, giving generously to worthwhile causes, and living a Christian lifestyle.

6. I will be truthful in my speech, never plagiarizing another's work, exaggerating the facts, misusing personal experiences, or communicating gossip.

7. I will seek to be Christlike in attitude and action toward all persons regardless of race, social class, religious beliefs, or position of influence within the church and community.

Responsibilities to Family

1. I will be fair to every member of my family, giving them the time, love, and consideration they need.

2. I will understand the unique role of my spouse, recognizing that his or her primary responsibility is as marital partner and parent to the children and secondarily as church worker and assistant to the pastor.

3. I will regard my children as a gift from God and seek to meet their individual needs without imposing undue expectations on them.

Responsibilities to the Congregation

1. I will seek to be a servant-minister of the church by following the example of Christ in faith, love, wisdom, courage, and integrity.

2. I will faithfully discharge my time and energies as pastor, teacher, preacher, and administrator through proper work habits and reasonable schedules.

3. In my administrative and pastoral duties, I will be impartial and fair to all members.

4. In my preaching responsibilities, I will give adequate time to prayer and preparation so that my presentation will be biblically based, theologically correct, and clearly communicated.

5. In my pastoral counseling, I will maintain strict confidentiality, except in cases in which disclosure is necessary to prevent harm to persons and/or is required by law.

6. In my evangelistic responsibilities, I will seek to lead persons to salvation and to church membership without manipulating converts, proselytizing members of other churches, or demeaning other religious faiths.

7. In my visitation and counseling practices, I will never be alone with a person of another sex unless another church member is present nearby.

8. I will not charge fees to church members for weddings or funerals; for nonmembers I will establish policies based on ministry opportunities, time constraints, and theological beliefs.

9. As a full-time minister, I will not accept any other remunerative work without the expressed consent of the church.

10. In leaving a congregation, I will seek to strengthen the church through proper timing, verbal affirmation, and an appropriate closure of my ministry.

Responsibilities to Colleagues

1. I will endeavor to relate to all ministers, especially those with whom I serve in my church, as partners in the work of God, respecting their ministry and cooperating with them.

2. I will seek to serve my minister colleagues and their families with counsel, support, and personal assistance.

3. I will refuse to treat other ministers as competition in order to gain a church, receive an honor, or achieve statistical success.

4. I will refrain from speaking disparagingly about the person or work of any other minister, especially my predecessor or successor.

5. I will enhance the ministry of my successor by refusing to interfere in any way with the church I formerly served.

6. I will return to a former church field for professional services, such as weddings and funerals, only if invited by the resident pastor.

7. I will treat with respect and courtesy any predecessor who returns to my church field.

8. I will be thoughtful and respectful of all retired ministers and, upon my retirement, I will support and love my pastor.

9. I will be honest and kind in my recommendations of other ministers to church positions or other inquiries.

10. If aware of serious misconduct by a minister, I will contact responsible officials of that minister's church body and inform them of the incident.

Responsibilities to the Community

1. I will consider my primary responsibility to be pastor of my congregation and will never neglect ministerial duties in order to serve in the community.
2. I will accept reasonable responsibilities for community service, recognizing that the minister has a public ministry.
3. I will support public morality in the community through responsible prophetic witness and social action.
4. I will obey the laws of my government unless they require my disobedience to the law of God.
5. I will practice Christian citizenship without engaging in partisan politics or political activities that are unethical, unbiblical, or unwise.

Responsibilities to My Denomination

1. I will love, support, and cooperate with the faith community of which I am a part, recognizing the debt I owe to my denomination for its contribution to my life, my ministry, and my church.
2. I will work to improve my denomination in its efforts to expand and extend the kingdom of God.

Associate Minister Code (Education/Music/Youth/Etc.)

I will be supportive of and loyal to the senior pastor or, if unable to do so, will seek another place of service.

I will be supportive of and loyal to my fellow staff ministers, never criticizing them or undermining their ministry.

I will recognize my role and responsibility to the church staff and will not feel threatened or in competition with any other minister of the church.

I will maintain good relationships with other ministers of my special area of ministry.

If single, I will be discreet in my dating practices, especially in relation to members of my congregation.[2]

Pastoral Counselor Code

I will have a pastor/counselor to whom I can turn for counseling and advice.

I will be aware of my own needs and vulnerabilities, never seeking to meet my personal needs through my counselees.

I will recognize the power I hold over counselees and never take advantage of their vulnerability through exploitation or manipulation.

I will never become sexually or romantically involved with a client or engage in any form of erotic or romantic contact.

I will demonstrate unconditional acceptance and love toward all counselees, regardless of their standards, beliefs, attitudes, or actions.

If I am unable to benefit a client, I will refer them to another professional who can provide appropriate therapy.

I will maintain good relationships with other counselors and therapists, informing them and conferring with them about mutual concerns.

I will keep confidential all matters discussed in a counseling setting unless the information is hazardous for the client or another person or by law must be disclosed.

I will offer my assistance and services to fellow ministers and their families whenever needed.

I will support and contribute to the ministry of my church through personal counseling, seminars, lectures, workshops, and group therapy.

I will seek to support the policies and beliefs of my church without unduly imposing them on any counselee.[3]

Military Chaplain Code

I will be an ethical example of a Christian lifestyle in a military setting.

I will perform my service duties according to the military codes of conduct, recognizing that my ultimate allegiance is to God.

I will be truthful in my reports to my senior officers without divulging unnecessary confidential information.[4]

Notes

Preface

1. Joe E. Trull developed a seminary course titled "Ministerial Ethics" in 1992, as well as coauthored a text by that title (Nashville: Broadman & Holman, 1993; 2nd ed., Grand Rapids: Baker Academic, 2004) during his first sabbatical, returning to New Orleans Baptist Theological Seminary to continue teaching as professor of Christian ethics. The seminary course became the most popular "second ethics course" required of MDiv students. The coauthor of both texts, Dr. James E. Carter, was a pastor in Texas and Louisiana, and for two decades the counselor to ministers for the Louisiana Baptist Convention. Some readers may be aware that James Carter died on January 26, 2015, just a few months after his wife had died unexpectedly following surgery—both losses were personal and painful.

2. For example: Walter Wiest and Elwyn A. Smith, *Ethics in Ministry: A Guide for the Professional* (Minneapolis: Fortress, 1990); James P. Wind, Russell Burck, Paul F. Camenisch, and Dennis P. McCann, eds., *Clergy Ethics in a Changing Society: Mapping the Terrain* (Louisville: Westminster John Knox, 1991); Richard M. Gula, *Ethics in Pastoral Ministry* (New York: Paulist Press, 1996); and William H. Willimon, *Calling and Character: Virtues of the Ordained Life* (Nashville: Abingdon, 2000).

3. R. Robert Creech teaches at Baylor University's George W. Truett Theological Seminary. Although the seminary has no required MDiv courses in Christian ethics or ministerial ethics, it offers electives in both and addresses the subject of ethics in ministry in pastoral ministry and pastoral leadership courses.

4. Russell Moore, "What to Do When a Pastor Falls," RussellMoore.com, April 15, 2016, www.russellmoore.com/2016/04/15/what-to-do-when-a-pastor-falls/. Moore studied ministerial ethics with Trull at New Orleans Baptist Theological Seminary.

Chapter 1 Walking with Integrity

1. Walker Percy, *The Thanatos Syndrome* (New York: Farrar, Straus & Giroux, 1987), 75.

2. James P. Wind, "Clergy Ethics in Modern Fiction," in *Clergy Ethics in a Changing Society: Mapping the Terrain*, ed. James P. Wind, Russell Burck, Paul F. Camenisch, and Dennis P. McCann (Louisville: Westminster John Knox, 1991), 99.

3. The pastor of First Baptist Church of Dallas, Dr. Robert Jeffress, traveled to Dordt College in Iowa to endorse Donald Trump; Jeffress also introduced Trump the previous September at a rally in Dallas. See http://www.dallasvoice.com/jeffress-endorse-trump-endorses-10212614.html/.

4. For example, see the various denominational codes of conduct in appendix B and appendix C.

5. Martin E. Marty, "Drift Away," *Sightings* (blog), Sept. 8, 2014, https://divinity.uchicago.edu/sightings/drift-away-martin-e-marty.

6. George Bullard, "Are Millennials Different Than Boomers 40 Years Ago?," *Baptist Standard*, September 15, 2014, 2–3.

7. A. James Rudin, "Opinion: A Top 10 List of Religion Stories for 2014," *Baptist Standard*, December 29, 2014, 3–4.

8. For example, in every one of the three full-time churches in which I was the pastor, over a period of twenty years, I dealt with sexual transgressions of ministers. In the first church, a minister of music was romantically involved with two choir members and his secretary. In the second church, the previous pastor was forced to leave due to romantic and sexual relationships with several members, and while I was pastor I learned the youth minister had been involved with several college students, and the part-time counselor was caught in a sexual act with a counselee. In my third full-time church, an associate music minister (whom we learned was homosexual) made advances to several young men during an overnight stay at his apartment.

9. Oliver Sacks, *The Man Who Mistook His Wife for a Hat* (New York: Summit Books, 1985).

10. I am indebted to James F. Drane, *Becoming a Good Doctor* (Kansas City: Sheed & Ward, 1988), 1, for the application of this story to ethics.

11. James M. Gustafson, "The Clergy in the United States," in *The Professions in America*, ed. Kenneth Lynn (Boston: Beacon, 1967), 70.

12. James F. Fishburn and Neil Q. Hamilton, "Seminary Education Tested by Praxis," *Christian Century*, February 1–8, 1984, 108–12.

13. Gaylord Noyce, *Pastoral Ethics: Professional Responsibilities for the Clergy* (Nashville: Abingdon, 1988), 11.

14. Stanley Hauerwas and William H. Willimon, *Resident Aliens: Life in the Christian Colony* (Nashville: Abingdon, 1989), 113–14.

15. William F. May, "Vocation, Career, and Profession," *Institute for the Study of American Evangelicals*, November 17–19, 1988, 3, 6.

16. Barbara Zikmund, "Changing Understandings of Ordination," in *The Presbyterian Predicament*, ed. Milton Coulter, John Mulder, and Louis Weeks (Louisville: John Knox, 1990), 154.

17. John Piper, *Brothers, We Are Not Professionals* (Nashville: Broadman & Holman, 2002).

18. "Minnesota Pastor Urges Colleagues to Stop Being Professionals," *Facts and Trends*, December 2002, 15.

19. Darrell Reeck, *Ethics for the Professions: A Christian Perspective* (Minneapolis: Augsburg, 1982), 33.

20. James Luther Adams, "The Social Import of the Professions," *American Association of Theological Schools Bulletin* 23 (June 1958): 154.

21. Reeck, *Ethics for the Professions*, 35.

22. Anthony Russell, *The Clerical Profession* (London: SPCK, 1980), 6.

23. Ibid.

24. Kenneth S. Lynn, ed., *The Professions in America* (Boston: Beacon, 1967), xii.

25. Robert N. Bellah and William M. Sullivan, "The Professions and the Common Good: Vocation/Profession/Career," *Religion and Intellectual Life* 4 (Spring 1987): 8.

26. "Expectations for Baptist Clergy a Source of Stress," *Baptist Messenger*, October 31, 1991, 6.

27. Dennis Campbell, *Doctors, Lawyers, Ministers: Christian Ethics in Professional Practice* (Nashville: Abingdon, 1982), 18–19.

28. Ibid., 20–21. However, Martin Marty notes that other models have shaped the American clergy: (1) the public role in a congregational-territorial context (1492–1830s), (2) the congregational-denominational role, and (3) the emergent private-clientele expression. See "The

Clergy," in *The Professions in America*, ed. Nathan O. Hatch (Notre Dame, IN: University of Notre Dame Press, 1988), 76–77.

29. Reeck, *Ethics for the Professions*, 38.

30. Lisa Newton, "The Origin of Professionalism: Sociological Conclusions and Ethical Implications," *Business and Professional Ethics Journal* 1 (Summer 1982): 3.

31. Adams, "Social Import of the Professions," 156.

32. Edmund D. Pellegrino, "Professional Ethics: Moral Decline or Paradigm Shift?," *Religion and Intellectual Life* 4 (Spring 1987): 27.

33. Michael D. Bayles, *Professional Ethics*, 2nd ed. (Belmont, CA: Wadsworth, 1989), 8–9.

34. Patrick D. Miller, "Work and Faith," *Theology Today* 59 (October 2002): 67.

35. Paul Camenisch has noted, however, that even professional characteristics such as "specialized skills" must be qualified for the clergy, because ministers must often be a jack-of-all-trades, standards of admission to the profession are not uniform, and their skills are not consistently valued in the larger society. See Paul F. Camenisch, "Clergy Ethics and the Professional Ethics Model," in Wind et al., *Clergy Ethics in a Changing Society*, 121–25.

36. Ibid., 68.

37. Ibid.

38. A. M. Carr-Saunders and P. A. Wilson, *The Professions* (New York: Oxford University Press, 1933), 290.

39. Adams, "Social Import of the Professions," 153.

40. Bayles, *Professional Ethics*, ix.

41 James Wind and Gil Rindle, *The Leadership Situation Facing American Congregations* (Bethesda, MD: Alban Institute, 2001).

42. Max L. Stackhouse, *Public Theology and Political Economy* (Washington, DC: University Press of America, 1991), 172.

43. Pellegrino, "Professional Ethics," 21.

44. Nathan O. Hatch, "The Perils of Being a Professional," *Christianity Today*, November 11, 1991, 27.

45. Campbell, *Doctors, Lawyers, Ministers*, 31–36.

46. Ibid., 36.

47. Ibid., 38.

48. Tony Cartledge, "What People Want from the Church," *Biblical Recorder*, January 17, 2003.

49. James D. Glasse, *Profession: Minister* (Nashville: Abingdon, 1968), 13.

50. Ibid., 14–16.

51. James M. Gustafson, "An Analysis of the Problem of the Role of the Minister," *Journal of Religion* 34 (July 1954): 187.

52. Martin E. Marty, "Clergy Ethics in America: The Ministers on Their Own," in Wind et al., *Clergy Ethics in a Changing Society*, 24.

53. Ibid., 24–35.

54. Gilbert L. Rendle, "Reclaiming Professional Jurisdiction," *Theology Today* 59 (October 2002): 419.

55. Reeck, *Ethics for the Professions*, 14.

56. Campbell, *Doctors, Lawyers, Ministers*, 24–25.

57. David L. Sills, ed., *International Encyclopedia of the Social Sciences* (New York: Macmillan, 1968), s.v. "professions."

58. Ibid.

59. Noyce, *Pastoral Ethics*, 198.

60. Peter Jarvis, "The Ministry: Occupation, Profession, or Status?," *Expository Times* 86 (June 1975): 264–66.

61. Ibid., 267.

62. Adams, "Social Import of the Professions," 162.

63. Ibid., 162–63.

64. Jacques Ellul, "Work and Calling," in *Callings*, ed. W. D. Campbell and J. Y. Halloway (New York: Paulist Press, 1974), 33.

65. Hauerwas and Willimon, *Resident Aliens*, 121.

66. Adams, "Social Import of the Professions," 163.

67. Glasse, *Profession*, 38.

68. Ibid., 38–43, where the author discusses each in detail.

69. Noyce, *Pastoral Ethics*, 21.

70. Ibid., 23–24.

71. Gaylord Noyce, "The Pastor Is (Also) a Professional," *Christian Century*, November 2, 1988, 976.

72. Glasse, *Profession*, 47.

73. Although the underlying assumption of this chapter seems to be that professionalism is a characteristic each minister develops, the reality is that social institutions, such as the church and education, play a significant role in determining ministerial professionalism, even though ultimately each minister must decide whether to accept that vocational identity.

74. Miller, "Work and Faith," 352, who also provided the illustration.

75. Camenisch, "Clergy Ethics and the Professional Ethics Model," 131.

Chapter 2 Being Good and Doing Good

1. Lyman Abbott, *Henry Ward Beecher* (Hartford: American Pub. Co., 1887), 210.

2. Frederick Buechner, *Telling the Truth* (New York: Harper & Row, 1977), 2.

3. Ibid. In his autobiography, *The Americanization of Edward Bok*, a member of Beecher's church related what the pulpiteer told Edward Bok years after the trial, in which the jury voted nine to three in favor of Beecher. Beecher reportedly said, "And the decision of the nine was in accord with the facts."

4. Robert J. Young, "Ethics in Ministry," http://www.surfinthespirit.com/church/ethics-ministry.html. See also his earlier article "Ministry and Ethics in Crisis: Implications for 21st-Century Ministers," *Enrichment* (Fall 2004): 16–21.

5. Michael Levin's article of November 15, 1989, was titled "Ethics Courses Useless" and was published along with three typical responses from ethicists in *Update* 6 (November 1990): 3.

6. Ibid., 4–6.

7. For a discussion of these three elements, see Bruce Birch and Larry Rasmussen, *Bible and Ethics in the Christian Life*, rev. ed. (Minneapolis: Augsburg, 1989), 43–62.

8. T. B. Maston, *Why Live the Christian Life?* (Nashville: Broadman, 1974), 98. See also Bill Tillman et al., eds., *Both-And: A Maston Reader* (Dallas: T. B. Maston Foundation, 2011), for an excellent compilation of the life and teachings of Maston, considered by many to be the greatest biblical ethicist that Southern Baptists produced, and also the major professor of Joe E. Trull.

9. See, for example, Glen H. Stassen and David P. Gushee, *Kingdom Ethics*, 2nd ed. (Grand Rapids: Eerdmans, 2016), which centers on the life and teachings of Jesus, and Richard Higginson, *Dilemmas* (Louisville: Westminster John Knox, 1988), 55–77, where he details the use of deontological rules and consequentialist principles for moral reasoning in both Testaments, as well as the use of story, imitation, key themes, and scale of values.

10. Birch and Rasmussen, *Bible and Ethics*, 14–16.

11. See also Thomas Ogeltree, *The Use of the Bible in Christian Ethics* (Philadelphia: Fortress, 1983); H. Edward Everding Jr. and Dana Wilbanks, *Decision Making and the Bible* (Valley Forge, PA: Judson, 1975); and T. B. Maston, *Biblical Ethics* (Macon, GA: Mercer University Press, 1982).

12. Higginson, *Dilemmas*, 76.

13. See Wayne G. Boulton, Thomas D. Kennedy, and Allen Verhey, eds., *From Christ to the World: Introductory Readings in Christian Ethics* (Grand Rapids: Eerdmans, 1994), for excellent articles by these authors and many other leading ethicists.

14. See Jeff Holloway, *The Politics of Grace: Christian Ethics as Theodicy* (Eugene, OR: Wipf and Stock, 2013).

15. Sam Wells, *Introducing Christian Ethics* (Oxford: Wiley-Blackwell, 2010).

16. Birch and Rasmussen, *Bible and Ethics*, 42–65.

17. Albert Knudson, *The Principles of Christian Ethics* (New York: Abingdon, 1942), 39.

18. Stanley Hauerwas, *Character and the Christian Life* (San Antonio: Trinity University Press, 1975), 115.

19. William Willimon, *The Service of God* (Nashville: Abingdon, 1983), 28–29.

20. Sondra Ely Wheeler, "Virtue Ethics and the Sexual Formation of Clergy," in *Practice What You Preach: Virtue, Ethics, and Power*, ed. James F. Keenan, SJ, and Joseph Kotva Jr. (Franklin, WI: Sheed & Ward, 1999), 102–3.

21. D. Glen Saul, "The Ethics of Decision Making," in *Understanding Christian Ethics*, ed. William Tillman Jr. (Nashville: Broadman, 1988), 90.

22. Walter E. Wiest and Elwyn A. Smith, *Ethics in Ministry: A Guide for the Professional* (Minneapolis: Fortress, 1990), 182.

23. Stanley Hauerwas, *A Community of Character* (Notre Dame, IN: University of Notre Dame Press, 1981), 10.

24. Darrell Reeck, *Ethics for the Professions: A Christian Perspective* (Minneapolis: Augsburg, 1982), 43.

25. Richard M. Gula, *Ethics in Pastoral Ministry* (New York: Paulist Press, 1996), 33.

26. Daniel Taylor, "In Pursuit of Character," *Christianity Today*, December 11, 1995, 31.

27. Hauerwas, *Community of Character*, 111.

28. Birch and Rasmussen, *Bible and Ethics*, 46.

29. Reinhold Niebuhr, *The Nature and Destiny of Man* (New York: Scribner's Sons, 1943).

30. Karen Lebacqz, *Professional Ethics: Power and Paradox* (Nashville: Abingdon, 1985), 76, italics in original.

31. Ibid., 77–91.

32. Ibid., 114.

33. Lewis Smedes, "How the Bible Is Used in Moral Decision Making" (lecture, New Orleans Baptist Theological Seminary, March 7, 1971).

34. Gaylord Noyce, *Pastoral Ethics: Professional Responsibilities for the Clergy* (Nashville: Abingdon, 1988), 30–31.

35. Wiest and Smith, *Ethics in Ministry*, 21.

36. Ibid., 23.

37. Dennis P. McCann, "Costing Discipleship: Clergy Ethics in a Commercial Civilization," in *Clergy Ethics in a Changing Society*, ed. James P. Wind, Russell Burck, Paul F. Camenisch, and Dennis P. McCann (Louisville: Westminster John Knox, 1991), 137.

38. Lewis Smedes, *A Pretty Good Person* (San Francisco: Harper & Row, 1990), 3.

39. Ibid., 172.

40. Nolan Harmon, *Ministerial Ethics and Etiquette* (Nashville: Abingdon, 1978), 34, italics in original.

41. Dudley Strain, *The Measure of a Minister* (St. Louis: The Bethany Press, 1964), 159.

42. John B. Coburn, *Minister: Man-in-the-Middle* (New York: Macmillan, 1963), 159.

43. David K. Switzer, *Pastor, Preacher, Person: Developing a Pastoral Ministry in Depth* (Nashville: Abingdon, 1979), 16.

44. Lebacqz, *Professional Ethics*, 64. See also Henlee Barnette, "The Minister as a Moral Role-Model," *Review and Expositor* 86 (Fall 1989): 513.

45. Reeck, *Ethics for the Professions*, 47.

46. William Willimon seems to chide ethicists Wiest and Smith for "approaching clergy ethics as dilemmas and situations" (*Calling and Character: Virtues of the Ordained Life* [Nashville: Abingdon, 2000], 121); however, Willimon could receive equal criticism for a naïveté that assumes ministers need only to shape their character in order to make good ethical decisions.

47. Richard Foster, *Money, Sex, & Power: The Challenge of the Disciplined Life* (San Francisco: Harper & Row, 1985), 15.

48. Ibid.

49. Wiest and Smith, *Ethics in Ministry*, 37–54.

50. Birch and Rasmussen, *Bible and Ethics*, 50.

51. Hauerwas, *Community of Character*, 92.

52. Stanley Hauerwas and William H. Willimon, *Resident Aliens: Life in the Christian Colony* (Nashville: Abingdon, 1989), 12.

53. Higginson, *Dilemmas*, 107, also notes that Niebuhr agreed that a more accurate title would be *The Not-So-Moral Man in His Less-Moral Communities*.

54. Niebuhr, *Nature and Destiny of Man*, 248.

55. Reeck, *Ethics for the Professions*, 47.

56. L. H. Marshall, *The Challenge of New Testament Ethics* (London: Macmillan, 1960), 100.

57. John Macquarrie, ed., *Dictionary of Christian Ethics* (Philadelphia: Westminster, 1967), s.v. "Kant and Kantian Ethics," by A. C. Ewing.

58. W. D. Ross, *The Right and the Good* (Oxford: Oxford University Press, 1946), 19–21.

59. Lebacqz, *Professional Ethics*, 24.

60. Ibid., 75.

61. Maston, *Biblical Ethics*, viii, 168. See also Tillman, *Both-And*, esp. 19–21, 30–31, 33–34, 36–40, and 253–55.

62. Higginson, *Dilemmas*, 55–69.

63. Smedes, *Pretty Good Person*, 85.

64. Birch and Rasmussen, *Bible and Ethics*, 59.

65. George Wharton Pepper, *A Voice from the Crowd* (New Haven: Yale University Press, 1915), 23.

66. Strain, *Measure of a Minister*, 50.

67. Lebacqz, *Professional Ethics*, 89.

68. Birch and Rasmussen, *Bible and Ethics*, 62.

69. Charles Swindoll, *Rise & Shine: A Wake-Up Call* (Portland, OR: Multnomah, 1989), 190.

70. Ibid., 191.

71. Hauerwas, *Community of Character*, 91.

72. Saul, "Ethics of Decision-Making," 94. An excellent example of narrative ethics written in a "baptist theology" is James McClendon's *Systematic Theology: Ethics* (Chicago: Moody Press, 1956).

73. Charles M. Sheldon, *In His Steps* (Chicago: Moody Press, 1956).

74. Hauerwas, *Community of Character*, 131.

75. T. B. Maston, *To Walk as He Walked* (Nashville: Broadman, 1985), 9–11.

76. Lebacqz, *Professional Ethics*, 103.

77. Reeck, *Ethics for the Professions*, 55.

78. Higginson, *Dilemmas*, 230.

79. Quoted in Lewis Smedes, *Choices: Making Right Decisions in a Complex World* (San Francisco: Harper & Row, 1986), 81.

Chapter 3 Looking in the Mirror

1. William Arndt, Frederick W. Danker, and Walter Bauer, *A Greek-English Lexicon of the New Testament and Other Early Christian Literature* (Chicago: University of Chicago Press, 2000), 93.

2. William H. Willimon, *Pastor: The Theology and Practice of Ordained Ministry* (Nashville: Abingdon, 2009), 326.

3. Wendell Berry, "The Body and the Earth," in *The Art of the Commonplace: The Agrarian Essays of Wendell Berry*, ed. Norman Wirzba (Emeryville, CA: Shoemaker & Hoard, 2003), 99.

4. Ibid., 93.

5. Richard B. Hays, *The Moral Vision of the New Testament: Community, Cross, New Creation; A Contemporary Introduction to New Testament Ethics* (San Francisco: Harper-SanFrancisco, 1996), xi.

6. James William McClendon Jr., *Systematic Theology*, 2nd ed., vol. 1, *Ethics* (Nashville: Abingdon, 2002), 43.

7. "Americans' Faith in Honesty, Ethics of Police Rebounds," Gallup.com, Dec. 21, 2015, http://www.gallup.com/poll/187874/americans-faith-honesty-ethics-police-rebounds.aspx.

8. Diana R. Garland, "Clergy Sexual Misconduct Study: Executive Summary," May 18, 2016, http://www.baylor.edu/clergysexualmisconduct/index.php?id=67406.

9. Glenn E. Ludwig, *In It for the Long Haul: Building Effective Long-Term Pastorates* (Bethesda, MD: Alban Institute, 2002), 24.

10. Ronald Stuart Thomas, *The Minister* (Montgomeryshire, UK: Montgomeryshire Printing Company, 1953).

11. Ibid., 2.

12. Ibid.

13. Clinical psychologist Herman Kagan argues for the existence of a "psychological immune system" that is part of the evolutionary development of the human brain. This system helps us identify and respond to threats and dangers, as the biological immune system does. The psychological immune system, like the biological, can be both beneficial and deadly. This system is held in check, he argues, by the development of moral and ethical standards (*The Psychological Immune System: A New Look at Protection and Survival* [Bloomington, IN: Author House, 2006], 246). The "moral immune system" referred to here is a metaphorical description of our capacity to respond to challenges to our most important ethical standards when under pressure to compromise them.

14. Henri J. M. Nouwen, *The Wounded Healer: Ministry in Contemporary Society* (Garden City, NY: Image Books, 1979), 81–96.

15. Ibid., 85.

16. Ibid.

17. Ibid., 87.

18. Ibid.

19. David K. Pooler, "Pastors and Congregations at Risk: Insights from Role Identity Theory," *Pastoral Psychology* 60, no. 5 (March 22, 2011): 708.

20. Ibid., 707.

21. Ibid., 708.

22. Harvard Health Publications, "How to Boost Your Immune System," *Harvard Health*, June 15, 2016, http://www.health.harvard.edu/staying-healthy/how-to-boost-your-immune-system.

23. Wendell Berry writes, "I believe that the community—in the fullest sense: a place and all its creatures—is the smallest unit of health and that to speak of the health of an isolated individual is a contradiction in terms." "Health as Membership," in *Art of the Commonplace*, 146.

24. R. Paul Stevens and Phil Collins, *The Equipping Pastor: A Systems Approach to Congregational Leadership* (Washington, DC: Alban Institute, 1993), 75–91.

25. Richard M. Gula argues for the appropriateness of the covenant model over the contractual one in *Ethics in Pastoral Ministry* (New York: Paulist Press, 1996), 15–21.

26. Thomas, *Minister*, 2.

27. Pooler, "Pastors and Congregations at Risk," 711.

28. R. Robert Creech, "Sustainable Church: Practices That Make for a Lifetime of Service," *Review and Expositor* 113, no. 3 (August 1, 2016): 285–302, doi:10.1177/0034637316656424.

29. Eugene H. Peterson refers to the development of a "vocational holiness" to counteract the dangers of a "vocational idolatry" that threatens a pastor's integrity, an interior adequate to our exterior (*Under the Unpredictable Plant: An Exploration in Vocational Holiness* [Grand Rapids: Eerdmans, 1994], 3).

30. Ludwig, *In It for the Long Haul*, 60.

31. Charles B. Bugg, "Professional Ethics among Ministers," *Review and Expositor* 86, no. 4 (September 1989): 562–63.

32. Roy M. Oswald, *New Visions for the Long Pastorate* (Washington, DC: Alban Institute, 1983), 91.

33. Robert A. Sizemore, "Calling, Affinity, and Personal Growth: Key Factors in Long-Term Ministries" (DMin diss., Trinity International University, 2014), 115, http://search.proquest .com.ezproxy.baylor.edu/docview/1648430986/abstract.

34. Janet Maycus, "Condition: Critical: Exploring the Causes of Poor Clergy Health," *Sustaining Pastoral Excellence*, https://www.faithandleadership.com/programs/spe/articles/200601 /critical.html?printable=true.

35. Stephanie Paulsell, *Honoring the Body: Meditations on a Christian Practice*, Practices of Faith Series (San Francisco: Jossey-Bass, 2002).

36. Bob Wells, "Which Way to Clergy Health?," *Pulpit and Pew*, 2002, http://pulpitandpew .org/which-way-clergy-health.

37. Kathryn Greene-McCreight, *Darkness Is My Only Companion: A Christian Response to Mental Illness*, rev. ed. (Grand Rapids: Brazos Press, 2015).

38. Lewis Brogdon, *Dying to Lead: The Disturbing Trend of Clergy Suicide* (Bowie, MD: Seymour Press, 2015).

39. Sharon L. Miller, Kim Maphis Early, and Anthony Ruger, *Taming the Tempest: A Team Approach to Reducing and Managing Student Debt*, Auburn Studies 19 (New York: Auburn Theological Seminary, 2014), 5–6.

40. Ibid., 18.

41. Becky R. McMillan and Matthew J. Price, *How Much Should We Pay the Pastor? A Fresh Look at Clergy Salaries in the 21st Century*, Pulpit and Pew: Research on Pastoral Leadership, no. 2 (Durham, NC: Duke Divinity School, 2003), 3.

42. Angela H. Reed and R. Robert Creech, *Sustainability in Congregational Vocational Ministry among Texas Baptists: An Oral History Research Project* (Waco: Baylor University Department of Oral History, 2014), transcript.

43. Elizabeth Ann Jackson-Jordan, "Clergy Burnout and Resilience: A Review of the Literature," *Journal of Pastoral Care & Counseling (Online)* 67, no. 1 (March 2013): 1–5.

44. Dean R. Hoge and Jacqueline E. Wenger, *Pastors in Transition: Why Clergy Leave Local Church Ministry*, Pulpit and Pew Series (Grand Rapids: Eerdmans, 2005), 198–99.

45. Richard J. Foster, *The Challenge of the Disciplined Life: Christian Reflections on Money, Sex, and Power* (San Francisco: HarperOne, 1989), 5.

46. Garland, "Clergy Sexual Misconduct Study."

47. H. B. London and Neil B. Wiseman, *Pastors at Greater Risk: Real Help for Pastors from Pastors Who Have Been There* (Ventura, CA: Gospel Light, 2003), 238.

48. Ed Stetzer, "My Pastor Is on the Ashley Madison List," *The Exchange: A Blog by Ed Stetzer*, Aug. 27, 2015, http://www.christianitytoday.com/edstetzer/2015/august/my-pastor-is -on-ashley-madison-list.html.

49. The suicide was reported at http://money.cnn.com/2015/09/08/technology/ashley -madison-suicide/ and the resignation at http://www.usatoday.com/story/tech/2015/08/31/ash ley-madison-christian-theologian-robert-craig-sproul-jr/71489636/.

50. A widely circulated anonymous article from 1982 demonstrated the danger that pornography posed to ministers long before the internet became available (name withheld, "The War Within: An Anatomy of Lust," *Leadership Journal*, Fall 1982, http://www.christianitytoday .com/le/1982/fall/warwithinanatomylust.html).

51. William H. Willimon, *Pastor: The Theology of Ordained Ministry* (Nashville: Abingdon, 2009), 325–26.

52. Ibid., 326–27.

53. For testimony of the impact of an extended pastoral sabbatical on both pastor and congregation, see Eugene H. Peterson, *The Contemplative Pastor: Returning to the Art of Spiritual Direction* (Grand Rapids: Eerdmans, 1993), 141–54.

54. Timothy Fry, Timothy Horner, and Imogene Baker, eds., *RB 1980: The Rule of St. Benedict in English* (Collegeville, MN: Liturgical Press, 1981).

55. For an example of such a code, see Clergy Ethics Committee, "Ministerial Ethics: A Covenant of Trust" (Dallas: Baptist General Convention of Texas Christian Life Commission, 2005).

56. The concept of congruence in life is found in Charles Hobbs, *Time Power: The Revolutionary Time Management System That Can Change Your Professional and Personal Life* (New York: HarperCollins, 1987), 32.

57. Peterson, *Contemplative Pastor*, 22.

58. Ibid., 23.

59. Stephen R. Covey, A. Roger Merrill, and Rebecca R. Merrill, *First Things First* (New York: Free Press, 1996), 88–92.

Chapter 4 Looking at the Church

1. Wendell Berry, *A Place on Earth: A Novel* (Berkeley: Counterpoint, 2001), 103.

2. R. Paul Stevens and Phil Collins, *The Equipping Pastor: A Systems Approach to Congregational Leadership* (Washington, DC: Alban Institute, 1993), 7.

3. Berry, *A Place on Earth*, 104.

4. Randall Everett, "Pastor and Staff to Congregation Relationships," in *Pastor, Staff, and Congregational Relationships: Through Servant Leadership and Quality Administration*, ed. Bernard M. Spooner (Coppell, TX: CreateSpace, 2014), 73–75.

5. Wes Jackson, *Consulting the Genius of the Place: An Ecological Approach to a New Agriculture* (Berkeley: Counterpoint, 2010), ix.

6. For a model for such a covenant, see Clergy Ethics Committee, "Ministerial Ethics: A Covenant of Trust" (Dallas: Baptist General Convention of Texas Christian Life Commission, 2005).

7. Eugene H. Peterson, *The Contemplative Pastor: Returning to the Art of Spiritual Direction* (Grand Rapids: Eerdmans, 1993), 144–45.

8. Kennon L. Callahan, *Twelve Keys to an Effective Church: Strong, Healthy Congregations Living in the Grace of God* (San Francisco: Jossey-Bass, 2010), 100, 127.

9. Lyle E. Schaller, *The Pastor and the People* (Nashville: Abingdon, 1986), 88.

10. Donald A. Schön, *The Reflective Practitioner: How Professionals Think in Action* (New York: Basic Books, 1983).

11. Craig Dykstra, "Pastoral and Ecclesial Imagination," in *For Life Abundant: Practical Theology, Theological Education, and Christian Ministry*, ed. Dorothy C. Bass and Craig Dykstra (Grand Rapids: Eerdmans, 2008), 41–61.

12. Ronald D. Sisk helps pastors with two important questions: (1) What does it mean to be *competent?* and (2) How does a competent minister *function?* See *The Competent Pastor: Skills and Self-Knowledge for Serving Well* (Herndon, VA: Rowman & Littlefield, 2005).

13. Allan Hugh Cole, "What Makes Care Pastoral?," *Pastoral Psychology* 59, no. 6 (July 9, 2010): 715.

14. Jürgen Moltmann, *In the End, the Beginning: The Life of Hope* (Minneapolis: Fortress, 2004), 105.

15. Wendell Berry, "An Argument for Diversity," in *What Are People For? Essays* (Berkeley: Counterpoint, 2010), 116.

16. Wallace Stegner and T. H. Watkins, *Where the Bluebird Sings to the Lemonade Springs: Living and Writing in the West* (New York: Modern Library, 2002), xxvii.

17. Wendell Berry, *It All Turns on Affection: The Jefferson Lecture and Other Essays* (Berkeley: Counterpoint, 2012), 12.

18. Wendell Berry, "Economy and Pleasure," in *What Are People For?*, 136.

19. Martin B. Copenhaver, "Staying Power: Reflections on a Long Pastorate," *Christian Century*, March 20, 2013, 29.

20. Dietrich Bonhoeffer, *Life Together* (London: SCM, 1954), 29.

21. "It's Okay to Go There: The Place of Friendship in Ministry," *Pulpit and Pew*, reprinted from the Winter 2003 issue of *Divinity*, the alumni magazine of Duke Divinity School, http://pulpitandpew.org/its-okay-go-there-place-friendship-ministry.

22. Marilynne Robinson, *Gilead* (New York: Farrar, Straus & Giroux, 2004), 6–7.

23. Gaylord Noyce, *Pastoral Ethics: Professional Responsibilities for the Clergy* (Nashville: Abingdon, 1988), 91.

24. Gaynor Yancey, Beth R. Kilpatrick, and Kimberly Stutts, "Confidentiality in the Church," *Family and Community Ministries* 23, no. 4 (2010): 61–69.

25. Craig Meissner makes a case theologically and biblically for the importance of confidentiality on the part of ministers in "The Seal of the Confessional and Maintenance of Confidentiality in Pastoral Practice," *Logia* 20, no. 3 (2011): 25–33.

26. Office for Civil Rights, "Summary of the HIPAA Privacy Rule," HHS.gov, May 7, 2008, http://www.hhs.gov/hipaa/for-professionals/privacy/laws-regulations/index.html.

27. Christopher Lind, "Keeping and Sharing: Confidentiality in Ministry," *Journal of Pastoral Care & Counseling* 60, nos. 1–2 (2006): 117–31. Lind interviews pastors, chaplains, and other ministers about their understanding and practice of confidentiality.

28. "Legal Statutes Regarding Confidential Clergy Communications Privilege," http://www.denver.goarch.org/clergy/resources/statutes/confidential_communications.html#texas.

29. Texas Rules of Evidence Article V. Privileges Rule 505. Communications to Members of the Clergy, http://texasevidence.com/article-v-privileges/rule-505-communications-to-members-of-the-clergy/.

30. Ibid.

31. Michael Clay Smith, "Pastor on the Witness Stand: Toward a Religious Privilege in the Courts," *Catholic Lawyer* 29 (1984): 1–21.

32. Ronald K. Bullis, "Child Abuse Reporting Requirements: Liabilities and Immunities for Clergy," *Journal of Pastoral Care* 44, no. 3 (September 1990): 244–48.

33. Texas Family Code Section 261, http://www.statutes.legis.state.tx.us/Docs/FA/htm/FA.261.htm.

34. Ronald K. Bullis and Cynthia S. Mazur, *Legal Issues and Religious Counseling* (Louisville: Westminster John Knox, 1993), 96; William W. Rankin, *Confidentiality and Clergy: Churches, Ethics, and the Law* (Harrisburg, PA: Morehouse, 1990), 47–61.

35. Rankin, *Confidentiality and Clergy*, 61.

36. Donald Dale Freeman, "Confidentiality in the Practice of Authorized Ministry: A United Church of Christ Perspective," *Prism* 24, nos. 1–2 (September 2010): 121.

37. W. Dow Edgerton, "Confidentiality," *Prism* 19, no. 1 (2004): 60.

38. The most notable is the *Nally v. Grace Community Church* case in California in 1984. That case eventually made its way to appeal to the US Supreme Court, which refused to hear it, leaving it with the California State Supreme Court's decision to support the original verdict of the trial court, exonerating the pastors involved from charges of malpractice or negligence (Rankin, *Confidentiality and Clergy*, 23–30).

39. Ibid., 31.

40. William H. Willimon, *Pastor: The Theology and Practice of Ordained Ministry* (Nashville: Abingdon, 2009), 60.

41. This is a term used in the context where the author served, to be clear that none of the pastors on the staff were qualified, trained "counselors."

42. See Eugene Peterson's description of the pastoral work of spiritual direction in *Working the Angles: The Shape of Pastoral Integrity* (Grand Rapids: Eerdmans, 1987), 149–92.

43. Will D. Campbell, *Brother to a Dragonfly* (New York: Continuum, 2000), 212.

44. Ibid., 213. Campbell suggests that his conscience might eventually lead him to refuse to sign the document at all, asking the couple to go first to a justice of the peace to sign the "contract of Caesar." He also confesses to having performed weddings with no documents at all, defying Caesar to question that the couple is married.

45. "Texas Baptists—Christianity & Same-Sex Marriage," http://txb.life/article/prepare-you r-church-for-same-sex-marriage-ruling; Kara Bettis, "Same Sex Marriage Is Legal: How Pastors Are Responding in This Crucial Moment," *Leadership Journal*, June 2015, http://www.christianity today.com/le/2015/june-web-exclusives/same-sex-marriage-is-legal-how-pastors-are-respond ing-in-th.html; The Ethics & Religious Liberty Commission, "Explainer: What You Should Know about the Supreme Court Same-Sex Marriage Ruling," *ERLC*, June 26, 2015, http://erlc .com/resource-library/articles/explainer-what-you-should-know-about-the-supreme-court -same-sex-marriage-ruling; Leith Anderson, Jo Anne Lyon, Stephen Monsma, and anonymous pastor, "Same-Sex Marriage: New Challenges, New Opportunities," *Leadership Journal*, July 2015, http://www.christianitytoday.com/le/2015/july-web-exclusives/same-sex-marriage-new -challenges-new-opportunities.html.

46. Marriage laws can vary drastically from state to state. Pastors need to be clear about the requirements for officiants before performing a wedding. See "Marriage Laws," Legal Information Institute, https://www.law.cornell.edu/wex/table_marriage.

47. "Industry Statistical Information," Cremation Association of North America, http:// www.cremationassociation.org/?page=IndustryStatistics.

48. Raymond H. Bailey, "Ethics in Preaching," *Review and Expositor* 86, no. 4 (September 1989): 536.

49. Joseph R. Jeter Jr., "'Posturing in Borrowed Plumes': An Introduction to Preaching and Plagiarism," *Encounter* 66, no. 4 (Autumn 2005): 293–300; Thomas G. Long, "Stolen Goods: Tempted to Plagiarize," *Christian Century*, April 17, 2007, 18–21; Carter Shelley, "'Stolen Words': A Brief History and Analysis of Preaching and Plagiarism," *Encounter* 66, no. 4 (Autumn 2005): 301–16.

50. O. Wesley Allen Jr., "Liar, Liar, Pulpit on Fire: Homiletical Ethics and Plagiarism," *Lexington Theological Quarterly* 41, no. 2 (2006): 66. Allen, of Lexington Theological Seminary, provides a thorough treatment of the ethics of plagiarism.

51. Rev. Gerard A. Herklots was the curate (1858) and later vicar (1872) of St. Saviour's, Hampstead, the Hopkins's family's church. Gerard Manley Hopkins, *The Poetical Works of Gerard Manley Hopkins*, ed. Norman H. MacKenzie (Oxford: Clarendon, 1990), 44.

52. One such case involving a prominent pastor made national news. "Pastor Resigns after Admitting Plagiarism," *Christian Century*, June 15, 2004, 16.

53. Not everyone considers such plagiarism an ethical issue. For example, Bil Cornelius and Bill Easum offer this advice to pastors who desire to "Go Big":

> Sometimes pastors are so busy writing messages that they have no energy left to focus on strategic pursuits like adding a service or staff member or advertising or getting out among the public. Instead of spending so much time in the office, we recommend buying another pastor's sermon series, whoever's teaching you happen to like, and teach his or her series for a month. Tell your people what you are doing. In his early years at Bay Area Fellowship, Bil C. used to regularly take other preachers' messages and use them from beginning to end, and give credit at the bottom of his message outlines. This way

he could use his time reaching people instead of creating a message from scratch. (Bil Cornelius and Bill Easum, *Go Big: Lead Your Church to Explosive Growth* [Nashville: Abingdon, 2006], 70)

54. Dirk Nelson, "Credibility in Preaching," *Covenant Quarterly* 72, nos. 1–2 (February 2014): 54–58.

55. William D. Barrick, "Exegetical Fallacies: Common Interpretive Mistakes Every Student Must Avoid," *Master's Seminary Journal* 19, no. 1 (2008): 15–27.

56. Tryon Edwards, *A Dictionary of Thoughts: Being a Cyclopedia of Laconic Quotations from the Best Authors of the World, Both Ancient and Modern* (Detroit: F. B. Dickerson Company, 1908), 436.

57. Phillips Brooks, *Lectures on Preaching, Delivered before the Divinity School of Yale College in January and February, 1877* (Boston: E. P. Dutton, 1877), 8.

58. Will Willimon takes preachers to task for abandoning the prophetic preaching of the Word for cultural accommodation in "Pastors Who Won't Be Preachers: A Polemic against Homiletical Accommodation to the Culture of Contentment," *Journal for Preachers* 29, no. 4 (2006): 37–42.

59. Ronald J. Allen has thoughtfully assembled a comprehensive code of ethics for preachers that provides a good starting place to think through one's own commitments to preaching ethically in "A Code of Ethics for Preachers," *Encounter* 66, no. 4 (Autumn 2005): 343–48.

60. Richard J. Foster, *The Challenge of the Disciplined Life: Christian Reflections on Money, Sex, and Power* (San Francisco: HarperOne, 1989), ix.

61. Wendell Berry, "Nature as Measure," in *What Are People For?*, 208–9.

62. Wendell Berry, "Damage," in *What Are People For?*, 8.

63. Richard J. Foster, *Celebration of Discipline: The Path to Spiritual Growth* (San Francisco: HarperSanFrancisco, 1998), 111.

64. Henri J. M. Nouwen, *In the Name of Jesus: Reflections on Christian Leadership* (New York: Crossroad, 1992), 85–90.

65. Susan Nienaber, "Getting Clear on Boundaries and Ethics," *Congregations* 31, no. 4 (September 2005): 44.

66. Robert K. Greenleaf, *The Servant as Leader* (Cambridge: Center for Applied Studies, 1973).

67. C. Gene Wilkes, "Servant Leadership: The Place to Begin," in *Pastor, Staff, and Congregational Relationships: Through Servant Leadership and Quality Administration*, ed. Bernard M. Spooner (Coppell, TX: CreateSpace, 2014), 23–26.

68. I am indebted to Eugene H. Peterson for this metaphor (*Working the Angles*, 2).

69. Max Depree, *Leadership Is an Art* (New York: Crown Business, 2004), 11.

70. For practical insight into equipping ministry, see Sue Mallory, *The Equipping Church* (Grand Rapids: Zondervan, 2001). For theological and theoretical background, see Findley B. Edge, *The Greening of the Church* (Waco: Word Books, 1971), and Stevens and Collins, *Equipping Pastor*.

71. Steve L. Woodworth, "We Are All Interim Pastors," *Leadership Journal*, May 2015, http://www.christianitytoday.com/le/2015/may-web-exclusives/we-are-all-interim-pastors.html.

72. James M. Antal offers a thorough consideration of the ethical issues surrounding the transition of ministry from one congregation to another in *Considering a New Call: Ethical and Spiritual Challenges for Clergy* (Bethesda, MD: Rowman & Littlefield, 2000).

73. Steven M. Johnson, "Running with Patience: Encouraging the Long-Term Pastorate," *Review and Expositor* 113, no. 3 (August 1, 2016): 359–68, doi:10.1177/0034637316658493.

74. Eugene H. Peterson, *Under the Unpredictable Plant: An Exploration in Vocational Holiness* (Grand Rapids: Eerdmans, 1994), 19. Peterson argues that "the *norm* for pastoral work is stability. Twenty-, thirty-, and forty-year-long pastorates should be typical among us (as they once were) and not exceptional. Far too many pastors change parishes out of adolescent boredom, not as a consequence of mature wisdom. When this happens, neither pastor nor congregations have access to the conditions that are hospitable to maturity in faith" (29).

75. Willimon, *Pastor*, 315.

76. Lawrence W. Farris, *Ten Commandments for Pastors Leaving a Congregation* (Grand Rapids: Eerdmans, 2006).

77. R. Robert Creech, "Bowen Theory and a Pastoral Transition," *Family Systems Forum* 12, no. 3 (Fall 2010): 1–2, 8–10.

78. Edwin H. Friedman, Gary Emanuel, and Mickie Crimone, *Generation to Generation: Family Process in Church and Synagogue* (New York: Guilford, 2011), 250–53.

Chapter 5 Looking at Fellow Ministers

1. Marilynne Robinson, *Gilead* (New York: Farrar, Straus & Giroux, 2004), 74.

2. Eugene H. Peterson, *The Pastor: A Memoir* (New York: HarperOne, 2011), 160.

3. Acts 16:10 begins the first of the well-known "we sections" of Acts, indicating that Luke has joined the team (John B. Polhill, *Acts*, The New American Commentary 26 [Nashville: Broadman & Holman, 1992], 346). The "we sections" include Acts 16:10–17; 20:5–15; 21:1–18; and 27:1–28:16.

4. Note Paul's references to those who worked with him: Rom. 16:1–24; 1 Cor. 1:1; 16:10–20; 2 Cor. 1:1, 19; 2:12–13; 7:5–7; 8:16–24; 12:18; Phil. 2:19–30; 4:2–3; Col. 1:1; 4:7–18; 1 Thess. 1:1; 3:1–3, 6; 2 Thess. 1:1; 1 Timothy; 2 Timothy; Titus.

5. David Capes, "Paul's Co-Workers," *A Word in Edgewise* (blog), January 24, 2013, https://davidbcapes.com/articles/brief-articles/pauls-co-workers/.

6. The same case could be made for some of the other apostles—Peter, James, and John, for example, who are portrayed as working together or with others

7. Jim Taylor, "Has America Become Too Competitive?," *Psychology Today*, April 2, 2013, http://www.psychologytoday.com/blog/the-power-prime/201304/has-america-become-too-competitive.

8. Kennon L. Callahan, *Effective Church Leadership: Building on the Twelve Keys* (San Francisco: Jossey-Bass, 1997), 13.

9. Ibid., 27.

10. For a fresh perspective on the radical nature of the kingdom narrative as a basis for living and ministering, see Donald B. Kraybill, *The Upside-Down Kingdom* (Harrisonburg, VA: Herald, 2011).

11. Edwin H. Friedman, Gary Emanuel, and Mickie Crimone, *Generation to Generation: Family Process in Church and Synagogue* (New York: Guilford, 2011), 268.

12. Mike Fleischmann, "Honor Thy Predecessor," *Leadership Journal*, April 2015, http://www.christianitytoday.com/le/2015/april-online-only/honor-thy-predecessor.html.

13. Ibid.

14. Ron Lyles (senior pastor at South Main Baptist Church, Pasadena, Texas) in an interview with the author, July 2016.

15. Bill Wilson, "A Healthy Handoff: The Crucial Relationship between Former and Current Pastor," *Center for Congregational Health*, April 29, 2011, https://cntr4conghealth.wordpress.com/2011/04/29/a-healthy-handoff-the-crucial-relationship-between-former-and-current-pastor/. For Glenn's entire interview with Wilson, see Bill Wilson, "A Healthy Handoff: Interview with Dr. Mike Glenn," *Center for Congregational Health*, April 29, 2011, https://cntr4conghealth.wordpress.com/2011/04/29/a-healthy-handoff-interview-with-dr-mike-glenn/.

16. Bill Wilson, "A Healthy Handoff: Interview with Michael Lea," *Center for Congregational Health*, April 29, 2011, https://cntr4conghealth.wordpress.com/2011/04/29/a-healthy-handoff-interview-with-michael-lea/; Bill Wilson, "A Healthy Handoff: Interview with Ken Morris," *Center for Congregational Health*, April 29, 2011, https://cntr4conghealth.wordpress.com/2011/04/29/a-health-handoff-interview-with-ken-morris/.

17. Wilson, "Healthy Handoff: The Crucial Relationship," 9.

18. Ibid.

19. Fleischmann, "Honor Thy Predecessor."

20. William M. Tillman, "The Congregation Relating Ethically to the Pastor, Staff, and Other Congregations," in *Pastor, Staff, and Congregational Relationships: Through Servant Leadership and Quality Administration*, ed. Bernard M. Spooner (Coppell, TX: CreateSpace, 2014), 120.

21. Ibid., 121.

22. Ron Ashkenas, "Jack Welch's Approach to Breaking Down Silos Still Works," *Harvard Business Review*, September 9, 2015, https://hbr.org/2015/09/jack-welchs-approach-to-break ing-down-silos-still-works.

23. Phil Lineberger, "The Pastor Relating to Staff," in *Pastor, Staff, and Congregational Relationships*, 39.

24. Exod. 3:19–22; Irenaeus, *Against Heresies* 4.30; Origen, *Letter to Gregory* 1; Augustine, *On Christian Teaching* 2.40.

25. See, for example, Mike Bonem, *In Pursuit of Great and Godly Leadership: Tapping the Wisdom of the World for the Kingdom of God* (San Francisco: Jossey-Bass, 2012).

26. Charles Duhigg, "What Google Learned from Its Quest to Build the Perfect Team," *New York Times*, Feb. 25, 2016, http://www.nytimes.com/2016/02/28/magazine/what-google-learned -from-its-quest-to-build-the-perfect-team.html?_r=0.

27. Doug Bixby, "Pastor in the Middle: Don't Avoid Conflict, Avoid Triangles," *Christian Century*, June 22, 2016, 24–26.

28. Larry C. Ashlock, "Practicing Christian Ethics in Pastor, Staff, and Congregational Relationships," in *Pastor, Staff, and Congregational Relationships*, 115.

29. Abe Levy, "Leader of the Future Already in Position at Oak Hills Church," *San Antonio Express-News*, Sept. 8, 2012, http://www.mysanantonio.com/news/local_news/article/2-sets -of-hands-on-reins-3850612.php.

30. Friedman, Emanuel, and Crimone, *Generation to Generation*, 265.

31. For a detailed account of the transition from the perspective of employing Bowen Family Systems Theory as a means of thinking through the succession, see R. Robert Creech, "Bowen Theory and a Pastoral Transition," *Family Systems Forum* 12, no. 3 (Spring 2010): 1–2, 8–10.

32. R. Paul Stevens and Phil Collins, *The Equipping Pastor: A Systems Approach to Congregational Leadership* (Washington, DC: Alban Institute, 1993), 1–2.

33. The story of W. A. Criswell's inability to "leave" First Baptist Church, Dallas, Texas, and the impact of that on his successor, Joel Gregory, is a dramatic example. See "The Rise and Fall and Rise Again of Joel Gregory," *Baptist News Global*, Sept. 16, 2014, https://baptistnews .com/article/the-rise-and-fall-and-rise-again-of-joel-gregory/.

34. Wilson, "Healthy Handoff: The Crucial Relationship," 9.

35. The term "intentional interim" is copyrighted by The Interim Ministry Network, Inc.

36. Ron Brown suggests that one or more of the following situations might call for a congregation's wisely engaging an intentional interim: the departure of a long-tenured pastor (seven or more years); the forced termination of a pastor; moral failure on the part of the departing pastor; severe conflict between the departing pastor and the congregation; the church has not conducted a self-study of structure, priorities, mission, or vision in the past five years; or the church has a pattern of the last two pastors serving for less than three years ("Interim or Intentional Interim©," *Review and Expositor* 100, no. 2 [2003]: 248).

37. Ibid., 253–54.

Chapter 6 Promoting Peace and Justice

1. Kennon L. Callahan, *Twelve Keys to an Effective Church: Strong, Healthy Congregations Living in the Grace of God* (San Francisco: Jossey-Bass, 2010), 53, bold in original.

2. Ibid., 53–54, bold in original.

3. Ibid., 54, bold in original.

4. See Stanley Hauerwas and William H. Willimon, *Resident Aliens: Life in the Christian Colony* (Nashville: Abingdon, 1989).

5. Cited in Jürgen Moltmann, *Theology of Hope: On the Ground and the Implications of a Christian Eschatology* (New York: Harper & Row, 1975), 20.

6. Ibid., 327.

7. See this thoroughly developed biblical theology in J. Richard Middleton, *A New Heaven and a New Earth: Reclaiming Biblical Eschatology* (Grand Rapids: Baker Academic, 2014).

8. Hauerwas and Willimon, *Resident Aliens*, 39.

9. Jim Wallis, *God's Politics: Why the Right Gets It Wrong and the Left Doesn't Get It* (San Francisco: HarperSanFrancisco, 2005), xvii.

10. Mark Galli, "Why We Need More 'Chaplains' and Fewer Leaders," ChristianityToday.com, Dec. 1, 2011, http://www.christianitytoday.com/ct/2011/decemberweb-only/morechaplains.html.

11. Ibid.

12. Thom S. Rainer, "Ten Signs a Pastor Is Becoming a Chaplain," ThomRainer.com, Sept. 7, 2015, http://thomrainer.com/2015/09/ten-signs-a-pastor-is-becoming-a-chaplain/.

13. Kennon L. Callahan, *Effective Church Leadership: Building on the Twelve Keys* (San Francisco: Jossey-Bass, 1997), 3.

14. Callahan, *Twelve Keys*, 22, 28–29. See also his *Preaching Grace: Possibilities for Growing Your Preaching and Touching People's Lives* (San Francisco: Jossey-Bass, 1999).

15. Callahan, *Effective Church Leadership*, 31.

16. As a pastor, I often reminded myself and the congregation I served that "if Jesus lived at 16106 Middlebrook Drive [the address of our church's building], people would know he was there and would miss him if he were gone."

17. Paul Hiebert, "Conversion, Culture and Cognitive Categories," *Gospel in Context* 11, no. 4 (October 1978): 24–29; Paul Hiebert, "The Category 'Christian' in the Mission Task," *International Review of Mission* 72, no. 287 (July 1983): 421–27.

18. Gary Corwin, "Bounded and Centered Sets," *Evangelical Missions Quarterly* 47, no. 4 (October 2011): 390–91.

19. Eric Swanson and Rick Rusaw, *The Externally Focused Quest: Becoming the Best Church for the Community* (San Francisco: Jossey-Bass, 2010), 112.

20. Ibid., 114.

21. Scot McKnight takes issue in the strongest terms with what he calls "the Skinny Jeans Kingdom People," who focus on social justice done by Christians alongside others in the public sector. The definition of "kingdom work" as "good deeds done by good people (Christian or not) in the public sector for the common good" is, in McKnight's terms "not what 'kingdom' *ever* means in the Bible." He also objects to the "Pleated Pants Kingdom People," who see the kingdom Jesus offered as being about personal redemption alone. McKnight argues for the terms *kingdom* and *church* being synonymous. Kingdom mission is local church mission, including evangelism, worship, catechesis, fellowship, edification, discipleship, and gifts of the Spirit. He concludes, "The only place kingdom work is and can be done is in and through the local church when disciples (kingdom citizens, church people) are doing kingdom mission." See *Kingdom Conspiracy: Returning to the Radical Mission of the Local Church* (Grand Rapids: Brazos, 2014), 5, 205–8.

22. Robert Lewis, *The Church of Irresistible Influence: Bridge-Building Stories to Help Reach Your Community* (Grand Rapids: Zondervan, 2001), 37.

23. For the story of Fellowship Bible Church, see ibid.

24. Rebecca Barrett-Fox, *God Hates: Westboro Baptist Church, American Nationalism, and the Religious Right* (Lawrence: University Press of Kansas, 2016).

25. John Beukema, "Like a Good Neighbor: Six Keys to Improve Your Church's Reputation within the Community," *Leadership* 24 (Spring 2003): 56.

26. Eric Swanson, "Is Your Church a Good Neighbor? Why Some Communities Resist Churches—and Others Welcome Them," *Leadership* 23 (Summer 2002): 80.

27. Swanson recounts the experience of churches in Little Rock, Arkansas, that cooperated to serve their city: "For the past four years, more than 100 Little Rock congregations and over 5,000 volunteers have served their communities by building parks and playgrounds and refurbishing nearly 50 schools. They set records for Red Cross blood donations and have signed up thousands of new organ donors. They began reaching out to the community through 'life skill' classes (on marriage, finances, wellness, aging, etc.) in meeting rooms at banks, hotels, and other public forums (with more than 5,000 people attending). Together the churches have donated nearly a million dollars to community human service organizations that are particularly effective in meeting the needs of at-risk youth. They have renovated homes and provided school uniforms, school supplies, winter coats, and Christmas toys for hundreds of children." Ibid., 81.

28. Swanson and Rusaw, *Externally Focused Quest*, 185.

29. Swanson, "Is Your Church a Good Neighbor?," 80.

30. See Elmer John Thiessen, *The Ethics of Evangelism: A Philosophical Defense of Proselytizing and Persuasion* (Downers Grove, IL: IVP Academic, 2011). Thiessen argues for the ethical validity of evangelism, or proselytizing, in a pluralistic society.

31. Charles S. Kelley Jr., "Ethical Issues in Evangelism: A Pyramid of Concerns," *Theological Educator* 46 (September 1992): 38.

32. For an example of ethical principles applied to social ministry, see "FAQs," World Vision International, September 13, 2012, http://www.wvi.org/faqs.

33. Paul Tillich, *Love, Power, and Justice: Ontological Analyses and Ethical Applications* (New York: Oxford University Press, 1960), 84.

34. Roger S. Greenway, "The Ethics of Evangelism," *Calvin Theological Journal* 28, no. 1 (April 1993): 152.

35. Kelley, "Ethical Issues in Evangelism," 38.

36. Gaylord B. Noyce, "The Ethics of Evangelism," *Christian Century*, October 10, 1979, 976.

37. J. B. Smith, "Group Calls for Waco Payday Loan Regulations," WacoTrib.com, Nov. 17, 2015, http://www.wacotrib.com/news/city_of_waco/group-calls-for-waco-payday-loan-regulations/article_b1687cb7-28e0-54b4-837c-5921b33765d8.html.

38. Gregory Ripps, "Eight-Liner Opponents Face Deadline," *Wilson County News*, February 3, 2016, http://www.wilsoncountynews.com/article.php?id=70548&n=section-general-news-eight-liner-opponents-face-deadline; and William J. Gibbs, "Eight-Liners: 'Game Over,'" *Wilson County News*, February 24, 2016, http://www.wilsoncountynews.com/article.php?id=71015&n=section-general-news-eight-liners-game-over.

39. Lewis, *Irresistible Influence*, 36.

40. Ibid., 36–37.

41. Edwin H. Friedman, Gary Emanuel, and Mickie Crimone, *Generation to Generation: Family Process in Church and Synagogue* (New York: Guilford, 2011), 38.

42. This occurred most recently in the 2016 presidential campaign as Republican nominee Donald Trump met with a large group of evangelical leaders to garner their support. Emma Green, "Trump Is Surrounding Himself with Evangelical Pastors," *Atlantic*, June 21, 2016, http://www.theatlantic.com/politics/archive/2016/06/trump-is-surrounding-himself-with-evangelical-pastors/488114/.

43. "The Restriction of Political Campaign Intervention by Section 501(c)(3) Tax-Exempt Organizations," Sept. 13, 2016, https://www.irs.gov/charities-non-profits/charitable-organizations/the-restriction-of-political-campaign-intervention-by-section-501-c-3-tax-exempt-organizations. After his election, President Trump announced his intent to "destroy" the Johnson Amendment (Mark Landler and Laurie Goodstein, "Trump Vows to 'Destroy' Law Banning Political Endorsements by Churches," *The New York Times*, February 2, 2017, https://www.nytimes.com/2017/02/02/us/politics/trump-johnson-amendment-political-activity-churches.html).

44. "Religion and Politics," Pew Research Center, http://www.pewforum.org/topics/religion-and-politics/.

45. Tyler Fleming, "Going 'against the Grain,' Black Church Backs Trump for President," *Charlotte Observer*, Aug. 20, 2016, http://www.charlotteobserver.com/news/local/article 94274037.html.

46. David Gushee, "Winning God's Vote: Boundaries for the Candidate/Clergy Courtship in '16," *Religion News Service*, Dec. 30, 2015, http://religionnews.com/2015/12/30 /candidates-clergy-god-politics/.

47. Hauerwas and Willimon, *Resident Aliens*, 47–48.

48. Email from Chris McBride, director of movement mobilization, Antioch Movement of Churches, August 20, 2016.

49. Russell Moore, *Onward: Engaging the Culture without Losing the Gospel* (Nashville: B&H, 2015), 69.

Chapter 7 Facing Clergy Sexual Abuse

1. "Working Together," A Newsjournal of the Center for the Prevention of Sexual and Domestic Violence, Marie Fortune, Dir., Seattle, WA 98103. Cited in Joy Jordan-Lake, "Conduct Unbecoming a Preacher," *Christianity Today*, February 10, 1992, 26. For contemporary examples, see Diana R. Garland, "Clergy Sexual Misconduct Study: Executive Summary," May 18, 2016, http://www.baylor.edu/clergysexualmisconduct/index.php?id=67406.

2. "Religion News Writers Pick Their Top Stories of 2002," *Baptist Message*, January 2, 2003, 4. For an extensive article on one view of "the cause of the Catholic clergy's sex abuse scandal," see Lisa Miller, "A Woman's Place Is in the Church," *Newsweek*, April 12, 2010, 36–43.

3. Laurie Goodstein, "Decades of Damage: Trail of Pain in Church Crisis Leads to Nearly Every Diocese," *New York Times*, January 12, 2003. The survey, the most complete compilation of data on the problem available, contains the names and histories of 1,205 accused priests and 4,268 people who have claimed publicly to have been abused by priests.

4. "Clergy Ratings at Lowest Point Ever," *Christianity Today*, February 2003, 21.

5. See Garland, "Clergy Sexual Misconduct Study."

6. Diana R. Garland, "Clergy Sexual Misconduct: Don't Call It an Affair," *Journal for Family and Community Ministries* 26 (2013): 68–69. After her untimely death in 2015, the school was named the Diana R. Garland School of Social Work by Baylor University.

7. Ibid., 69.

8. Teresa Watanabe, "Problem of Clergy Abuse Extends to All Denominations," *Austin American-Statesman*, March 31, 2002, A13.

9. Ibid., A15.

10. When Dee Ann Miller first told church officials she was assaulted in Africa by a fellow Southern Baptist missionary, two leaders replied it was partly her fault! Read her story in *How Little We Knew: Collusion and Confusion with Sexual Misconduct* (Lafayette, LA: Prescott, 1993) and her novel *The Truth about Malarkey* (Bloomington, IN: 1stbooks.com, 2000), or visit her website at http://members.tripod.com/~NoColluding.

11. Peter Rutter, *Sex in the Forbidden Zone: When Men in Power—Therapists, Doctors, Clergy, Teachers, and Others—Betray Women's Trust* (Los Angeles: Jeremy P. Tarcher, 1986), 15–16.

12. Ibid., 15.

13. Stanley J. Grenz and Roy D. Bell, *Betrayal of Trust: Confronting and Preventing Clergy Sexual Misconduct*, 2nd ed. (Grand Rapids: Baker, 2001), 19.

14. Tom Economus, "Buzz-Words That Put Victims over the Edge!," *Missing Link* (Spring/ Summer 1998): 1.

15. Rutter, *Sex in the Forbidden Zone*, 17.

16. The basic outline and some of the content in the following sections are based on the author's seminal contribution (pp. 10–26) in the 44-page publication *Broken Trust: Confronting Clergy Sexual Misconduct*, published by the Christian Life Commission (CLC) of the Baptist

General Convention of Texas (BGCT), 7557 Rambler Park Rd., Suite 1200, Dallas, TX 75246, where copies may be acquired.

17. David E. Garland and Diana R. Garland, *Flawed Families of the Bible* (Grand Rapids: Brazos, 2007).

18. D. R. Garland, "Clergy Sexual Misconduct," 69.

19. Thomas S. Giles, "Coping with Sexual Misconduct in the Church," *Christianity Today*, January 11, 1993, 49.

20. See the discussion of this issue in David Rice, *Shattered Vows: Exodus from the Priesthood* (Belfast: Blackstaff, 1990), 3.

21. Dee Miller, "The Kingdom Is Not Served by Self-Serving Secrecy," *Baptists Today*, May 4, 1995, 7.

22. Jeff T. Seat, "The Prevalence and Contributing Factors of Sexual Misconduct among Southern Baptist Pastors in Six Southern States," *Journal of Pastoral Care* (Winter 1993): 363–64.

23. See David Briggs, "No Longer Silent," *Christian Century*, April 4, 2001, 7, which reports a study by a consortium of eight major missionary organizations randomly surveying 1,200 former missionary children. Of more than 600 responding, 6.8 percent experienced sexual abuse during primary school, and 4 percent said they were sexually abused during grades 7 through 12.

24. Quoted in Gerald L. Zelizer, "Sex Scandals Rock Trust in All Religions' Leaders," *USA Today*, April 23, 2002, 11A.

25. G. Loyd Rediger, "Clergy Moral Malfeasance," *Church Management—The Clergy Journal* (May–June 1991): 37–38.

26. A. Shupe, *Spoils of the Kingdom: Clergy Misconduct and Religious Community* (Urbana: University of Illinois Press, 2007), 7.

27. This is partly due to the fact that most ministers are male, but also due to the nature of sexual abuse: "In a U.S. survey, 80% of professional sexual abuse cases involved a male therapist and a female client." Carl Sherman, "Behind Closed Doors: Therapist-Client Sex," *Psychology Today* (May–June 1993): 13.

28. See Grenz and Bell for their development of these two aspects of CSA in chaps. 3 and 4 of *Betrayal of Trust*.

29. Ibid., 83.

30. John D. Volgelsang, "From Denial to Hope: A Systemic Response to Clergy Sexual Abuse," *Journal of Religion and Health* (Fall 1993): 197. See also "Study Finds Clergy Sexual Misconduct Widespread," *Christian Century*, October 20, 2009, 14.

31. Rutter, *Sex in the Forbidden Zone*, 124.

32. Karen Lebacqz and Ronald J. Barton, *Sex in the Parish* (Louisville: John Knox, 1991), 199. The authors note that sexual contact during or after any counseling relationship is considered grossly unethical by all counseling associations.

33. The Roman Catholic Church scandals concerning priests and children have underscored an important distinction between pedophiles (sexual desire for children) and ephebophiles (desire for postpubescent adolescent boys), the target of about 80 percent of abusing priests (Jennifer Daw, *Monitor on Psychology* [June 2002]).

34. See Grenz and Bell, *Betrayal of Trust*, 203n4, which lists the sources of the seven profiles.

35. Ibid., 42–47.

36. Marie Fortune, *Is Nothing Sacred? When Sex Invades the Pastoral Relationship* (New York: Harper & Row, 1989), 47.

37. Ibid., 156.

38. One of the authors of this text was the "after pastor" to these incidents.

39. Cited by Greg Warner, "Sexual Misconduct by Ministers—A Cause for Concern," *Baptist Message*, February 17, 1994, 5.

40. An archdiocese in Minnesota filed for bankruptcy in response to lawsuits by victims of CSA, becoming the twelfth in the United States to do so in the face of sex abuse claims. See "Archdiocese Files Bankruptcy," *Dallas Morning News*, January 17, 2015, 8A. About the same time, the Florida Baptist Convention had a $12.5 million abuse award levied against it. See "SNAP Leader Terms $12.5 Million Abuse Award against Florida Baptist Convention Historic," *Associated Baptist Press News*, January 26, 2014, 1–2.

41. Grenz and Bell, *Betrayal of Trust*, 27.

42. Herbert S. Strean, *Therapists Who Have Sex with Their Patients: Treatment and Recovery* (New York: Brunner/Mazel, 1993), 4.

43. Fortune, *Is Nothing Sacred?*, 103–6.

44. David R. Brubaker, "Secret Sins in the Church Closet," *Christianity Today*, February 10, 1992, 30–32.

45. Lebacqz and Barton, *Sex in the Parish*, 224–25.

46. See Allen Roy Johnston, "Wounded Churches: Causes and Long Term Curative Suggestions for Congregations and Afterpastors," a published DMin project with extensive bibliography (60 Lyle Lane, Selah, WA 98942).

47. David Cramer et al., "Theology and Misconduct," *Christian Century*, August 20, 2014, 20.

48. Sarah Pulliam Bailey, "Ministry Leader Gothard Quits after Abuse Allegations," *Christian Century*, April 2, 2014, 17.

49. "Priest Firings Climbed in '11–12," *Dallas Morning News*, January 18, 2014, A14.

50. "Ex-Pastor Gets 12 Years," *Dallas Morning News*, February 13, 2014, B1.

51. "Ex-Youth Minister Gets 22 Years for Sex Abuse," *Dallas Morning News*, October 8, 2015, B2.

52. Annette Lawson, *Adultery: An Analysis of Love and Betrayal* (New York: Basic Books, 1988), 221.

53. Grenz and Bell, *Betrayal of Trust*, 33.

54. Task Force on Sexual Abuse of Patients (Ont.) and Marilou McPhedran, *The Preliminary Report of the Task Force on Sexual Abuse of Patients* (Toronto: College of Physicians and Surgeons of Ontario, 1991), 12.

55. Pamela Cooper-White, "Soul-Stealing: Power and Relations in Pastoral Sexual Abuse," *Christian Century*, February 20, 1991, 197.

56. Jack Balswick and John Thoburn, "How Ministers Deal with Sexual Temptation," *Pastoral Psychology* 39, no. 5 (1991): 285.

57. Dee Miller, "How Could She?" (1998), an unpublished article used by permission.

58. Survivor advocate Dee Miller writes, "The demons are not the perpetrators. They aren't the colluders, and certainly not the survivors. I've named the collective demons in an acronym—DIM thinking—Denial, Ignorance, and Minimization," in "Moving beyond Our Fears" (1998), unpublished article used by permission.

59. See especially the entire issue of the *Baptist Standard*, June 11, 2007, which includes the articles "Cloak of Secrecy That Protects Abusers" (p. 1), "The Trap of Recycling Sex Abusers" (p. 9), "Sexual Predators" (p. 10), "Sex-Abuse Victims" (p. 11), and "Should . . . Clergy Be Restored" (p. 13).

60. Cited by Greg Warner, "With Sexual Misconduct, All Suffer in Blame Game," *Associated Baptist Press*, December 23, 1993, 6–8.

61. Ibid.

62. Grenz and Bell, *Betrayal of Trust*, 134.

63. Warner, "With Sexual Misconduct," 4.

64. Rutter, *Sex in the Forbidden Zone*, 223.

65. Lebacqz and Barton, *Sex in the Parish*, 107–8.

66. Ibid., 65.

67. Fortune, *Is Nothing Sacred?*, 106–7, 148–53.

68. Grenz and Bell, *Betrayal of Trust*, 147.

69. Balswick and Thoburn, "How Ministers Deal with Sexual Temptation," 280, 270.

70. Garland, "Clergy Sexual Misconduct," 67.

71. For an explanation of "accountability groups," see *Broken Trust: Confronting Clergy Sexual Misconduct* (Dallas: Christian Life Commission, Baptist General Convention of Texas, 2001), 28.

72. See Barbara A. Williams, "Clergy Sexual Misconduct: A Primer for Denominational Church Leaders," *American Baptist Churches in the USA* (Spring 1995); Peter Rogness, "Making the Church a Safe Place," *Lutheran: ELCA* (June 2002); *Broken Trust*; and the United Methodist Church's extensive program in Donald C. Houts, *Clergy Sexual Ethics: A Workshop Guide* (Decatur, GA: Journal of Pastoral Care Publications, 1991).

73. Fortune, *Is Nothing Sacred?*, 106.

74. Ray Furr, "Churches Can Prevent Sexual Abuse by Screening Staff and Volunteers," April 12, 2002, http://www.ethicsdaily.com/churches-can-prevent-sexual-abuse-by-screening -staff-and-volunteers-cms-600.

75. Marie Fortune closes her text with a model of the procedure developed by the American Lutheran Church for responding to complaints of unethical behavior by clergy (*Is Nothing Sacred?*, 135–53).

76. Greg Warner (ABP), "Breaking the Cycle," *Baptist Standard*, June 11, 2007, 9.

77. Marv Knox, "Hold Churches Accountable for Abuse," *Baptist Standard*, June 11, 2007, 5. This action followed a two-year study of CSA and the publishing of a 45-page resource booklet (see *Broken Trust*, endnote 16).

78. Ken Camp, "BGCT Sexual Misconduct Policy Replaces File with Prevention," *Baptist Standard*, March 9, 2016, 1. The executive board voted to "implement a sexual abuse prevention program, . . . provide training opportunities, . . . extend compassion, . . . and initially focus on protection for children." Many, including this author, feel this is a step backward from addressing the problem of CSA.

79. For a full discussion of the pros and cons of a code of ethics for ministers, see chap. 8 and a sample contemporary code in app. C.

80. Bob Allen, *Baptist News Global*, June 21, 2016, 1.

81. Grenz and Bell, *Betrayal of Trust*, 115–18.

82. Fortune, *Is Nothing Sacred?*, 66.

83. Grenz and Bell, *Betrayal of Trust*, 118.

84. "Convention Resolution Addresses Sexual Integrity for Spiritual Leaders," *Baptist Press*, June 12, 2002.

85. Nancy R. Heisy, "Another Look at Matthew 18," *The Mennonite*, October 27, 1992, 466–67.

86. Fortune, *Is Nothing Sacred?*, 99.

87. Grenz and Bell, *Betrayal of Trust*, 156.

88. Toby A. Druin, "Ridding the Ministry of Sexual Predators," *Baptist Standard*, September 30, 1998, 4.

Chapter 8 Developing a Personal Code of Ethics

1. Dennis Campbell, *Doctors, Lawyers, Ministers: Christian Ethics in Professional Practice* (Nashville: Abingdon, 1982), 23.

2. Nolan B. Harmon lists Congregational, Disciples, Methodist, Presbyterian, and Unitarian codes of ethics in *Ministerial Ethics and Etiquette*, rev. ed. (Nashville: Abingdon, 1979), 201–8.

3. See the "National Capital Presbytery Code of Ethics," in William H. Willimon, *Calling and Character: Virtues of the Ordained Life* (Nashville: Abingdon, 2000), 151–64.

4. Arthur H. Becker, "Professional Ethics for Ministry," *Trinity Seminary Review* 9 (Fall 1987): 69.

5. James Allen Reasons, "The Biblical Concept of Integrity and Professional Codes of Ethics in Ministerial Ethics" (PhD diss., Southwestern Baptist Theological Seminary, 1990), 1.

6. James M. Aldurf, review of *Is Nothing Sacred? When Sex Invades the Pastoral Relationship*, by Marie Fortune, *Christianity Today*, July 16, 1990, 53.

7. Seminary professors Walter E. Wiest and Elwyn A. Smith state that such codes are "inherently legalistic" and "will not do." *Ethics in Ministry: A Guide for the Professional* (Minneapolis: Fortress, 1990), 12.

8. Reasons, "Biblical Concept of Integrity," 4.

9. For example, the author of this chapter made a motion at the 2002 annual convention of the Baptist General Convention of Texas (the largest Southern Baptist state convention) that a representative committee of 9 to 15 persons be appointed "to study and develop for consideration by the 2004 Convention a 'Code of Ethics for Baptist Ministers' which could serve as a model for ministers, churches, and Baptist institutions to utilize, adapt, and adopt if they so choose, as guidelines which reflect basic ethical obligations for ministry, define the ministerial profession, and serve as a support to protect the individual minister." However, the denominational leader who appointed and directed this committee was strongly opposed to "codes" as being "too legalistic and dangerous" for Baptists and led the group to develop an alternative document, "Ministerial Ethics: A Covenant of Trust," stating this approach was "more consistent with Baptist ecclesiology and polity."

Needless to say, this author was disappointed by the disregard of the original motion by this denominational leader, but he decided not to create chaos at the 2004 convention, which faced other major decisions. "Ministerial Ethics: A Covenant of Trust" explains the history of the document in the foreword, followed by a 7-page statement on various "covenant" responsibilities. As this author explained to the CLC director, a "covenant" is personal, between the minister and God or some other group, and would make little impact on the ethical practices of most ministers. Though the glossy publication was sent to all Texas Baptist ministers, to my knowledge it was rarely read or used.

10. Amitai Etzioni, "Money, Power, and Fame," *Newsweek*, September 18, 1989, 10.

11. Alasdair MacIntyre, *A Short History of Ethics* (New York: Macmillan, 1966), 266.

12. Jane A. Boyajian, ed., *Ethical Issues in the Practice of Ministry* (Minneapolis: United Theological Seminary, 1984), 82.

13. Michael D. Bayles, *Professional Ethics*, 2nd ed. (Belmont, CA: Wadsworth, 1989), 197.

14. Karen Lebacqz, *Professional Ethics: Power and Paradox* (Nashville: Abingdon, 1985), 66, italics in original.

15. Lisa Newton, "The Origin of Professionalism: Sociological Conclusions and Ethical Implications," *Business and Professional Ethics Journal* 1 (Summer 1982): 40.

16. Lebacqz, *Professional Ethics*, 18.

17. Bayles, *Professional Ethics*, 84.

18. Darrell Reeck, *Ethics for the Professions: A Christian Perspective* (Minneapolis: Augsburg, 1982), 64.

19. Reasons, "Biblical Concept of Integrity," 12–13.

20. Campbell, *Doctors, Lawyers, Ministers*, 23. Reeck also notes many "unspoken purposes," such as "to give an air of professionalism, to embrace public relations, and to enable bureaucratization" (*Ethics for the Professions*, 64).

21. Lebacqz, *Professional Ethics*, 68.

22. William F. May, "Code and Covenant or Philanthropy and Contract?," *Hastings Center Report* 5 (December 1975): 29–38.

23. A. M. Carr-Saunders and P. A. Wilson, *The Professions* (New York: Oxford University Press, 1933), 421.

24. Reasons, "Biblical Concept of Integrity," 17.

25. C. S. Calian, *Today's Pastor in Tomorrow's World* (New York: Hawthorne Books, 1977), 104–5.

26. Bayles, *Professional Ethics*, 177.

27. Ibid., 166–67.

28. Lebacqz, *Professional Ethics*, 68.

29. Bayles, *Professional Ethics*, 185.

30. May, "Code and Covenant," 38.

31. Reasons, "Biblical Concept of Integrity," 46–54, provides a detailed discussion of this topic.

32. Lebacqz has made a significant contribution by focusing on the importance of roles for professional relationships (*Professional Ethics*, 135).

33. Lisa H. Newton, "A Professional Ethic: A Proposal in Context," in *Matters of Life and Death*, ed. John E. Thomas (Toronto: Samuel Stevens, 1978), 264.

34. Gaylord Noyce, *Pastoral Ethics: Professional Responsibilities for the Clergy* (Nashville: Abingdon, 1988), 198.

35. Susan Bryant, "'Didn't Mean It' Is No Excuse," *Richmond Times Herald*, February 24, 1992, B5.

36. James D. Berkley, "Turning Points: Eight Ethical Choices," *Leadership* 9 (Spring 1988): 32, italics added.

37. Z. N. Morrell, *Flowers and Fruits in the Wilderness*, 3rd ed. (St. Louis: Commercial Printing, 1882), 33.

38. Boyajian, *Ethical Issues*, 85.

39. Nolan B. Harmon, *Ministerial Ethics and Etiquette* (Nashville: Abingdon, 1928).

40. "Focus on the Family Now Promoting 'Shepherd's Covenant' for Pastors," *Baptist Standard*, February 24, 2003, 8.

41. Chris Lisee, "Evangelical Body Proposes Code of Ethics for Pastors," *Christian Century*, July 25, 2012, 10.

42. *Richmond Times-Dispatch*, October 19, 1991, B10.

43. Boyajian, *Ethical Issues*, 85.

44. Paul F. Camenisch, "Clergy Ethics and the Professional Ethics Model," in *Clergy Ethics in a Changing Society: Mapping the Terrain*, ed. James P. Wind, Russell Burck, Paul F. Camenisch, and Dennis P. McCann (Louisville: Westminster John Knox, 1991), 125.

45. Minnesota State Statue 148A requires all employers of counselors to make an inquiry of previous employers for the last five years to determine whether there have been any occurrences of illegal sexual contact.

46. Boyajian, *Ethical Issues*, 79.

47. Henlee H. Barnette, "The Minister as a Moral Role-Model," *Review and Expositor* (Fall 1989): 505–16.

48. W. Ward Gasque, "God's Assistant Watchdog," *Christianity Today*, November 5, 1990, 19.

49. Archibald D. Hart, "Being Moral Isn't Always Enough," *Leadership* 9 (Spring 1988): 25.

50. Boyajian, *Ethical Issues*, 90.

51. Harmon, *Ministerial Ethics and Etiquette*, 202.

52. Noyce, *Pastoral Ethics*, 193. As previously noted, however, a minister's multiplicity of roles makes competency in all areas virtually impossible.

53. See appendix II in Joe E. Trull and James E. Carter, *Ministerial Ethics* (Nashville: Broadman & Holman, 1993), 226ff.

54. Hart, "Being Moral Isn't Always Enough," 26.

55. "Policy on Sexual Ethics in the Pastoral Relationship as Recommended to the Board of Directors of the Potomac Association," unpublished document of the UCC in Virginia.

56. Becker, "Professional Ethics for Ministry," 70.

57. Lebacqz, *Professional Ethics*, 68.

58. Richard A. Hunt, John E. Hinkle Jr., and H. Newton Maloney, eds., *Clergy Assessment and Career Development* (Nashville: Abingdon, 1990), 40–41.

59. M. Pabst Battin, "Professional Ethics and the Practice of Religion: A Philosopher's View," in Boyajian, *Ethical Issues*, 17–20.

60. Margaret Battin, *Ethics in the Sanctuary: Examining the Practices of Organized Religion* (New Haven: Yale University Press, 1990), 3–4.

61. Hart, "Being Moral Isn't Always Enough," 27–29, focuses on four principles: accountability, confidentiality, responsibility, and integrity.

62. Reasons, "Biblical Concept of Integrity," 134–38.

63. Becker, "Professional Ethics for Ministry," 75.

64. Becker notes a Lutheran Council recommendation not to divulge "unless it is reasonably anticipated that such persons may do great harm to themselves or others." He also suggests that pastors ought never to agree to *secretiveness*, only to confidentiality (ibid., 74).

65. "Report for the Task Force on Ministerial Ethics: Eastern Oklahoma Presbytery," adopted by Presbytery, February 13, 1990.

66. See "When a Pastoral Colleague Falls," *Leadership* 11 (Winter 1991): 102–11.

67. "NRB Moves Slowly to Enforce Ethics Code," *Christianity Today*, March 9, 1992, 59.

68. Robert Spanier, "Anti-Board Sentiment Rouses Mass. Physicians," *American College of Physicians Observer* 9 (December 1989): 7.

69. Rudolph W. Nemser, "Guidelines for the Unitarian Universalist Ministry: A History," in Boyajian, *Ethical Issues*, 70–75, which explains the function of these "Guidelines."

70. Rev. Wayne Arnason of Charlottesville, Virginia, in an interview with the author on February 14, 1992, and UUMA *Guidelines*, 28.

71. Ron Sisk, "More Groups Embrace Ethics Codes For Ministers," EthicsDaily.com, March 3, 2003, http://www.ethicsdaily.com/more-groups-embrace-ethics-code-for-ministers-cms -2237.

72. Chris Lisee, "Evangelical Body Proposes Code of Ethics for Pastors," *Christian Century*, July 25, 2012, 18.

73. Hunt, Hinkle, and Maloney, *Clergy Assessment and Career Development*, 40.

74. Pamela Cooper-White, "Soul-Stealing: Power Relations in Pastoral Sexual Abuse," *Christian Century*, February 19, 1991, 199.

75. H. Newton Maloney, "Codes of Ethics: A Comparison," *Journal of Psychology and Christianity* 5 (Fall 1986): 94.

76. Jane Clapp, *Professional Ethics and Insignia* (Metuchen, NJ: Scarecrow, 1974); and Rena A. Gorlin, ed., *Codes of Professional Responsibility*, 2nd ed. (Washington, DC: Bureau of National Affairs, 1990).

77. Thomas Schaffer, "Work and Faith," *Theology Today* 59 (October 2002): 351–52.

78. Reeck, *Ethics for the Professions*, 61–62.

79. Arthur L. Caplan, "Cracking Codes," *Hastings Center Report* 8 (August 1978): 18.

80. Reasons, "Biblical Concept of Integrity," 40–41.

81. Reeck, *Ethics for the Professions*, 61.

82. C. S. Lewis, *Mere Christianity* (New York: MacMillan, 1960), 71.

83. Lewis Smedes, *A Pretty Good Person* (San Francisco: Harper & Row, 1990), 86.

84. Reeck, *Ethics for the Professions*, 66.

85. Berkley discusses eight areas of ethical concern for pastors who construct their own codes: beliefs, service, morality, competence, compensation, colleagues, confidentiality, and friendships ("Turning Points," 32–41).

86. Smedes, *Pretty Good Person*, 86.

87. Reeck, *Ethics for the Professions*, 69.

88. Ibid., 72.

89. Joy Jordan-Lake, "Conduct Unbecoming a Preacher," *Christianity Today*, February 10, 1992, 30.

90. Bob Smietana, "Proceed with Care," *Facts & Trends* (Summer 2016): 36–39.

91. See endnote 9 for an explanation of this author's unsuccessful attempt to initiate such a code of ethics for ministers in his own Southern Baptist denomination.

92. Richard Spann, *The Ministry* (New York: Abingdon-Cokesbury, 1959), 44–48.

Appendix A A Procedure for Responding to Charges of Clergy Sexual Abuse

1. This model is adapted from Stanley J. Grenz and Roy D. Bell, *Betrayal of Trust: Confronting and Preventing Clergy Sexual Misconduct* (Grand Rapids: Baker Books, 2001), 162–74. Originally published in *Broken Trust: Confronting Clergy Sexual Misconduct* (Dallas: Christian Life Commission, Baptist General Convention of Texas, 2001), 25–26.

Appendix B Early Denominational Codes of Ethics

1. Nolan B. Harmon, *Ministerial Ethics and Etiquette*, rev. ed. (Nashville: Abingdon, 1983), 201, states that the code was adopted by the New Haven, Connecticut, Association for Congregational Ministers and published in *Church Administration* by Cokesbury Press in 1931.

2. Harmon states that this code was adopted "by a group of Methodist ministers meeting in conference at Rockford, Illinois," and it was published in *Christian Century,* December 16, 1926 (ibid., 204).

3. Harmon notes that this code was adopted by the New York Presbytery and quoted in an article by William H. Leach in *The Methodist Quarterly Review* (July 1927) (ibid., 205).

4. Harmon indicates that this code was adopted by the Unitarian Ministerial Union and quoted in *Church Management* (August 1926) (ibid., 206).

Appendix C Contemporary Denominational Codes of Ethics

1. Comparing this contemporary Disciples Code with the one printed in Nolan B. Harmon, *Ministerial Ethics and Etiquette*, rev. ed. (Nashville: Abingdon, 1983), 202–4, reveals only one word change: "Kingdom of God" to "Realm of God."

2. "My Ministerial Code of Ethics" (Indianapolis: Department of Homeland Ministries—Christian Church [Disciples of Christ], 1990). The foreword, written by an executive, states, "Since its publication in 1944, more than 30,000 copies of the code have been distributed. . . . With each successive reprint, a general committee was given the possibilities of change in the code. When all the suggestions were received, it was determined that they were sufficient only to effect editorial changes. The code has stood well the test of time and is commended to all ministers as a high code of professional conduct."

3. As published in the *Guidelines: Unitarian Universalist Ministers Association* (Boston: UUMA, 1988), 11–14.

4. Provided by the First Congregational Church, Chesterfield, Virginia, affiliated with the United Church of Christ. Similarities to the Disciples Code are quite obvious.

5. Provided by Harley D. Hunt, executive director of the Ministers Council, American Baptist Churches, USA, and dated May 1991. Also available is "A Process for Review of Ministerial Standing," adopted by the National Commission on the Ministry, January 18, 1991, which defines the procedures for handling allegations and enforcing the code.

6. Sexual exploitation is defined as, but not limited to, all forms of overt and covert seduction, speech, gestures, and behavior. Harassment is defined as but not limited to repeated unwelcome comments, gestures, or physical contacts of a sexual nature.

7. *Ethics in Ministry Relations—1992,* approved by the 1992 Annual Conference of the Church of the Brethren, Elgin, Illinois, September 1992. The 23-page document also includes an excellent section titled "A Theology of Ministerial Ethics" (4–9) and one titled "Process for Dealing with Allegations of Sexual Misconduct" (11–18).

8. Richard M. Gula, *Ethics in Pastoral Ministry* (New York: Paulist Press, 1996), 142–52.

9. "Report from the Task Force on Ministerial Ethics," Eastern Oklahoma Presbytery.

10. In the appendix of William H. Willimon, *Calling and Character: Virtues of the Ordained Life* (Nashville: Abingdon, 2000), 151–64.

Appendix D Sample Codes of Ethics

1. These sample codes are generic examples of ministerial codes, and they have been edited to include the most significant emphases, both principles and specific guidelines, in each category. To write a personal code of ethics, ministers should evaluate their own ministry obligations in light of the discussions in the text, then refer to these sample codes as broad statements of possibilities for a personal code of ethics.

2. The sample codes of the associate ministers and others that follow include only those obligations, in addition to the senior minister code, that uniquely apply to each special ministerial role.

3. See also Joe E. Trull and James E. Carter, *Ministerial Ethics: Moral Formation for Church Leaders* (Grand Rapids: Baker Academic, 2004), 250–56, for the code of the Christian Association of Psychologists and Counselors, which, although it has many obvious weaknesses, does deal with the primary issues facing pastoral counselors.

4. See also Joe E. Trull and James E. Carter, *Ministerial Ethics: Moral Formation for Church Leaders* (Grand Rapids: Baker Academic, 2004), 256–57, for the Covenant and Code of Ethics for Chaplains of the Armed Forces. These statements have been suggested by military chaplains as possible additions to that code.

Subject Index

abuse. *See* child abuse, reporting of; clergy sexual abuse (CSA)
abusers, types of, 158–60, 168
accountability
  codes of ethics and, 70, 181–82, 184–85, 188–90, 196–99
  ensuring, 205–6
  pastoral, 64–68, 173–76
accusation, clergy sexual abuse, 211–12
administration, leadership and, 94–98
affection, pastoral care and, 79–82
agnosia, 3–4
American Baptist code, 230–32
anomie, 4
associate minister code, 238
associations, ministerial, 119–20
atypical moral commitment, 187
authority, 27–28, 94–96
authorship, code of ethics, 201–2
autonomy, professional, 13, 22
availability, community and, 138–39
awareness, personal, 167–68

background checks, clergy, 171–72, 175
Baptist code, 230–32
Beecher, Henry Ward, 25–26, 29–30, 244n3
Bible, the
  clergy sexual abuse and, 154, 173–74
  community and, 128–30
  ethics and, 27–28
  the pastor and, 60, 79, 96–97
blackout, clergy, 68–69. *See also* burnout, clergy
blame, inappropriate, 162

boomers, 80
boundaries, 115–16, 122, 132–33
Brethren code, 232–34
Brooks, Phillips, 207
burnout, clergy, 6, 68–69

calendar, appointment, 70–71
calling
  career and, 7, 9, 14–15
  ministry as, 5–7, 17
  professionalism and, 8, 19
care, pastoral, 79–89, 132
career, calling and, 7, 9, 14–15
centered sets, 132–33, 137–38
change, power and, 95–96
chaplain, pastor as, 132, 148–49
chaplain code, military, 239
character
  centrality of, 34–35
  defined, 30–31
  ethics and, 29–35, 185, 203–5
  God's, 36–37, 43
  virtues and, 31–34
  See also integrity
Chicago school, professionalism and, 12
child abuse, reporting of, 83–84
church, the
  clergy sexual abuse and, 161–63, 170–72, 174–76
  codes of ethics and, 193
  as local, 74–75
  values and, 36
  vocation and, 5–7
  See also congregation, the

Scripture Index